EMBRACING THE VOID

EMBRACING THE VOID

Rethinking the Origin of the Sacred

Richard Boothby

Northwestern University Press
Evanston, Illinois

Northwestern University Press
www.nupress.northwestern.edu

Brief passages included in this book were originally published in "The No-Thing of God: Psychoanalysis of Religion after Lacan" in *The Oxford Handbook of Philosophy and Psychoanalysis*, edited by Michael Lacewing and Richard Gipps (Oxford: Oxford University Press, 2018), and have been reproduced by permission of Oxford University Press.

Printed in the United States of America

10 9 8 7 6 5 4 3 2 1

Library of Congress Cataloging-in-Publication Data

Names: Boothby, Richard, 1954– author.
Title: Embracing the void : rethinking the origin of the sacred / Richard Boothby.
Other titles: Diaeresis.
Description: Evanston, Illinois : Northwestern University Press, 2023. | Series: Diaeresis | Includes bibliographical references and index.
Identifiers: LCCN 2022023700 | ISBN 9780810145382 (paperback) | ISBN 9780810145399 (cloth) | ISBN 9780810145405 (ebook)
Subjects: LCSH: Psychoanalysis and religion. | Philosophy and religion. | Holy, The. | Nothing (Philosophy) | BISAC: PHILOSOPHY / Religious | PHILOSOPHY / Movements / Post–Structuralism
Classification: LCC BF175.4.R44 B67 2023 | DDC 200.1/9—dc23/eng/20220824
LC record available at https://lccn.loc.gov/2022023700

For my wife, Rebecca Nichols,
my darling, die-hard atheist

Contents

Preface

Is Nothing Sacred?

The soul has to go on loving in the void.
　　—Simone Weil

Over the centuries, human beings have probably expended more thought, time, energy, and passion entangled with religion than with any other enterprise beyond brute survival. Were Martian explorers to visit Earth, they would report to their fellow Martians that the two-legged animal is also, and maybe above all, the animal that worships. But what exactly is worship? Throughout human history, the dizzying array of cultic, ritual, and spiritual practices have failed to coalesce into any palpable unity. If anything, tensions between differing religious viewpoints now seem more pitched than ever. One might well ask whether it is possible to conceive of the notion of the sacred as a unitary phenomenon.

This book risks the assertion that the "varieties of religious experience," as William James called them, do indeed share a common core. Yet the task of excavating that common nucleus must contend with two major challenges that are internal to the effort. The first challenge accompanies the central premise of the argument that follows, which proposes that the religious impulse is uniquely illuminated by the lessons of psychoanalysis. For any reader acquainted with Freud's scathing critique of religious belief that choice of approach will certainly seem dubious, if not downright nonsensical. Exposed to Freud's unrelenting hostility, readers with even a modest religious inclination are inevitably tempted to ask: "Is *nothing* sacred?"

Also problematic is the fact that psychoanalysis itself has for a long time been a target of critique by a wide range of detractors, among them droves of feminists, humanists, behaviorists, geneticists, neuroscientists, and pharmacologically inclined psychiatrists. In many corners of the academy, and nearly everywhere on the street, Freudian theory seems to be a stock in decline. One wonders: Does the Freudian legacy still have anything valuable to offer?

For most readers, however, the second big challenge is probably even more daunting than the first. It concerns the book's unlikely conclusion, which answers the question "Is nothing sacred?" with a resounding "Yes!"—though not in the sense that there is nothing that deserves to be esteemed as holy, but rather in the sense that the experience of the sacred, the inclination to bow before something mysteriously elevated, something we are tempted to call more-than-human, arises precisely from our being primally oriented toward . . . Nothing. In what follows, I will argue that the core of the religious impulse resides in our relation to what we do not know, that at the most primitive level of human consciousness we remain in thrall to an unencompassable Void. The strangest fact, however, is that this Nothing is far from being merely nothing. On the contrary, relation to the pregnant Void is the most decisive, enabling feature of the human being. As Martin Heidegger famously put it, we are creatures "held out into the nothing."[1]

The aim of this book is to show how and why that is so.

Introduction

Reposing Freud's Final Question

We leave Heaven
To the angels and the sparrows.
—Heinrich Heine, quoted by Freud in *The Future of
an Illusion*

Sigmund Freud did not go gentle into his good night. At the age of eighty-one, having fled the Nazis for London, he grappled with his growing anxieties about the darkening fascist menace, with the challenges of living in exile, and with his own impending death from cancer of the jaw. Yet during those final, intensely fraught years, Freud's intellectual work not only continued but achieved a kind of crescendo. His labors were centered on the biblical figure of Moses and resulted in his last book, *Moses and Monotheism.*

The book proposed an extraordinary double thesis, asserting that Moses was not an Israelite but an Egyptian, and that the Jewish religion was born when his followers murdered him. Despite the hesitations of his supporters about the credibility of the core argument, Freud remained adamant about pressing ahead with publication. Just before he died and amid considerable furor, he called it "quite a worthy exit."[1]

The focus of Freud's final book suggests that he recognized religion as a special field for psychoanalytic theorization. *Moses and Monotheism* was the fourth of a series of studies, preceded by the foundational 1907 essay "Obsessive Actions and Religious Practices," *Totem and Taboo* of 1911, and *The Future of an Illusion*, which appeared in 1927. But what remained an important sidebar for Freud appears to be a much more central point of reference in the thought of Freud's most inventive and insightful interpreter, the French psychoanalyst and theorist Jacques Lacan. Throughout his writings and seminars, Lacan refers repeatedly to religious figures, concepts, and themes, indeed so much so that we are tempted to conclude that Lacan regarded religion as a problem in which the basic concepts of psychoanalysis are adumbrated with special clarity.

My aim in this book is to draw on a series of Lacan's statements toward the goal of outlining a distinctly Lacanian theory of religion. We can anticipate even now that such a perspective will offer a more suggestively open viewpoint than the ferociously critical judgment advanced by Freud. At the same time, however, Lacan remains committed to an atheistic conclusion. The result can often appear to reflect a strangely mixed or suspended judgment. Lacan compressed the key point into a terse adage. "The true formula for atheism," he says, "is that God is unconscious."[2] My intention is to clarify the conceptual frame within which such a claim becomes understandable.

Reaching that goal will require identifying the points at which Lacan breaks with Freud while also revealing the core meaning of Freud's discoveries in completely new and striking ways. Lacan's crucial move is a shift from a *thematic* to a *structural* analysis. There is no better place to introduce the difference between the two approaches than in relation to the Oedipus complex. What Freud conceived as love for the mother and murderous rivalry with the father is recast by Lacan in terms of the dynamics of the child's entry into language.

What is at stake for Lacan can still be related to the triangle of mother, child, and father. The mother is the original human partner, the primal link for the infant's organic sustenance and the addressee of the child's first words. The paternal role is then identified with the lawful regularizing of the symbolic function that stabilizes meaning. What Freud had related to the tyrannical "no" of the father thereby becomes for Lacan a matter of "symbolic castration," by means of which the child's vocalizations are lifted out of the relation to the mother alone and related to standards of meaning that govern the linguistic community at large. This background makes sense of one of Lacan's favorite pieces of wordplay, that of *le Nom du Père*—"the Name of the Father"—where the French word *Nom* (Name) is homophonic with the word *Non* (No).

When the triadic dynamics of the Oedipus complex are conceived in terms of the child's insertion into language, castration ceases to be tied to any physical threat, real or imagined. But it is precisely this theoretical shift that allows Lacan to rejoin Freud's most basic claim in *Moses and Monotheism* about the bridge between the dynamics of individual and group psychology. For Lacan, the speaking subject is always already linked to the human community at large by the rule-governed operation of language. If fantasies arise in the group—say, about a castrating, tyrannical patriarch—they are preceded and made possible by the way the law of language was established in the first place by reference to a third party that stands outside the bond between the child and the mother, stabilizing a degree of separation between them.

This brief sketch of Lacan's theoretical innovations will be familiar to those modestly acquainted with his work. But many Lacanian concepts remain confoundingly obscure, even for dedicated readers. Accordingly, a further objective of this study is to reexamine a handful of key points of Lacan's thought that are often given short shrift. The need for such special labors of interpretation is increased by the fact that Lacan's style of writing and speaking, indeed his whole style of thinking, constantly skirts the unstable boundary between clarity and obscurity, even between sense and nonsense.[3]

If Lacan's discourse can often be maddeningly difficult, it remains exciting and valuable for the way it denies us refuge in comfortable assumptions and preconceptions, forcing us to reengage the most basic questions as if for the first time. In this respect, Lacan's method is deeply appropriate to a discourse about the unconscious, for which any claim to understand completely is by definition an overreach. In fact, Lacan's work can be said to be everywhere oriented toward the *strange*. And not for nothing. One could do worse than to define the unconscious as the way the strange is permanently, intimately, and insistently inscribed at the heart of ourselves.

It is thus entirely in line with my purposes in this book that, in a brief aside in his twentieth seminar, the seminar that probably dabbles in the religious more than any other, Lacan indulges in a play on words about the strange. In the midst of discussing the paradoxical fact, the very *strange* fact, that "sexual *jouissance* [or excessive enjoyment] has the privilege of being specified by an impasse," Lacan reminds us that the French word for "'strange' offers an amusing pun—*étrange, être-ange.*"[4] When one says "strange" in French, one also unavoidably says "angel-being" or "to be an angel." Lacan's *jeu de mots* suggests that, just as the appearance of an angel is something exceedingly strange, there might be something angelic about the strange itself.

This book tries to clarify what Lacan meant by saying something so strange.

Part 1

Rereading Lacan
(or, What Is the Other?)

The challenge in what follows is to piece together a coherent account of religion from a Lacanian viewpoint. The potential payoff is a radically new interpretation of the human disposition toward worship. To unfold that interpretation, we need first to map a handful of key coordinates in Lacan's theoretical frame. The aim is not to provide any comprehensive accounting of his thought. I make no claim to canvas the full breadth and depth of Lacan's contributions. The much more modest goal in part 1 is, first, to trace exactly how Lacan's cardinal problematic of the *Other* is positioned in relation to his triad of prime categories: imaginary, symbolic, and real. The second, complementary task is to clarify more precisely the relationship between the little other of the fellow human being and the "big Other" of the symbolic code—a problematic that is all too often merely taken for granted by commentators on Lacan's thought. Only when that preliminary work is done will the tools be at hand to venture an account of the religious phenomenon in a Lacanian perspective.

1

Religion from Freud to Lacan

You would be wrong to think that the religious authors aren't a good read. I have always been rewarded whenever I have immersed myself in their works.
  —Jacques Lacan

On the topic of religion, it's clear that Lacan doesn't merely repeat Freud's critique. Not so clear is the meaning of what Lacan says on his own.[1] At different points in his teaching, Lacan associates the ancient gods with the unthinkable real,[2] he identifies the "I am what I am" of the burning bush with the pure subject of speech,[3] and he insists that his own *Écrits* should be compared with the writings of the great mystics.[4] The aim of this book is to offer an account of Lacan's rewriting of psychoanalytic theory that allows these claims to make sense. To achieve that aim it will be indispensable to orient ourselves, at least briefly, toward the main elements of Freud's view.

Freud's Three-Pronged Spear

Freud's best-known treatment of religion, *The Future of an Illusion*, almost completely ignores familiar atheistic arguments about the lack of evidence for an invisible supernatural power. Freud focuses not on the *object* of belief, but rather on the *subject* who believes. The problem is the *motive* for believing. The core claim is brutally simple: "It would be very nice if there were a God who created the world and was a benevolent providence, and if there were a moral order in the universe and an afterlife; but it is a very striking fact that all this is exactly as we are bound to wish it to be."[5]

Freud backs up this damning alignment of wish and belief with two other considerations. The first appeals to the history of primitive religions, in which divinities merely personify blind natural forces. The reason, Freud argues, is that "impersonal forces and destinies cannot be approached; they remain eternally remote. But if the elements have passions that rage as they do in our own souls, if death itself is not something spontaneous but the violent act of an evil Will, if everywhere in nature there are Beings around us of a kind that we know in our own society, then we can breathe freely, can feel at home in the uncanny and can deal by psychical means with our senseless anxiety."[6] Further evidence for the wish-fulfilling function of faith is provided by the psychical history of the individual. That history decisively tips the personifying tendency toward the figure of the father. Religious belief thus appears to be based on "an infantile prototype. . . . [O]nce before one has found oneself in a similar state of helplessness: as a small child, in relation to one's parents."[7]

Freud's critique thus poses religious belief as a sugarcoating of reality, a childish faith in notions that are simply too good to be true. Just as most maturing grade-schoolers undergo a progressive abandonment of their childhood faith in candy-dispensing beings like the tooth fairy, the Easter bunny, and Santa Claus, a fully consistent adolescent would eventually draw the conclusion that faith in God, too, must eventually be given up. As Freud puts it, "Men cannot remain children for ever; they must in the end go out into 'hostile life.' We may call this *'education to reality.'* Need I confess to you that the sole purpose of my book is to point out the necessity of this forward step?"[8]

The call for intellectual maturity lies at the heart of Freud's critique in *The Future of an Illusion.* Religious faith is bad for one's intellectual health. Here again, Freud inverts a common argument, this time the argument that science is about determinate observations and hard facts while religion indulges in squishy, untestable fancies, the stuff of bad poetry. Freud's claim is almost the reverse. What is bad about religious belief is its intractable rigidity. What most characterizes religious consciousness is its unwillingness to leave room for the admission of doubt. As Freud thinks of it, religion is a form of malignant certainty. When Freud at one point pauses to "moderate my zeal and admit the possibility that I, too, am chasing an illusion," he is thereby demonstrating the greatest difference between his own posture as a scientist and that of the religious believer.

In *Civilization and Its Discontents,* too, Freud characterizes religious belief as a means for easing the pains of existence. Faith, he claims, is a kind of narcotic. But this notion of religion as a painkiller seems immediately contradicted by religious outlooks that don't make life easier. Recalling examples of religiously inspired heroes and martyrs like Harriet Tubman, Mahatma Gandhi, Dorothy Day, Martin Luther King Jr., or, for that matter, the itinerant rabbi from Nazareth who so famously ran afoul of the authorities, one could make a case for religion as a stimulant to ever greater exertions, ever weightier responsibilities, ever heightened demands for action. Within the compass of *The Future of an Illusion*, Freud has no defense against such a counterexample. His argument simply doesn't apply to it. His best rejoinder might be simply to ask how many among the faithful could plausibly count themselves with the likes of Tubman, Gandhi, Day, and King. No doubt, the results of such a tally would be a cold shower for the champions of belief.

Beyond the pages of *The Future of an Illusion*, however, Freud surely does have something significant to say about the moral challenge and spiritual ascesis of religion. Here we arrive at the second main prong of Freud's treatment of religion, laid out in *Totem and Taboo* and expanded in *Moses and Monotheism*. It elaborates upon the identification of the deity with a father figure, tensed with powerful ambivalences of love, fear, and hatred, while also making the relation with the father the model for the superego and its painful levy of guilt and self-recrimination. This second line of argument is well capable of accounting for self-sacrifice in the name of religious commitment. The self-inflicted sufferings of the monastics who kneel upon little stones while praying, who flagellate themselves on long pilgrimages, who fast, sleep upon oak-hard beds, or labor in the fields wearing agonizing hair shirts all testify to the ferocity of the superego. Unlimited self-punishment is its essential demand. This Freudian analysis is bad news for saints. The self-denying, righteous do-gooder may just be a neurotic.

Freud's account of religion thus unfolds along two lines: childish wish fulfillment and superegoic masochism. How are the two strands related? And what prevents the disparate dynamics at stake from creating an unbridgeable, unsustainable antagonism?

To see why no such internal contradiction arises it is helpful to make a brief detour through Nietzsche's theory of bad conscience. Expounded in the second essay of his *Genealogy of Morals*, bad conscience is Nietzsche's answer to the riddle of the human being as the animal capable of beating itself. The riddle is especially challenging for Nietzsche because it appears to contradict so dramatically his fundamental thesis about the will to power as the universal motive of all creatures.

Nietzsche's answer is that when its outward-tending expression is blocked, the will to power gratifies its lust for cruelty on the only other object available: *itself*. He thus claims that "all instincts that do not discharge themselves outwardly *turn inward*—this is what I call the *internalization* of man: thus it was that man first developed what was later called his 'soul.'"[9] The will to power remains the ground and source of all activity, "only here the material upon which the form-giving and ravishing nature of this force vents itself is man himself, his whole ancient animal self—and not, as in that greater and more obvious phenomenon, some *other* man, *other* men."[10]

Nietzsche's formulation of bad conscience is echoed to a remarkable extent in Freud's description of the activity of the superego. Compare, for instance, this passage from *Civilization and Its Discontents*:

> What means does civilization employ in order to inhibit the aggressiveness which opposes it, to make it harmless, to get rid of it, perhaps?
> . . . What happens to him to render his desire for aggression innocuous? Something very remarkable, which we should never have guessed and which is nevertheless quite obvious. His aggressiveness is introjected, internalized; it is, in point of fact, sent back to where it came from—that is, it is directed towards his own ego. There it is taken over by a portion of the ego, which sets itself over against the rest of the ego as super-ego, and which now, in the form of "conscience," is ready to put into action against the ego the same harsh aggressiveness that the ego would have liked to satisfy upon other, extraneous individuals.[11]

Freud and Nietzsche both envisage a current of aggression that is turned back upon the aggressor itself. And both recognize such a turning-inward upon the self as enabling the interior life of the "soul," from which arise the fruits of art, literature, music, and so on. Nietzsche even uses the same word to describe such products: "sublimation." "This uncanny, dreadfully joyous labor of a soul voluntarily at odds with itself that makes itself suffer out of joy in making suffer—eventually this entire active 'bad conscience'—you will have guessed it—as the womb of all ideal and imaginative phenomena, also brought to light an abundance of strange new beauty and affirmation, and perhaps beauty itself."[12]

Back now to our problem about the dynamics of Freudian infantile wish fulfillment and superego self-punishment. The underlying reason why they don't conflict is that both mitigate helplessness. Like the two possible deployments of Nietzsche's will to power, both are modes of securing control: the one against outward threats, the other over inward ones. The wish fulfillments of *The Future of an Illusion* defend against external dangers: the destructive forces of nature and the ultimate inescapability of death. The self-denial and asceticism enforced by the superego are aimed at dangers from within, threats posed to self-control by one's own desires and appetites.

If Freud's theories here run parallel to those of Nietzsche, there remains a crucial point on which Freud marks an important advance.

What Freud enables us to see better than Nietzsche is the way the two very different dynamics of the religious sensibility are not only different forms of the same underlying need for control but may readily combine and reinforce one another, as if the sugar of wishful illusion blends happily with the salt of superegoic self-punishment to produce a supremely satisfying dish. It is with respect to this point that we come upon the third prong of Freud's critical analysis of religion: the function of the symptom as a compromise formation.

Worshipful Obsession, Obsessional Worship

However compelling, the first two strands of Freud's critique of religion—the wish-fulfilling and the superegoic—also have an obvious limitation in their focus on gods. How, then, to account for nontheistic systems of religious practice like Buddhism or Taoism? Must we conclude that they are not really religions at all?

Freud's first foray into a psychoanalytic interpretation of the religious, his 1907 essay "Obsessive Actions and Religious Practices" offers a far-reaching argument that is more widely applicable to the range of religious life. It is also more closely based on clinical observations and more explicitly theorizes an intrinsically complex dynamic at the heart of the religious phenomenon. That dynamic is the essentially two-sided function of the symptom, which is at once *repressive* and *expressive* of some impulse. A prime value of that interpretation is its power to explain the stubborn attachment of worshippers to their religious practice. Operating like a neurotic symptom, the real miracle of the religious posture is the way that it can mix renunciation with gratification, salt with sugar. It is worth noting that this more elemental and more broadly applicable argument is Freud's *earliest* attempt at comprehending the religious. In the light of a Lacanian perspective, it can also be interpreted to be the most *profound.*

Freud's point of departure is the baseline resemblance of religious ritual to the quasi-ceremonial fastidiousness of obsessive behavior. "We shall not expect to find a sharp distinction between 'ceremonials' and 'obsessive actions,'" he remarks. "As a rule obsessive actions have grown out of ceremonials."[13] In effect, obsessional neurosis is "a private religion."[14] Both cases, neurosis and religion, display a conspicuous attention to detail in which objects are handled with extreme care and actions adhere to a precise order and execution. Failure to re-create the prescribed form of the ritual triggers anxiety. Freud then moves quickly to identify the psychical mechanism that underlies the outward likeness. Both obsessive neurosis and religion are centrally concerned with renouncing gratification of the two most elemental drives, aggressive and sexual.

At this point Freud makes a crucial move, specifying exactly how the agency of repression operates in the obsessive symptom. The content of the symptom is typically arrived at by displacement, as when a newly married wife compulsively fusses over a gravy stain on the tablecloth when the original occasion for anxiety arose in the sexual sphere—a blood stain on the honeymoon sheets. The result of the displacement is to allow the symptomatic object or action to be at the same time *like and unlike the original*.[15] The symptom in some way resembles what it symbolizes and yet remains in some respect different from it. By consequence, the repetition of the symptom serves to repress the drive, but simultaneously functions at least partly to gratify it. The stubborn attachment to obsessional behavior owes to this double function. The symptom serves two masters: the necessity for repression *and* gratification. It is this double function that Freud calls a "compromise formation." He compares it to a tourist in Egypt being helped to the top of the pyramids, simultaneously pulled from above and pushed from below. Obsessive symptoms thus "fulfill the condition of being a compromise between the warring forces of the mind. They thus always reproduce something of the pleasure which they are designed to prevent; they serve the repressed instinct no less than the agencies which are repressing it."[16]

The central symptom of Freud's most famous case of obsession, the case of the Rat Man, illustrates the dynamic. The obsessional idea derived from a story told by a fellow soldier about an Oriental torture in which a cage of starving rats is affixed to the naked buttocks of the victim, allowing the rats to gnaw their way into the anus. The Rat Man became consumed with a recurring dread that such horrifying treatment might be applied to the two most important figures in his life: his father and his fiancée. In the frightful shudder that accompanied each of the patient's compulsive reimaginings, Freud recognized a struggle to defend against a sexually charged desire combined unmistakably with a partial satisfaction of that very desire.

It is not difficult to see how key religious phenomena can be interpreted in parallel fashion. In the opening of *The Future of an Illusion*, Freud cites three elemental drives with which religion (in this case, Christianity) crucially concerns itself: cannibalism, incest, and lust for killing.[17] The first instance is perhaps the most obvious inasmuch as the Christian Eucharist can be taken to stage a ritual act of cannibalism. The ritual simultaneously enfolds the participants in a community of love while symbolically inviting them to feast on human flesh and blood. With respect to incest the Christian Church similarly renounces sexual relations within the family, in fact renounces all sexual relations outside of marriage, yet implicitly imagines universal incest to the extent that all members of the church are understood to be a single family of brothers and sisters. As regards lust for killing, Christianity would seem to be unequivocal in its condemnation of violence. And yet Christian spiritual life not infrequently centers upon the goriest details of crucifixion. Such contemplation is particularly conspicuous among some mystics—Julian of Norwich is a well-known example—in which the worshipper is elevated to a sublime experience of loving union and forgiveness precisely by means of the fixing the attention upon the spectacle of a naked, bleeding body, pierced in the entrails by a spear and nailed hand and foot to a wooden cross.[18]

The symptomatic compromise that we glimpse here in mainstream religious rituals and practices, at once repressive and gratifying of primitive drives, appears more spectacularly in the behavior of religious extremists. One thinks, for example, of the treatment of witches and heretics by the functionaries of the Inquisition. Under the careful supervision of officers of the church who compiled precise, day-by-day, hour-by-hour records of the agonies inflicted by the inquisitors, the victims, very frequently women, would be tortured for long periods by methods whose cruelty was exceeded only by their perverse imaginativeness. The initial treatment of such victims, by far less brutalizing than what followed, was itself telling from a psychoanalytic point of view. In what was ostensibly an attempt to discern marks on the body left by the Devil, all hair would be burned off the victims' bodies, rendering them ultra-naked. The almost incomprehensibly sadistic torments that ensued—all manner of burnings, piercings, joint dislocations, crushing of fingers and thumbs, and so on—were justified as temporary harms to the body in the service of saving the immortal soul.

Freud also relies on the bifold character of symptomatic enjoyment to sketch a theory of the historical evolution of religions. The crucial idea is that of balancing "the warring forces of the mind." The tendency toward displacement favors repression, but when taken too far it starves the symptom of its enjoyable proximity to the drive. The solution is a measured restoration of that proximity. Freud therefore claims that "the petty ceremonials of religious practice gradually become the essential thing and push aside the underlying thoughts. That is why religions are subject to reforms which work retroactively and aim at a re-establishment of the original balance of values."[19] When an overabstracted ritual has become bloodless and moribund, it can be revitalized by ramping up the sensuous dimension of the experience. The history of baptism provides a suggestive example. When the practice first emerged early in the Christian era, baptism was performed by pouring or sprinkling water over the recipient. During the early modern period, however, some sects adopted total immersion, thus inaugurating the familiar riverbank scenes of penitent initiates in white robes being dunked full-length into the water. The history of Pentecostalism in Appalachia offers another example. Freud would not have found it surprising that these ultraconservative sects, the very ones who barred tobacco and alcohol, insisted on ankle-length skirts for women and long-sleeve shirts for men, and strenuously prohibited all cosmetics, also goosed up the excitement of the worship experience by introducing the handling of poisonous snakes into the liturgy.

Lacanian Heresy

In a simple but elegant pun, the title of Lacan's twenty-second seminar, "R.S.I."—which pronounced in French sounds like "heresy"—suggests both a measured departure from Freudian orthodoxy and, more subtly but palpably, the promise of a new angle of interpretation on the problem of religion. The three letters stand for the three fundamental registers—Real, Symbolic, and Imaginary—with which Lacan rewrites the essentials of psychoanalytic theory. We can roughly introduce them by returning briefly to the case of the Rat Man.

The fantasy of bodily violation presented by the rat torture recalls the dynamics of the imaginary. What is at stake for Lacan is not imaginary in the sense of being a mere illusion or fanciful construction. His interest lies rather in the role played by the body image in laying down the most primordial contour of psychic identity. During the period of late infancy that Lacan calls the "mirror stage," the unifying gestalt of the body image provides the primitive model for the coherence of one's sense of self.[20] His point of departure is the prematurity of human birth, what embryologists call "fetalization." The oversize cranium of the human being requires that the infant be born some months prior to its full maturation. Without such an early exit, the fetal head would not pass through the pelvic cradle of the mother. Over the course of millennia, untold numbers of mothers and infants have died for this reason, as many still do where cesarean delivery is unavailable.

Thanks to its prematurity of birth, the human being arrives in the world long before the instinctual mechanisms that might guide its movements are consolidated. It is the role of the imaginary to provide a compensatory crutch. Where instinctual control of movement is absent, the perceptual automatisms that enable the discrimination of gestalt unities step in to fill the deficit. The infant's motor incoordination leans upon imitating the body image of the other. The imago thereby becomes the primitive template for what Freud called "ego."

To this quick sketch of the positive, enabling role of the body image we have to add its downside. Reliance on an external image has the effect of alienating the human subject from itself. On this point Lacan rests a central postulate of his entire outlook: the opposition between the *ego* as the seat of one's conscious sense of self and the *subject* of unconscious desire, an opposition that Lacan expresses in the contrast between the *moi* and the *je*, the "me" and the "I." However indispensable at the outset, the imaginary organization of the psyche must eventually be overcome. Without the pacifying benefit of sublimation, the tension of the internal split between the controlling ego and the subject of desire generally takes one of two forms. Either it is projected outward as aggression toward the other or it is turned inward upon the subject itself in the form of what Freud called the "primordial masochism" of the death drive. Either way, the resulting fantasies imagine a *corps morcelé*—the body torn to pieces.[21]

These dynamics are readily observable in the Rat Man's "great obsessive fear."[22] The horrifying fantasy of rats chewing their way into the victim's anus is first of all a scenario of bodily violation that implies a rupture of the ego. On this side of the obsessive idea, it is the Rat Man himself who is gnawed open, his own sense of identity breached under the pressure of a repressed idea. But then again, he is obsessed with the fear that the torture will be applied to someone else, and not just random others: his father and his fiancée. Here we arrive at the aggressive dimension, the energy of a violent declaration of independence from the two most important people in his life. Lacan's theory of the mirror stage enables us to see how both aspects—self-lacerating and aggressive—are crucially involved. They are structurally inseparable.

If identification and the stability of the ego are the primary functions of the imaginary, the unconscious desire of the subject emerges in pulsations of the "symbolic," Lacan's catchall for the resources and functions of language. Drawing on the legacy of structuralist linguistics, especially on the work of Ferdinand de Saussure and Roman Jakobson, Lacan launches a radical reinterpretation of Freud's essential discovery under the rallying cry that "the unconscious is structured like a language." Rejecting the naive conception of words as mere tags for things in a one-to-one correspondence, the structuralist breakthrough conceived of the meaning of words as constituted less by their relation to things than by their relation to other words. Language functions by virtue of being an interconnected network. This interconnectedness means that every entry into language, every speaking of a particular word, tacitly implicates a host of other words. Language is a kind of spider's web in which tugging at one side of the web produces vibrations across the whole lattice. Shifting to a musical metaphor, Lacan claims that "it suffices to listen to poetry, which Saussure was certainly in the habit of doing, for a polyphony to be heard and for it to become clear that all discourse is aligned along the several staves of a musical score. Indeed, there is no signifying chain that does not sustain—as if attached to the punctuation of each of its units—all attested contexts that are, so to speak 'vertically' linked to that point."[23]

Lacan deploys this conception of the unavoidable overrichness of linguistic signification to reinterpret Freud's many analyses of wordplay in dreams, slips of the tongue, bungled actions, and symptomatic complexes. The basic dynamics are spectacularly displayed in the case of the Rat Man. Once we attend to the signifiers involved, a complex thicket of connections emerges that illuminates the underlying conflicts that animate the obsessive idea. That idea crystallizes around the morpheme "Rat," which functions like a kind of switch point in a constellation of emotionally loaded issues: the starving, gnawing rodents (*Ratten*), but also monetary debts (*Raten*), a gambler (*Spielratte*), and marriage (*Heiraten*). The key thing Lacan adds to Freud's own elaborate analyses (and what he adds to the linguistic theory of Saussure as well) is a more general theory of the signifier centered on its unconscious dimension. The signifier always passes into the speech stream an indeterminate excess. Lacan refers to this margin of excess as a "slippage of the signified beneath the signifier."[24] The consequence is that we always say more than we intend. It is in the space of the unsaid and unintended that unconscious effects unfold.

The knot of signifiers compacted in the rat fantasy forms the skeleton of what Freud called the "complexive sensitiveness" of the neurosis.[25] The issues of money and gambling were related to the patient's father. During his own hitch in the army, the father had been temporarily entrusted with the regimental funds but had carelessly gambled them away. He was then forced to borrow money from a friend to cover his loss, a debt he never repaid. In the patient's mind, the father was a *Spielratte*, literally a "game-rat" burdened with debts (*Raten*). The money with which he played, along with the money he borrowed to make up his loss, were morally tainted and thus appropriately associated with rats. "So many florins, so many rats," the patient found himself saying.[26] This background of doubt about the father's integrity became specially activated when the patient was himself in the army and suffered a loss of his own. A major onset of symptoms immediately followed upon his losing his pince-nez while on maneuvers. Later, struggling with the question of marrying the girl with whom he had fallen in love, the symptoms were only exacerbated. The taint of the father's debt (*Raten*) then contaminated the son's prospects of marriage (*Heirat*).

What, then, of the third of Lacan's categories, that of the "real"? The first and cardinal point is that the Lacanian real has nothing whatever to do with what we ordinarily refer to as "reality." On the contrary, the "real" as Lacan thinks of it is the impact of something unthinkable. Neither imaginable nor nameable, the real fundamentally escapes representation. As something unassimilable for the ego, the real is closely associated with the experience of trauma. And yet this impossible, intractable impact of something unknowable and uncanny animates the pulse of unconscious desire. The real is thus not merely an encounter with something incomprehensible in the outside world, but an engagement with what is incomprehensible in oneself.

The unthinkable kernel of the real lies somehow at the heart of the unconscious. The closest parallel in Freud's theory is to the disruptive perturbations of the death drive that remain "beyond the pleasure principle." Its subjective impact Lacan calls *jouissance*, rather tepidly translated by the English term "enjoyment." The French word derives from the verb *jouir*, which is, among other things, slang for the experience of orgasm, also referred to as *la petite mort*, "the little death." The term already alerts us to the role of the other person in unconscious enjoyment. The French word *jouissance* calls up questions of ownership or possession, particularly relevant to the right of using what belongs to somebody else, as when one lays claim to enjoying, or using, the house of another.

What is at issue in *jouissance* concerns violations of what is "proper." It may therefore be closer to pain than to pleasure but nevertheless delivers an obscure satisfaction. Here, too, the Rat Man provides us with a suggestive example. As the patient described the dreadful rat torture, he appeared animated by a weird mix of horror and fascinated gratification. "While he was telling his story," Freud remarked, "his face took on a very strange, composite expression. I could only interpret it as one of *horror at pleasure of his own of which he himself was unaware.*"[27]

Far from being locatable within the coordinates of ordinary reality, the Lacanian real is precisely what the predictable fabric of everyday reality functions to keep at a distance. We depend on "reality" to spare us from the real. The real escapes our every attempt at signification, something that occurs at the limit of the law, at the point where the symbolic function reveals itself to be incomplete, interrupted, or inconsistent. The real is a completely novel and unexpected twist that changes everything.

The upsurge of the real cannot be predicted, nor can its effects be assayed in advance. It is partly for this reason that Lacan refers to the real as not only unthinkable but "impossible."

Rethinking Religion

Given this primer of Lacanian concepts, what can we now say about Lacan's theory of religion? Let us begin by putting the bad news up front—he doesn't offer one, at least not explicitly. Despite the myriad references he makes to theologians and mystics, to religious beliefs and practices through history and around the globe, Lacan prescinds from venturing an overarching theory. Nor does he appear to put forward any unequivocal judgment.

The contrast with Freud's view is striking. Though Freud adopts a handful of interpretive angles, he gives every indication of having circumscribed the subject matter. His damning assessment appears to pronounce a final verdict. One rarely if ever gets the same sense from Lacan. On the contrary, reading Lacan, one repeatedly gathers the impression that he regards the problem of the sacred not only as particularly profound and complex but as somehow consubstantial with the distinctiveness, even the very definition, of the human being.

It is the thesis of this book that, despite his own reticence to put forward a comprehensive account of the religious, Lacan's rethinking of the Freudian unconscious supplies resources that are uniquely suited to radically interpreting the essential posture of worship. Relying on those resources, it is possible to sketch the broad outlines of an ambitious and far-reaching answer to the fundamental question: What *is* religion? In the remaining two chapters of part 1, we seek to equip ourselves with a battery of indispensable interpretive tools by clarifying a handful of key points of Lacan's thought. Part 2 draws on the results to unfold analyses of specific religious formations—Greek polytheism, Judaism, and Christianity, followed by briefer considerations of Hinduism, Buddhism, and Islam.

Before launching on that trajectory, let us sketch in rough outline the two most common interpretations of Lacan's relevance for the problem of religion.

The first identifies God with an aspect of the unthinkable real. Divinity is to be situated in a domain utterly beyond human conception, a zone that forever outstrips all capacities to image or name it.[28] Equating God with the real offers some obvious attractions, prime among them the satisfaction of locating the divine in a dimension of radical transcendence.[29] Lacan's claim that "the defining characteristic of the real is that one cannot imagine it" thus recalls the long tradition of "negative" or "apophatic" theology.[30] According to that tradition, we cannot approach the nature of God by any positive means. The best we can do is to locate God by negation, resolutely denying the applicability to the divine of all finite and definite categories. God, as Rudolf Otto put it, is the *mysterium tremendum*.[31]

It is easy to suppose that Lacan simply shares the standpoint of negative theology. He expressly associates his writings with those of the mystics.[32] But to leave the matter there would hardly open up a novel perspective. Why bother to labor through the obscurities of Lacan's discourse if there is so little that is really new to be gotten from it?

Other, more substantive questions pop up when we turn to the second, most commonly adopted angle of approach to Lacan's treatment of religion, which identifies the divine with the symbolic. It is a theme that is audible throughout Lacan's work. In one of his earliest seminars, he proposes that "the Holy Spirit is the entry of the signifier into the world."[33] Almost twenty years later, he roundly declares: "It is indubitable that the symbolic is the basis of what was made into God."[34] A kindred claim appears in a late interview in which Lacan reiterates his fondness for the opening line of the Gospel of John. "I am in favor of John and his 'In the beginning was the Word,'" he says.[35]

Yet the challenge is to make sense of Lacan's appeal to the Word. He is himself acutely aware of the difficulty in conceptualizing it. "'In the beginning was the Word,' I couldn't agree more," he says, "but, before the beginning, where was it? That's what is truly impenetrable."[36] One of our principal tasks in what follows will be to delve more deeply into the nature of the signifier as Lacan conceives it. We will need to clarify what he meant by claiming to "have defined the signifier as no one else has dared."[37]

The problem of the signifier is closely linked with another crucial concept of Lacanian theory—that of the symbolic *grand Autre*, or "big Other." It is hard not to imagine that Lacan had the concept of God at least partly in mind when he coined the phrase. The "big Other" is the nameless and faceless regulator who oversees the written and unwritten rules that direct our lives. Of course, part of what is at stake are the properly linguistic rules governing grammar, syntax, and semantics. But it is much more than that. The big Other also monitors our polite behavior, inspects our adherence to fashion, defines for us what is funny (sometimes actually laughing for us in the laugh track of TV sitcoms), insists on our silent decorum at one moment and calls for our full-throated patriotic fervor at another. The power of this symbolic big Other resides in part precisely in the fact that it exists everywhere and nowhere, that it is both "all and none."[38]

In this supposition of something subject-like in the symbolic code we rightly discern a shadow of the Freudian primal father who haunts monotheism. The big Other issues from the child's entry into language by means of what Lacan calls the "paternal metaphor" because it crucially involves a third party who triangulates the child's relation to the mother. It is this function that underlies the promotion of master signifiers, the legitimacy of which are warranted by the big Other in the role of *le sujet supposé savoir*, the "subject supposed to know." And what is God but the ultimate form of such supposition? If we mortals fail to grasp the meaning of our lives, the same is not true of the divine agency whose plan for Creation is assumed to be complete in every detail. "The subject supposed to know," says Lacan, "is God, full stop, nothing else."[39]

God in the real or in the symbolic. Must we make a choice? And what, more precisely, do each of these approaches amount to?

In the rest of part 1, I lay the groundwork for answering the question of the religious from a Lacanian perspective—a perspective that involves both the real and the symbolic—by carefully analyzing Lacan's conception of our relations with the *fellow human being*. The key lies in posing what might initially sound like a flat-footed, even naive question: what relation obtains between Lacan's notion of the symbolic *big Other* and the "little other," the actually existing individual who stands before me? Lacan remarks that "the connection between the subject and the little other and the connection between the subject and the big Other don't live separate lives."[40] But what does he mean? What precisely do those connections consist of?

2

The Abyss of the Other

Das Ding has to be posited as exterior, as the prehistoric Other that is impossible to forget—the Other whose primacy of position Freud affirms in the form of something *entfremdet,* something strange to me.
   —Jacques Lacan

The core focus of my argument in this book, a focus not always given the attention it deserves by commentators, concerns the precise intersection between what Lacan called the "big Other" and the "little other." The terms are intended to name, on the one side, the regularized structures that enable symbolic exchange and, on the other, the fellow human being, the unique individual with whom we speak.

We've already introduced Lacan's notion of the big Other and sketched in crude outline some of its relevance to the problem of religion. But we here encounter the problem of the little other for the first time. The immediate question, quite naturally, is why there is a *problem* at all. For common sense, nothing could be more obvious, more simply given, and more immediately comprehensible than our relations with such little others. If we have a problem with the little others—simply put, *other people*—it mostly consists of the ways we find them to be tediously overpredictable, mildly annoying, or downright repulsive. Or else we are troubled by the pesky challenge of getting them to do what we want. In fact, one might readily think that Lacan's very choice of the term "*little* other" already hints at a slightly dismissive, disparaging tone, a prejudgment about the relative insignificance and inconsequentiality of the other people that surround me. Nothing could be further from the case.

In the Shadow of the Thing

To adopt Lacan's view of the fellow human being, we have to recognize that our routine, everyday relations with others are not only deceptively superficial but function to conceal an abyssal confrontation with something unknown and unnerving. The little other is the locus of a disturbing mystery. Lacan's thesis is that the foundation of subjectivity is established in a complicated reaction to a quasi-traumatic encounter with the little other. Lacan theorizes it in his concept of *das Ding*—"the Thing."

Lacan introduces *das Ding* in his 1959–60 seminar, *The Ethics of Psychoanalysis*—and he unmistakably signals its central importance. The Thing is nothing less than the primordial pivot around which the effects of the unconscious revolve.[1] "*Das Ding,*" he says, "is a primordial function which is located at the level of the initial establishment of the gravitation of the unconscious *Vorstellungen.*"[2] Precisely because the Thing occupies the most obscure core of the unconscious, it deserves to be identified as the most elemental motive *cause* of human behavior. Lacan resorts to a salad of Latin and Greek to describe it: "At the heart of man's destiny is the *Ding* . . . the *causa pathomenon,* the cause of the most fundamental human passion."[3] *Das Ding* names the inaccessible yet potent engine of desire. As such, it is the constitutive core of subjectivity itself.

Lacan insists that we are dealing here with an absolutely central concept of far-reaching significance. What, then, does he mean by it? The immediate temptation is to associate the Lacanian "Thing" with Kant's famous *Ding-an-sich*—the Thing-in-itself—which names the unthinkable reality of entities, not as they appear to our organs of perception, ordered by our categories of understanding, but as they truly are in and of themselves. Kant's noumenal kernel of things would seem to align well with Lacan's notion of the unthinkable real. The parallel with Kant's philosophy even extends to the notion of the sublime. Sublimation is achieved, Lacan says, when "the object is elevated to the dignity of the Thing."[4]

Yet such a Kantian posing of the Lacanian Thing needs to be resisted at least long enough to recognize that the crucial dimension of *das Ding* concerns not objects but *other people*. The original unthinkable object is the fellow human being. This conclusion is obvious when we return to the text from which Lacan takes his clue, a brief but profoundly suggestive flight of theorizing in Freud's early unpublished essay *Project for a Scientific Psychology*. Freud notes how the child divides the figure of the *Nebenmensch*, the "neighbor" or fellow human being, between what the child can recognize on the basis of similarities to its own body—precisely the sort of mirror recognition that Lacan associates with the imaginary—

and a locus of something that is "new and non-comparable," a zone of something unknown. This unrepresentable excess Freud calls *das Ding*. It is this division of the human other—a division that reserves at the heart of the familiar a locus for something excessive and as yet unknown—that will serve as the template for all of the child's future attempts to interrogate the nature of objects. "It is in relation to the fellow human-being," says Freud, "that a human-being learns to cognize."[5] The key point is not merely that there remains an inaccessible, noumenal core of all objects but that the original schema locating such an unknown dimension is modeled on what is unknown in the human Other. To mark the distinctive importance of this conception of the Other, I spell it here with a capital "O."[6]

In taking up Freud's discussion of *das Ding*, Lacan begins by making explicit what Freud clearly implied but never directly stated. The experience of the *Nebenmensch* is first of all the experience of the maternal Other. Freud makes the point with an oddly oblique reference, saying only that "an object like this was simultaneously the [subject's] first satisfying object and further his first hostile object, as well as his sole helping power."[7] Lacan makes it unambiguous: what we are talking about is the relation with one's own mother.

Three years after first introducing it, Lacan develops a new and crucially important dimension of his idea. In the 1962–63 seminar *Anxiety* he proposes that the enigmatic locus of something uncognized in the mother is the root source of anxiety. "Not only is [anxiety] not without object," he says, "but it very likely designates the most, as it were, profound object, the ultimate object, the Thing."[8] The challenge of the neighbor-Thing consists not simply in the discovery of an inaccessible kernel at the heart of the Other but in the way it raises the unsettling question of what object I am for that unknown desire. "Anxiety," says Lacan, "resides in the subject's fundamental relationship . . . with the desire of the Other."[9] "Anxiety is bound to the fact that I don't know which object *a* I am for the desire of the Other."[10] The question presses with particular force in the drama of toilet training, when the demand of the maternal caretaker for the regulation of the infant's bowels reenergizes anxiety about the unanswered question of what the (m)Other wants. The Lacanian thesis thus goes beyond merely locating the source of anxiety in the fellow human being. It asserts, contrary to the sweetest myth about childhood, that the hidden source of the deepest and most uncanny anxiety is related to the mother herself. "What provokes anxiety . . . is not, contrary to what is said, the rhythm of the mother's alternating presence and absence. The proof of this is that the infant revels in repeating this game of presence and absence. . . . The most anguishing thing for the infant is precisely . . . when the mother is on his back all the while, and especially when she's wiping his backside."[11]

We might note in passing how this Lacanian understanding of the dynamics of the mother-child relation at least partly resembles the explanation offered by Simone de Beauvoir. At a key point of her argument in *The Second Sex*, de Beauvoir reasserts the value of the Freudian Oedipus complex (albeit with crucial changes) for understanding the deep roots of ambivalence toward the feminine.[12] The core of the Oedipus complex is not, as Freud thought, that the child must be separated from the mother by a threat of castration, but rather that the child is motivated to bring about its own separation, seeking to achieve an autonomy that can be won only by a certain rejection of the maternal embrace. As de Beauvoir lays out the argument: "The attachment of the infant to the mother's breast is at first an attachment to Life in its immanent form, in its generality and its immanence; the rejection by weaning is the beginning of the rejection by abandonment, to which the individual is condemned once he emerges as a separate being from the Whole. It is from that point, and as he becomes more individualized and separate, that the term *sexual* can be applied to the inclination he retains for the maternal flesh henceforth detached from his."[13] De Beauvoir here poses separation from the mother as initiated by the child. Lacan echoes this key point. He could well be paraphrasing de Beauvoir when he insists that "it's not true that the child is weaned. He weans himself. He detaches himself from the breast."[14]

But the parallel here between Lacan and de Beauvoir is limited. Their point of convergence only makes it more essential to clarify Lacan's distance from de Beauvoir, who departs from Freud merely in claiming that the child's desire for the mother is disturbed not by a threat of paternal castration but rather by the child's own rejection. For Lacan, the problem isn't the desire of the child at all, but rather that of the mother, inasmuch as her desire is encountered as a vaguely ominous unknown. It is the inaccessible core of the mother's desire that Lacan names *das Ding*. "*Das Ding* is the element that is initially isolated by the subject in his experience of the *Nebenmensch* as being by its very nature alien, *Fremde*. . . . *Das Ding* has to be posited as exterior, as the prehistoric Other that is impossible to forget—the Other whose primacy of position Freud affirms in the form of something *entfremdet*, something strange to me."[15] It is in the light of this perspective that we can make sense of Lacan's unsettling comparison of the mother to the specter of a giant praying mantis.[16] Elsewhere, he invokes a similar metaphor, likening the mother to a crocodile and the phallic signifier to a stick with which to keep its jaws from snapping shut.[17]

My Mother, the Monster

Let us pause for a moment to absorb the shock of these claims. We here witness Lacan parting company with Freud on the primary pivot of his psychoanalytic theory—the Oedipus complex. For Lacan, the psychic challenge is not, as Freud thought, the pain of having to give up desire for the mother in the face of a paternal threat of castration. On the contrary, the primal challenge for the child is posed by the mother's own desire, insofar as it remains an unknown. The figure of the mother rears up as a fearful and monstrous specter, the unsettling abyss of a gigantic question mark. If there is a link to the myth of Oedipus in this Lacanian perspective it resides less in the familiar drama of murdering the father and marrying the mother than with Oedipus as the man who confronts a potentially fatal riddle. Lacan casts the mother in the role of the dreadful and enigmatic Sphinx.[18]

If Lacan here recasts the very foundations of Freud's theory, he also upends our deeply ingrained sense of the mother's embrace as the very definition of security and reassurance. By locating the primal origin of anxiety in the mother herself, Lacan shatters our fondest idyll of childhood, the very core of most people's deepest nostalgia. Is there anything closer to the pure gold of perfect contentment, anything more *calming* of anxiety, than the tender caress of mother's love? Not only does Lacan stake a violently counterintuitive claim, one that makes the Freudian postulates of castration anxiety and penis envy seem modest by comparison, but he also positions it as a cornerstone of his theoretical architecture. Is this theory really plausible?

Lacan's theory of the monstrous mother isn't just implausible. It is arguably the most implausible theory one could possibly imagine. It's the sort of travesty of common sense that prompts ordinary folks, unaccustomed to the high-flown cogitations of academics, to roll their eyes and whistle in disbelief.

Which is already one good reason why we should not dismiss it out of hand. One of Freud's greatest and most enduring legacies is his insistence on raising suspicion precisely about things that seem most completely beyond suspicion. Beginning with his extraordinary analysis of his own childhood recollections in his early essay "Screen Memories," Freud's signature gesture is to doubt precisely where certainty seems unassailable. Or, as he says in his essay "Negation": when the patient says "that figure in the dream, it's *not* my mother," you can be sure that it's his mother.[19] In fact, Freud had already cast his suspicious eye on the golden glow of mother love, theorizing that the developing child's relation to the mother undergoes a primordial division between two currents of libido, the "affectionate" and the fully "sensuous."[20] Psychologically speaking, the tender and the tawdry are worlds apart, and the masculine disposition toward the feminine is pervasively affected by the split between them. That split underlies the conspicuous tendency of traditional morality to divide the fair sex between "proper" and "loose" women, the division most dramatically reflected in the opposition between *mamma* and *putana*, Madonna and Whore. The rosy idealization of maternal love clearly conceals very powerfully ambivalent feelings.

The Freudian gesture of inserting doubt in the citadel of certainty is always and by its very nature a matter of weaving far-reaching conclusions from fragmentary and tenuous tissues of evidence. If Lacan is right that the maternal Thing forms the very nucleus of the unconscious, we can be sure that there is no simple proof of it. Here, the astronomical black hole is a helpful metaphor for the unconscious. So superdense as to exert a gravitational pull that even prevents light from escaping, the black hole is only detectable insofar as it disturbs the movements of other objects in its vicinity. If the dimension of the Thing in the mother somehow anchors the gravitation of the unconscious, it will be deducible only on the basis of indirect evidence.

So, is there any? One point of support is the account of the Other given by Jean-Paul Sartre. His central point is to distinguish the human Other as qualitatively different from all other objects. Sartre invites us to imagine strolling through a park or a wooded glade. My sphere of attention is distributed globally across the field of objects that surround me— expanses of grass punctuated by trees and rocks, birdsong occasionally piercing the silence. But suddenly, the rustle of leaves behind me announces the presence of another person. The upsurge of this new piece of sensory information immediately and radically reorders the entire sphere of my experience. All other objects instantly recede into the background, pushed aside by the awareness of a fellow human being. All possible vectors of my attention are instantaneously bent around the vortex of this new appearance. I am no longer the organizing center of my world but am displaced by another, irresistible locus of force that powerfully revalences the field of awareness. As Sartre puts it, "The appearance of the Other in the world corresponds therefore to a fixed sliding of the whole universe, to a decentralization of the world which undermines the centralization which I am simultaneously effecting."[21] The fellow human being exerts a uniquely destabilizing influence on the entire horizon of experience. The arrival of another person constitutes "the appearance among the objects of my universe of an element of disintegration in that universe."[22]

Sartre also makes the link to the upsurge of anxiety. The unexpected eruption of the other immediately rebounds on oneself, raising unmanageable questions about one's own being. "What I immediately apprehend when I hear the branches crackling behind me is not that *there is someone there*; it is that I am vulnerable, that I have a body which can be hurt, that I occupy a place and that I can not in any case escape from the space in which I am without defense—in short, that I *am seen.*"[23]

A further suggestive confirmation of Lacan's thesis about the anxiety-arousing power of the neighbor-Thing, a point that Sartre would no doubt have appreciated had he lived long enough to see it, might be taken from the relationship we have with androids. We all know that primitive robots that vaguely mimic human behavior can produce in us a charming effect. They may even elicit affection. Perhaps the world's all-time favorite is *Star Wars*' R2D2, the round-headed, beep-and-whistle, white tin can on wheels. But equally well known among robotics engineers is the phenomenon they call the "uncanny valley." At some point along the trajectory of greater and greater likeness to human appearance and behavior, robots cross a threshold and become strangely disturbing. No longer a cute machine, such eerily humanoid robots become zombie-like creatures that horrify us. In seeking an explanation, we might readily suppose that we become upset when a mere machine presumes to replace the human being, as if the more fully human robot embodies a sort of cosmic insult to our superiority. But what if the explanation is to be found not in the way a machine might encroach on uniquely human prerogatives but rather because the nearly human machine reminds us of the uncanny and disturbing dimension of the human itself, a dimension that in our everyday encounters with other people in the social world we are accustomed to controlling? What if the "uncanny valley" opens up when the robot begins to elicit a sense of the Thing in the Other, the dimension of the Other's intentions that remains unknown to us? What if robots become horrifying when they appear *too human*?

Alone Together

The difference between Lacan and Sartre should not be missed. For Sartre, the locus of pure negation resides in consciousness itself, the ground of subjectivity that Sartre calls *le pour-soi*, the for-itself. Sartrean anxiety is the dizzying experience of oneself as a void, the empty nothingness that enables freedom precisely because it is completely indeterminate. For Lacan, by contrast, the original upsurge of the unthinkable void is discovered in the Other and only in a second movement folds back upon the subject itself. Nevertheless, for both Sartre and Lacan, the fellow human being remains an absolutely unique object by virtue of its possession of consciousness and is, for that reason, an unparalleled source of anxiety. And, as Sartre makes clear, that special status is announced with particular intensity by the Other's *look*, the way I am *seen* by the Other.

The underlying point is already on display whenever we meet the eyes of another person. There is virtually no human culture in which this moment is not surrounded by unwritten yet powerful prohibitions. Indeed, it would not be too much to say that unguarded eye contact is a kind of uncodified but absolutely elementary human taboo. In most situations, meeting the gaze of the Other is not to be maintained for more than a second or two. If such a meeting lingers more than that, it inevitably raises unsettling questions about the Other's intentions. Otherwise said, the meeting of eyes raises the specter of *das Ding*.

Against the background of this Lacanian interpretation, a famous passage from Hegel's Jena manuscripts assumes renewed and poignant meaning, the passage in which Hegel compares the human Other to an inky Night of fearful apparitions. The point would seem very precisely to endorse the implication of Lacan's theory of the neighbor-Thing. The eyes of the fellow human being, Hegel argues, present us with a terrifying abyss.

> The human being is this Night, this empty nothing which contains everything in its simplicity—a wealth of infinitely many representations, images, none of which occur to it directly, and none of which are not present. This [is] the Night, the interior of [human] nature, existing here—pure Self—[and] in phantasmagoric representations it is night everywhere: here a bloody head suddenly shoots up and there another white shape, only to disappear as suddenly. We see this Night when we look a human being in the eye, looking into a Night which turns terrifying.[24]

If any sustained meeting of eyes immediately raises special challenges, the social space inhabited by human beings is also conditioned by a constant, if furtive, scanning of the eyes of others. We navigate the social space by remaining fleetingly but pointedly attentive to the direction of Others' gazes. Our inclination to check the direction of the Other's glance is aided by an anatomical anomaly. The whiteness of the optical sclera, the way in which the dark pupil of the eye floats in a little pool of contrasting white, appears to be unique to the human being. Even among our fellow primates, the tissue surrounding the pupil is dark or, if it is white, remains hidden behind the surrounding socket of tissue. The reason for the white sclera in human beings would appear to support the thesis that the question of the Other's intentions is perhaps the most primitive and powerful dimension of human sociality. There can be little doubt that the white framing of the pupils in human eyes allows the direction of the gaze to be read with impressive exactitude, even at considerable distances. From well across a crowded dance floor, for example, it is possible to see whether a potential partner has met our gaze, and to know precisely how long he or she is willing to sustain it. Any woman walking along a sidewalk can readily tell whether an oncoming man is scanning her body. In fact, she may readily be able to see quite clearly which parts of her body he is most interested in.

"Hold on!" pipes up a critic. "You characterize eye contact as a primal taboo but then immediately contradict yourself by saying that we constantly monitor the eyes of others."

Far from there being a contradiction here, the two phenomena are two sides of the same coin. Both instances centrally involve the disturbingly open question of the Other's intentions. In the first instance, the unguarded meeting of eyes risks the danger of a direct confrontation with our lack of certainty regarding those intentions. In the second instance, that of surreptitiously checking out the direction of the Other's gaze without actually engaging it, we attempt to allay anxiety by ferreting out a possible intention in advance, thereby stabilizing the relation to the Other by having already arrived some provisional reading of what they are up to.

Despite being wrongheaded in suspecting a contradiction, the critic's remark offers a clue to a more satisfying characterization of the mother-Thing. If eye-to-eye contact is our measure, we have to say that we're both unnerved by it *and attracted to it*. The larger implication is absolutely crucial for a fuller grasp of our topic. If the unknown dimension of the Other's desire is the primal source of anxiety, it also exerts a powerful allure. It is not for nothing that Lacan compares the Thing with a locus of gravitation. *Das Ding* is the primal locus of lack that sets desire in motion. "The question of *das Ding*," Lacan says, "is still attached to whatever is open, lacking, or gaping at the center of our desire."[25]

It is not difficult to see the two sides of this ambivalent posture at work in various behaviors. We might note, for example, that it is our disposition toward anxiety in the face of the unknown others that grounds our overwhelming tendency to reduce interactions with them to empty small talk. As everyone knows, mindless banter about the weather, the box scores, the latest gossip, and so on serves to provide a welcome dodge, a means of filling the otherwise awkward silences that might open up in our relation to other people.

The millennial generation has discovered a whole new means of achieving such an escape from anxious confrontation with the Other. As a college professor, I routinely witness the now-familiar phenomenon of three or four students gathered around a dining hall table, each of them huddled solipsistically over their cell phones. It is the slightly bizarre contemporary phenomenon that Sherry Turkle has dubbed "being alone together." Instead of interacting with one another, each member of such clusters is enclosed in a private gadget bubble. Indeed, here the word "avoid" assumes a charmingly meaning-laden signification: that of sidestepping the *void* in the Other. What we most truly "a-void" is the unknown dimension, the true void in the Other that consists of the Other's unknown and potentially anxiety-producing desire.

This way of perceiving the situation, oriented toward avoiding the anxiety of a more direct engagement, is reinforced when we remember that college students are late adolescents—that is, people passing through the period of life in which sensitivity to judgment by others is at its high-water mark. It is no accident that the primary intersubjective gesture offered to users of Facebook, for which the first generation of early adopters overwhelmingly consisted of young people, is the "Like" button. As its designers knew from the start, Facebook is a digital machine that is bound to elicit anxiety among its users about how others perceive them, and for precisely that reason they built in the perfect tool with which—very momentarily—to allay that anxiety.

If the "alone together" gadget distraction of millennials can be viewed as fundamentally defensive, it is also interesting for the way it brings us back to the other, *attractive* side of the ambivalence toward the Thing. The reason is that being online continually restimulates the plugged-in subject with the tantalizing prospect of encountering something new in the digital universe of Others. The user is constantly reseduced by the promise of an elusive but crucial something "out there" that hasn't yet been discovered. The power of this illusion—what makes it so totally different from a voyage of discovery to the local library—is the apparent immediacy of its delivery, the way the screen creates an illusion of an Other's real-time presence. Moreover, the as-yet-undiscovered world continually promised by social media is further tied to the Lacanian Thing by virtue of being focused on the question of Others' *enjoyment.* Nothing more reliably characterizes Facebook posts than depictions of enviable *jouissance.*

Taken together, these considerations allow us to understand in a new way how and why the digitally mediated link to the Other can be

almost irresistibly addictive. It provides a compelling, even fascinating
semblance of the Other-Thing while dulling the hard edge of its anxiety-
producing potential. The online experience delivers a tincture of the
unknown Other while allowing the screen gazer to remain cocooned in
a private space. The abyssal dimension of the Other is reduced to mere
tourism of the Unknown.

Ambivalence and the Falsely False

In tracing the two-sidedness of the relation to *das Ding*, anxious and alluring, we've already used the term "ambivalence." To my knowledge, Lacan
never makes the connection explicitly, but we can readily suspect that we
here locate the primal origin of the phenomenon. The tension between
anxiety and desire goes to the heart of Lacan's notion of *das Ding*. The
deepest source of ambivalence is the unknown we discover in the locus
of the fellow human being.[26]

We can enlarge on this point by means of Lacan's concept of the
falsely false. Lacan allows that, like human beings, "animals . . . efface
their traces and lay false traces." But, he then asks, "do they for all that
make signifiers?"

> There's one thing that animals don't do—they don't lay false traces to
> make us believe that they are false, that is, traces that will be taken for
> false. Laying falsely false traces is a behavior that is, I won't say quintes-
> sentially human, but quintessentially signifying. That's where the limit
> is. That's where a subject presentifies himself. When a trace has been
> made to be taken for a false trace, though in fact they are the traces of
> my true passage, we know that there's a speaking subject.[27]

What sense are we to make of this "falsely false"? One example is Freud's
famous joke about the two Jews who meet in a railway station in Galacia:
"'Where are you going?' asks one. 'To Cracow,' is the answer. 'What a liar
you are!' breaks out the first. 'If you say you're going to Cracow, you want
me to believe you're going to Lemberg. But I know that in fact you're
going to Cracow. So why are you lying to me?'" Freud remarks of this
joke that it attacks "not a person or an institution but the certainty of our
knowledge itself, one of our speculative possessions."[28] We can easily see
how it does so. The joke relies on the background assumption that one's
interlocutor will, as a matter of course, misrepresent himself. To lie about
oneself is the default position. The other interesting and puzzling aspect

of the joke is why the companion who posed the initial question, the one who later claimed to know already that the other was going to Cracow, asked his question in the first place. We have, it seems, a question that is not really a question (as the answer was known already) and an honest answer that is rejected as false (because it was assumed from the start that the other would lie).

Something precisely similar is at work in our most routine everyday intercourse. Take the standard greeting "Hi, how are you?" and its near-obligatory answer, "Fine, and you?" The exchange functions as a welcome social lubricant precisely because everyone knows that the initial question is not to be taken fully seriously, indeed that it is not a genuine question at all. For someone to actually respond to this question, embarking on one or another detailed account of one's state of health or feelings or fortunes, would reveal the respondent to be ignorant of the rules of the game. Equally telling is the fact that the most typical response—Fine!—is understood to be a mere pose, part of the standard coinage of politesse. No one familiar with the unwritten rules of social relations would take this monosyllabic pellet for any true indication of the Other's happiness.

The real purpose of this greeting game is the precise opposite of what it appears to be. Its real purpose, far from really soliciting some information from the Other, is to excuse both parties from having to speak honestly about themselves and, on the basis of that unspoken agreement, to allow them to slip by each other without having to tolerate any more substantive interaction. Translated into explicit terms, the exchange really says: "In sticking to this standard script, we both agree to skip talking about anything very meaningful concerning our own realities because, after all, we both know that we have other things to do, so let's just get on with it."

This familiar phenomenon returns us to Sartre, alerting us again to the differences between his existentialist sense of anxiety and that proposed by Lacan. In Sartre's view, such routinized exchanges of greeting are species of "bad faith," which functions to prevent the for-itself of human consciousness from encountering the vertigo of its own freedom.[29] Anxiety, in this view, is triggered by the profoundly unsettling confrontation with one's own dizzying possibilities. For Lacan, by contrast, the emphasis shifts from the subject to the Other. No doubt, as he says, "in anxiety, the subject is . . . held, concerned, involved in the innermost part of himself."[30] But the indispensable key is to see how this self-concern is circuited by way of what is questionable in the Other. "Anxiety," Lacan insists, is "a specific manifestation at this level of the desire of the Other as such."[31]

Back now to ambivalence. The "falsely false" character of politeness shows the degree to which ambivalence toward the neighbor-Thing gets worked out in remarkably fine grain. If the veneer of polite and mannered behavior allows us to dodge an encounter with the potentially anxiety-provoking dimension of the Thing, it also functions subtly to open up and preserve a space for the unknown in the interlocutor. Precisely by virtue of being obviously a contrivance of mere manners, polite exchanges like "Hi, how are you . . . fine!" leave open a margin in which we can at least vaguely imagine what might happen if the constraints of civility were suspended. We can always wonder, "Yes, but how does he really feel?" or "If she weren't being merely polite, what might she really be inclined to say?" In this way, the fictive character of the polite facade tends to open up, at least provisionally, the very space of interiority that it is supposed to deny. The recognition of a certain falseness is what establishes the horizon within which something more genuine might appear. It is an exemplary instance, as Lacan says, of finding "the structure of fiction at the origin of truth."[32]

The crucial point to recognize here is that the "falsely false" conventions of social intercourse enable us simultaneously to defend ourselves against anxiety in the face of Others while also preserving a limited openness toward a hidden excess. The result retraces the structure of the symptom as Freud defines it. The inner dynamics of politeness at once exert a repressive, defensive influence and maintain a certain opening toward the very thing—in this case, the unknown Other-Thing—that is being defended against. In fact, almost all of our examples point toward such a symptomatic compromise. "Alone together" millennials avoid exposure to the neighbor-Thing immediately across from them at the lunch table by means of miniscreen distraction, yet also they indulge a compulsive enjoyment of the Thing-like character of the internet as an opening to something unexpected.

" . . . It's Not My Mother"

"Your response to my objection is partly satisfying," the critic admits, "but so far you've dealt only with the generalized human Other, not with the mother in particular. Surely that is Lacan's most challenging claim."

The first and obvious response to this challenge is simply to observe that the mother presents the paradigmatic encounter with *das Ding* because she is the first such encounter. To go further, we've already sounded the necessary caution surrounding the demand for more explanation. Precisely if Lacan is right about the maternal-Thing forming the core of the unconscious, direct evidence remains in principle unavailable. But we've also anticipated the basic form that more indirect evidence might assume, at least if we take our clue from Freud's basic approach. The evidence will appear in the form of a complete inversion, a total reversal of values, that poses mother love as the very opposite of anxiety producing.

Following this line of interpretation, we are led to wonder whether the specifically maternal origin of the Lacanian Thing is to be discerned in what initially appears to be the most persuasive evidence against it: the *stranger anxiety* of early childhood. Taken at face value, the toddler's outburst of panic when confronted by a stranger would seem to be the ultimate proof that the child's psychic world is sharply and simply divided between the familiar and reassuring embrace of the mother and the jarring, fear-inspiring foreignness of the outsider. But what if, in conformity with so many of Freud's analyses, the truth is to be found only by directly inverting the immediate appearances of things? What if stranger anxiety represents a displacement outward of an anxiety originally aroused by the mother herself? Isn't a reversal of this sort an example of precisely the inversion of values that Freud repeatedly attributes to the workings of the unconscious? The monstrous dimension of the mother is rendered invisible by virtue of being relegated to a point outside the family unit altogether.

Slavoj Žižek is fond of making a parallel point with reference to the monsters of science fiction movies, everything from giant, disgusting blobs that fall from outer space to flying saucers that fascinatingly hover overhead. The monster that lurks "out there" and that constantly threatens to engulf us is in fact a projection of something from our most intimate life. In his essay "The Thing from Inner Space," Žižek observes that "the exemplary case of the Thing is, of course, the mysterious undead alien object falling from the universe, an object which is inhuman, but nonetheless alive and often even possessing a will of its own." He then continues:

> What better proof of the fact that this Thing comes from inner space than the very first scene of *Star Wars*? At first, all we see is the void— the infinite dark sky, the ominously silent abyss of the universe, with dispersed twinkling stars which are not so much material objects as abstract points, markers of space coordinates, virtual objects; then, all of sudden, in Dolby stereo, we hear a thundering sound coming from behind our backs, from our inner-most background, later rejoined by the visual object, the source of this sound—the gigantic spaceship, a kind of space version of the *Titanic*—which triumphantly enters the

frame of screen reality. The object-Thing is thus clearly rendered as a part of ourselves that we eject into reality.[33]

It is in these terms that we should interpret Lacan's neologism "extimate." He coins the term precisely in his introduction to the notion of *das Ding*, intending it to name the paradoxical switch point between what is most interior and "mine" versus what is completely, even spectacularly, exterior and alien. The blobs and zombies of B-rated movies are *extimate* objects. That is to say, we encounter in them something of our most intimate selves represented as completely outside ourselves.

In his twentieth seminar, *Encore*, Lacan refers in passing to a story by Guy de Maupassant, "Le Horla." The story presents a macabre fable of the Lacanian extimate. In day-by-day journal entries, the narrator relates his horror at the dawning realization that an invisible being now inhabits his bedroom. He first detects the presence of this uncanny companion when he is surprised to find his bedside water glass empty. "Somebody had drunk the water, but who? I? I without any doubt. It could surely only be I? In that case I was a somnambulist—was living, without knowing it, that double, mysterious life which makes us doubt whether there are not two beings in us." From that moment on, he is gripped by an unshakable dread. The very invisibility of the alien intruder becomes the surest evidence of its presence. "He does not show himself anymore," he says, "but I feel that He is near me, watching me, looking at me, penetrating me, dominating me, and more terrible to me when He hides himself thus than if He were to manifest his constant and invisible presence by supernatural phenomena."[34]

In the climax of the story, feeling assured that he has trapped his terrifying doppelgänger in his room, he sets fire to the house. Rushing out, he waits breathlessly, fearing that the fire might go out, or that it will somehow fail to fully engulf the house. When it succeeds, a new horror overtakes him as he hears the screams of the servants upstairs, whom he had neglected to warn. But that horror, however shattering, is immediately displaced by the realization of an even more terrible certainty: the Horla has *not* died. He now has no alternative, the narrator says. The only way to free himself from the alien intrusion of the Horla is to kill himself.

De Maupassant's story conveys a crucial Lacanian lesson about the Thing in the Other. The Other-Thing is outside us, but also *inside* us. Here we intersect with the cardinal postulate of Lacan's reappropriation of Freud's legacy: the notion that "human desire is the desire of the Other." Encountering the dimension of the unknown and uncognizable in the Other, we begin to pose the question of what is unknown and uncognized in ourselves. Inside or out, we are positively *haunted* by the Other-Thing.

If Lacan's theory of anxiety in relation to the mother herself reorients Freud's Oedipal dynamics, putting the accent more on the unknown desire of the mother than on the unrealizable desire of the child, it nevertheless makes new sense of Freud's famous reflections on the uncanny. A key point of that analysis turns on Freud's observation of the strange, mixed meaning of the German words for the homey and the strange. While the German word *heimlich,* by virtue of its reference to "home" (*Heim*), indicates what is safest and most familiar, it may also, according to its secondary meaning of what remains "concealed, kept from sight, so that others do not get to know of or about it," function as an equivalent for what is *unheimlich* or "uncanny."[35] The result is deeply appropriate for a psychology of the unconscious. The complex semantic potential of the word hints that what is most deeply upsetting and unnervingly alien slumbers unsuspected in the heart of what is most familiar. By locating the primal origin of anxiety in the mother herself, Lacan invites us to discern this paradox at its most absolutely fundamental level.

Love and Death

Lacan links the unknown Thing with the force of the death drive. Lacan thus insists that "Freud at the end of his thinking discovers once again the field of *das Ding,* and points out to us the space beyond the pleasure principle."[36] As the primal embodiment of the real, *das Ding* is the very signature of extremity, the abyssal dimension of an unknown that ineluctably attracts. Its gravitation never ceases to draw the subject toward darkness, risk, even self-destruction.

What makes Lacan's view so revolutionary is the way it locates the unthinkable real in precisely what is closest to us: the fellow human being. As such, it opens up a fresh appreciation of the way the sexual relation is charged with particularly intense anxiety. In sex, the reassuring fabric of everyday interactions that put the question of the Other's desire at a distance is disarmingly torn open. The subject is threatened by being reconfronted by the very unknown of the Other's desire from which the rules of public sociality are supposed to insulate us.

This perspective illuminates anew our sensitivity to nakedness. The first function of clothing is to create a social space from which the most obvious traces of the Other's desire, the bodily tokens of sexual arousal, have been subtracted. Modesty becomes recognizable as a bulwark against too raw—literally, too naked—a confrontation with the monstrous dimension of the neighbor. Clothes conceal the "real" person of private, quirky desires, thus allowing one or another standardized social role to step forward in all of its reassuring predictability. Clothing spares us the obscenity of too intimate a proximity to the Other's secret *jouissance.*

And yet the psychic function of clothing is also consistent with the dynamics of ambivalence that we traced in the "falsely false" character of conventional greetings. Clothes almost inevitably announce the very thing they are intended to conceal. Clothing, Lacan reminds us, "both shows and hides."[37] It doesn't take a psychoanalyst to know that the most interesting styles of clothing, particularly clothing for women, are the ones that most successfully work both sides of the street. The sexual piquancy of nudity is far more powerful when it is *partial* nudity. The reason is that the sexiness of nudity is at a maximum when it is presented less as a brute physical reality than as a tantalizing prospect, less a *perception* than an *anticipation.* It is for this reason that there are few aphrodisiacs more potent than the veil. One of the most ancient and most ubiquitous of human artifices, the veil attests to the existence of the Other-Thing in all its double-sidedness—something we can't live with but also can't live without. The diaphanous veil condenses the symptomatic duality of concealing and revealing. We are irresistibly drawn to imagine the very thing it covers over. In fact, it is tempting to suppose that the covering which disallows a direct view actually *creates* the object of desire that it conceals.

By contrast to the seductive power of the veil, total nudity can curiously deflate desire. Why? The reason becomes clear when we remember that the Thing in the Other is in fact something purely *supposed* by the observing subject. The Thing is a phantasmatic *positing* of the unknown of the Other's desire.[38] If clothing helps distance us from confronting the anxious question of that desire, if it tends to put the Thing under wraps, clothes simultaneously serve to create the invisible space *behind the clothing* in which the Thing can be even more effectively supposed to exist.

Let us add a final note relevant to sex in long-term relationships.[39] From a Lacanian standpoint, sex arouses anxiety because of the way it inevitably draws the subject back into a distressing proximity with *das Ding.* Which means that if the love relation must be built on trust, *sexual arousal, if it is to be satisfying, also depends upon a measured excitation of anxiety.* The great challenge for long-married couples thus consists in retaining some sense of the unknown dimension of the partner. The strained or failing relationship is most clearly flagged by frequently repeated phrases like "That's what you always do" or "You're so predictable" or "I'm so sick of you saying that." Such phrases point to a suffocating excess of (presumed) knowledge about the Other. Vitality in love and sex is maintained in no small measure by keeping in touch with what we *don't know* of our partner.

It's true that this analysis echoes a piece of commonplace wisdom, the stuff of Hallmark cards, about love stimulated by mystery. The spark of desire is struck in the space of something unknown. But the Lacanian view goes much farther, linking the incitement of desire to the sense of something not only hidden but even vaguely menacing. The overused cliché about some women's attraction to "bad boys" is not without a grain of validity. The ultimate implication of Lacan's theory of the Thing at the core of the unconscious points toward the linkage between sexual desire and the most obscure and primordial impulse of the human being, an impulse that plays with prospects of self-transformation that border upon self-destruction.

Finding Oneself in the Void

No wonder Lacan so emphatically signaled the importance of his concept of *das Ding*. The Thing animates the very core of Lacan's most elemental proposition: "Man's desire is the desire of the Other."[40] The subject's passage toward the assumption of its own desire must pass through the Other. One's own desire comes into being only by means of a detour, an essential being-outside-of-oneself. The "I" can step forward only from out of the void in the "You." As Žižek puts it, "the subject desires only insofar as it experiences the Other itself as desiring, as the site of an unfathomable desire, as if an opaque desire is emanating from him or her."[41] If it's true that desire must eventually find some vehicle of representation, it remains that the restlessness of desire is set in motion by what is not represented, what remains a lack or void. Lacan thus claims that "man finds his home at a point located in the Other that lies beyond the image from which we are fashioned. This place represents the absence where we stand."[42]

In the confrontation with the Other-Thing, what is ultimately at stake is the subject's own coming-to-be. The zone of the questionable in the Other is also that of the subject's own question. This more elusive but crucial stake of the game concerns the real of the subject's mute *jouissance*. Lacan's point is that the question of the Other always comes first, that the question of the subject's desire can be posed only in the locus of the Other.[43] "What anxiety targets in the real," he concludes, "includes the x of a primordial subject moving towards his advent as subject, . . . since the subject has to realize himself on the path to the Other. . . . [This subject] is the subject of *jouissance*. . . . [I]t can in no way be isolated as a subject, unless mythically."[44]

Taking account of this radically *ex-centric* character of the subject prepares us for understanding the indispensable companion to Lacan's dictum about desire as the desire of the Other: *the pulse of desire arises from the play of the signifier.* This theme, centered on the relation of *das Ding* to signification, will occupy us in the next chapter. Lacan is unequivocal about linking the abyssal enigma of *das Ding* with the function of language. He thus refers to "this field that I call the field of the Thing, this field onto which is projected something beyond, something at the point of origin of the signifying chain."[45] *Das Ding*, he says, "is the very correlative of the law of speech in its most primitive point of origin."[46] His conclusion is sweeping: "It is around *das Ding* that the whole adaptive development revolves, a development that is so specific to man insofar as the symbolic process reveals itself to be inextricably woven into it."[47]

To clarify these enigmatic claims we will need to understand how the signifier is related to the Other-Thing. To make a first step toward answering this crucial question let us take a two-stage approach, addressed first to the signifier spoken by the Other and then, opening a second dimension, to that spoken by the subject.

The first point, concerning what is spoken by the Other, is the easier to understand. Though the Thing is essentially a void, the zone of something unknown, it does not, so to say, come out of nowhere. The upsurge of the Thing follows upon one or another clue in the Other's behavior. For Lacan, the most important of those clues are unquestionably to be found in the mother's vocalizations. As Lacan says of it, "The Thing only presents itself to the extent that it becomes word."[48] The specter of the Thing arises with the signifier. Or rather, with the question about what exactly the signifier points to.

Once again, Lacan's formulation can be seen to take its clue quite precisely from Freud's original statement in the *Project for a Scientific Psychology*. What Freud calls "the perceptual complex" of the *Nebenmensch* is divided between two components: what the infant can recognize by the Other's likeness to its own body, and unrecognizable details that are "new and non-comparable." The figure of the mother might thus be said to fall into two parts, imaginary and symbolic. Her body image is familiar and reassuring, but her speech is destined increasingly to present the child with the question of what those sounds mean. From its very inception, in fact well before birth, the human infant is continually bathed in speech. "Man," as Lacan says, "is born into a sea of signifiers."[49] But what do they all signify? Even when the child has mastered the ability to speak, that fundamental question remains.

The special class of signifiers comprising proper names casts an interesting light on this discussion. By means of the infant's name, the child finds that "his place is already inscribed at his birth."[50] But why this name and not some other? It is no great stretch to assume that the choice of the child's name reflects the parents' most deeply held attitudes toward the world and their place in it—*almost certainly attitudes only partly known to the parents themselves.* To what place in the parents' joys and sorrows, victories and defeats, hopes and fears, has the child been assigned? How children accommodate themselves to their name and its unconscious cargo of obscure hopes and expectations will crucially shape their nascent sense of themselves.

My own name offers a suggestive example. Why did my parents name my one-year-older brother for a great-grandfather—James—while I, the second-born male child, received my father's name—Richard? To this day, years after my father's death at a ripe old age, I have no idea. But I would wager a great deal that those choices quite fatefully influenced the course of our lives. Was the intensity of my brother's lifelong struggle to win my parents' approval, matched only by the volatility of his rebellion against their expectations, energized by his awareness that I, not he, had been anointed with the father's name? Conversely, was my own quieter self-confidence born from the fact, voluble in its very silence, of having been given the name of the father?

The exceptional status of proper names bars us from relying on them for any general rule about our relation to language. But Lacan is convinced that a potential question attends all speech, at least to the extent that it is always possible to ask of any utterance, "Yes, I hear what you are saying, but what exactly are you trying to tell me?" This means that the specter of the Thing as the opaque enigma of the Other's desire can at any moment rear up behind whatever has just dropped from the Other's mouth. Lacan points to this crucial feature of speech when he defines the signifier as the minimum with which it is possible to lie.

The Birth of the Subject in the Ceded Object

What, then, of the other topic we promised to address, that concerning the emergence of the child's own speech? What is at stake in the infant's first vocalizations? While we will expand a great deal upon these questions in the following chapter, let us make a start here, as Lacan himself does in *Anxiety*, by reference to a key Freudian innovation: the theory of part objects. As is well known, Freud focuses on three component parts of the body—breast, feces, and penis—each associated with different organ systems and drive satisfactions. These three part objects underlie Freud's scheme of the three great periods of libidinal development: oral, anal, and phallic. Implicit in this theory is the idea that each of the part objects serves to mediate in a different way the relation between child and mother, the overall trajectory of which tends toward the achievement of increasing autonomy.

Lacan radicalizes the role of such mediation by linking the part object to *das Ding*. According to Lacan, a fragment of the body—what seems poised to escape the gestalt of the body's imaginary wholeness— functions in the child's mind as a stand-in for what remains unknown in the Other. The unthinkable "something or other" in the Other is primitively represented by means of focusing upon a mere part of the body. As Lacan puts this point: "Lack is radical, radical in the very constitution of subjectivity such as it appears to us on the path of analytic experience. I should like to set it out in the following formula—as soon as it becomes known, as soon as something comes to knowledge, something is lost and the surest way of approaching this lost something is to conceive of it as a bodily fragment."[51] With the focus on certain fragments of the body, the pivotal idea for Lacan becomes that of *the cut* that creates the part object. The cut produces the object but in so doing models the dynamics of separation from the mother, offering a schema for establishing an independent identity. The excremental object is of special importance because, unlike its predecessor, the breast, the feces are literally cut free from the infant's own body. Lacan especially emphasizes its significance for establishing the ground lines of autonomy. "Why single out the anus, if not for its decisive sphincter function, which contributes to cutting an object? This cut is what gives its value, its accent, to the anal object, with everything that it can come to represent, not simply, as they say, on the side of the gift, but on the side of identity."[52]

The most important function of infantile part objects is the way they implicitly serve as tokens of exchange between the emerging infant-subject and the maternal Other. But before they can serve that function they must first be given up into the space between the subject and the Other. In fact, they *create* that space. The part objects are, Lacan says, *objets cessible*, cedable or yieldable objects. Again, the excremental object is the clearest example. The feces are offered up as primitive counters in the game of relation to the mother. Lacan compares such ceded objects to Shylock's "pound of flesh," the exorbitant price of Antonio's freedom. "In the body there is always, by virtue of this engagement in the signifying dialectic, something that is separated off, something that is sacrificed, something inert, and this something is the pound of flesh."[53]

The ceded object furnishes a kind of pivot between the subject and the Other. It both introduces a space of separation from the Other and, on the basis of that separation, holds out the promise of some relation of exchange. It is along this line of argument that Lacan reverses Freud's conception of the infant who must be torn away from the breast by the threat of castration. Lacan insists, contrary to Freud, that the infant primordially regards the breast as an appendage of itself, which it subsequently gives up. "The most decisive moment in the anxiety at issue," Lacan says, "the anxiety of weaning, is not so much when the breast falls short of the subject's need, it's rather that the infant yields the breast to which he is appended as a portion of himself."[54] If the child has introduced a cut into the body of the mother, it has also submitted to the loss of a piece of its own body.

In Lacan's conception, each of the Freudian part objects—breast, feces, penis—materializes the function of what he comes to call the *objet petit a*, a function intimately linked with *das Ding*. As the "a" of its name indicates, the *objet a* is essentially related to the Other, or *Autre*. The "a" also suggests both an algebraic variable and the first letter of the alphabet, in both ways pointing toward a serial function of indeterminate content. Indeed, Lacan adds to Freud's initial trio of part objects a handful of others. The most notable among those additions—the voice and the gaze—are especially interesting because of the way they are so much more intimately related to the unknown void of the Other-Thing.[55] The *objet a* can be rightly understood as a stand-in or indicator of the Thing, a kind of reverberating trace of the Thing in the life of the subject.[56]

This discussion of the materialization of the *objet a* and its deployment in an economy of exchange provides a ready segue to the child's entry into language, the most highly elaborated economy of exchange. The part objects, cut apart from the body image, function as primordial nonverbal signifiers. But the linguistic signifier, too, has its place in this train of tokens of exchange. In the originary drama with the maternal Other, the inarticulate cry of the infant becomes in itself a ceded object, indeed the very first such object, yielded into the space between subject and Other. As Lacan says, "This manifestation of anxiety coincides with the very emergence in the world of he who is going to be the subject. This manifestation is his cry . . . this first effect of cession . . . the nursling can't do anything about the cry that slips out of him. He has yielded something and nothing will ever conjoin him to it again."[57]

Lacan here conjures up a profoundly mixed picture of something *done*, the inaugural achievement of the subject's first primitive action (as ceded, the object is given over into the space between the subject and the Other), but also something *suffered* (the object given up can never be fully recovered; it remains in some limbo between the subject and the Other). The act of ceding has its payoff in winning for the subject a measure of distance from the Other, a crucial degree of separation. And yet in the course of such ceding, the subject enlists itself in the dynamics of lack and, by the same stroke, in the prospect of reparation. The subject is now positioned in the space of desire.

Parting Is Sweet Sorrow

The most striking result of the foregoing discussion, as shockingly violent to common sense as it is to mainstream linguistics, is the notion that the most archaic function of language, usually thought to be aimed at *connection* with the Other, also and indispensably seeks to achieve a degree of *severance* from the fellow human being. If language finally relinks the subject to the Other, the primal entry into language forestalls anxiety by establishing a margin of detachment that puts the threatening unknown of the neighbor-Thing at a distance. In this view, the most primordial function of language is not connection but disjunction, not communication but separation. The first word of the human being is a declaration of independence.

Lacan buttresses this point about the separating and individuating function of the primal articulations of speech by observing its reflection in the phonemic structure of the words used to designate the primal Others. If the ground lines of identity are adumbrated by the cut that yields the part objects, the work of separation is also effected at the level of the phonemic microstructure of speech. "At an altogether different level," Lacan says, "the level of the signifying articulation, at the level of the most fundamental phonemes, those most firmly bound to the cut, the consonantal elements of the phoneme, are, as regards their most basal stock, essentially modulated at the level of the lips. . . . Mama and papa are labial articulations."[58] The names for the mother and father tend in most languages to be pronounced at the lips, the counterpart of the anus as a decisive anatomical borderline separating what is inside and what is outside of the body. The semipercussive effects of the consonants of "ma-ma" and "pa-pa" enact an embodied registration of separation.

Hannah Arendt opens her monumental work *The Human Condition* with a reference to the 1957 launching of the first orbital satellite, the Russian Sputnik. She then remarks that this unprecedented achievement was immediately recognized, in the words of one American reporter, as a first "step toward escape from men's imprisonment to the earth." The reporter's comment echoed the words of the pioneering Soviet physicist and rocket scientist Konstantin Tsiolkovsky, which came to be inscribed on his tombstone: "Mankind will not remain bound to the earth forever." To fully follow out the consequences of Lacan's concept of the relation of the signifier to the unknown Thing in the Other is to realize that Sputnik was merely a technologically elaborate successor to the most primordial example, as Arendt puts it, of an "object made by man launched into the universe."[59] For Lacan, the original such object is none other than the signifier, and it is launched for the same underlying reason, that of gaining a measure of escape, of achieving a margin of independence, from the gravitational bond of the Other.

An echo of the same point is audible in a remark by the primatologist Sue Savage-Rumbaugh. While most of Savage-Rumbaugh's work has aimed at closing the gap between humans and our simian relatives, she remains acutely cognizant of the distance between humans and the apes. "When I am with bonobos," she says, "I feel like I have something that I shared with them long ago but I forgot. As we've clothed ourselves and separated ourselves, we've gained a wonderful society, but we've lost a kind of soul-to-soul connection that they maintain."[60] Lacan's theory of the signifier in relation to *das Ding* points to the original moment of such a break with our closest fellow beings. The implication of the Lacanian view points to a certain loss of immediate creaturely communion, the replacement of an empathic link with a distinct measure of distance from the Other. This distancing is an indispensable condition of becoming human. The paradoxical conclusion to be drawn is that the acquisition of language in human beings relies first of all not on an addition to animal endowments but on a kind of subtraction from them. At some elemental level and in a crucial respect, the human child is always a stranger in a strange land.

3

The *Ex Nihilo* of the Signifier

> *Das Ding* . . . is the very correlative of the law of speech in its
> most primitive point of origin.
>
> The notion of creation *ex nihilo* is coextensive with the exact
> situation of the Thing as such.
> —Jacques Lacan

Despite his rallying cry of a "return to Freud," Lacan effects several radical departures from Freudian orthodoxy. Quite arguably, the most important of them is his rejection of Freud's posing of the Oedipus complex in favor of the *Komplex der Nebenmensch*, the complex of the neighbor-Thing.[1] The primal challenge for the maturing child is less a matter of having to painfully give up the attachment to the mother than of having to cope with the anxiety-producing unknown posed by the mother's desire. Yet Lacan insists that his innovations do indeed return to Freud's central insights. In this chapter we explore the ways Lacan's focus on *das Ding* led him to rediscover and radicalize the core idea of Freud's Oedipal theory: the notion that the constitution of the human subject ineluctably turns upon submitting the relation with the mother to the regulating influence of a third party. The structure of subjectivity is ineluctably triangular. It refers to not one Other but *two*. This third point of the triangle Lacan calls "the big Other." It remains to specify more precisely what he meant by it. We need to pose the question once again: What exactly is the relation between the little and the big Other?

The Disappearing Thing

Before I can resume my argument, my critic breaks in with a new question. "Your introduction to this chapter only further amplifies the central role you ascribe to *das Ding* in Lacan's thought. But if that role is really as pivotal as you claim, how do you account for the fact that Lacan barely mentions it after the seventh seminar?"

The critic has a point or, better, half a point. It's quite true that after the intensive focus on the Other-Thing in the *Ethics*, references to it in subsequent seminars are rare. Even in the second half of the Ethics seminar, it is mentioned only once or twice. Given the obvious emphasis with which the idea was introduced, this disappearing act is surely surprising. There are, however, a handful of striking exceptions that clearly suggest the enduring importance of the concept. The first occurs a year later, in the seminar *Transference*. In the *Ethics*, Lacan's claim was that sublimation elevates the object "to the dignity of the Thing." While he doesn't expand very much on this tantalizing tidbit, it is immediately tempting to presume that he is pointing to the way the art object, like the primal Other, withholds something from the one who experiences it. True art appears to harbor a mysterious aspect, a sense of something excessive, something unknown. In *Transference*, however, he puts the emphasis on the way the aura of the beautiful erects a defensive buffer of protection from it. He therefore points to "beauty rising up, such as it is projected at the extreme limit in order to stop us from going any further toward the heart of the Thing."[2] However, the most important subsequent reference to *das Ding* occurs three years after its first appearance, in *Anxiety*. There Lacan asserts the centrality of the Thing for the experience of anxiety. Anxiety, he says, "designates the most, as it were, profound object, the ultimate object, the Thing."[3]

These two later references are far from trivial. In fact, they put the unknown Thing at the heart of two of the most absolutely fundamental concerns of psychoanalysis: anxiety and sublimation.[4] Yet the fact remains that, after commanding the entire first half of the *Ethics* seminar, specific mention of *das Ding* recedes from Lacan's discourse.[5] Why? The biggest reason is that the Thing tends to be replaced in Lacan's mature period with his concept of the *objet petit a*. While specifying their relationship in detail would take us too far afield from our concerns here, we can readily say that they are internally related, in fact they are virtually inseparable.[6] The *objet a* appears as the *trace* of the Thing, like the "tell" of a poker player. In his sixteenth seminar, Lacan playfully and very suggestively refers to the *objet a* as "what tickles *das Ding* from the inside."[7]

We can identify several other paths along which the Thing and *objet a* are linked. The first and most obvious one concerns the part objects we connected to the Thing in the previous chapter. Lacan is clear that when breast, feces, and penis function as part objects they serve as elementary instantiations of the *objet a*. Another point of contact: Lacan typically identifies *objet a* with certain ancillary details, something marginal that doesn't quite fit the picture; a stain, tic, or blemish. Marilyn Monroe's beauty spot offers a good example. Far from detracting from her beauty, her obtrusive mole added something indefinable, something charming, precisely because it appeared to interrupt her otherwise flawless face. In eighteenth-century Europe, an artificially contrived facial spot was an element of high fashion. It is significant that when Lacan introduces *das Ding*, he likewise associates it with one or another strange detail. "*Das Ding*," he says, "is something that presents and isolates itself as the strange feature around which the whole movement of the *Vorstellung* turns."[8]

Freud himself offers in the *Project for a Scientific Psychology* a striking example of such a strange or incongruous detail only a few pages after introducing the concept of *das Ding*. A young woman reports being deeply distressed when she entered a shop and felt that the shop assistants were laughing at her clothes. Her intense embarrassment was strangely accompanied by a feeling of sexual arousal. Panic-stricken, she fled the shop, but afterward suffered increasingly debilitating effects. The key to the case, Freud discovers, was that the scene with the snickering shop assistants was associatively linked with a much earlier experience in childhood when she was groped through her skirts by an older shopkeeper. In that earlier incident, she felt no sexual arousal nor did she feel particularly traumatized. Yet the laughter of the assistants in the later scene reminded her of the strange grin of the older shopkeeper. Her sense that the assistants' laughter was aimed at her clothing further created an echo of the original incident. The elder shopkeeper had grabbed at her genitals *through her clothes*.

This tiny case-vignette is a perfect illustration of the subject's relation to *das Ding*. The shopkeeper's leering smile was a clue to an obscene enjoyment that remained completely mysterious for the young girl, in fact very likely an enjoyment that the shopkeeper could not fully acknowledge even to himself.[9] As such, it represented the traumatizing unknown of the Other-Thing. The outbreak of symptoms was triggered when the trace of the original encounter was reanimated by the experience of the shop assistants' laughter. The result was a dizzying, uncanny sensation in which the traumatic potential of the earlier scene was activated *après coup*.

If these considerations help clarify how the role assigned to *das Ding* in the seventh seminar comes increasingly to be assumed by the *objet a*, they nevertheless don't explain the shift. Was there something unsatisfying about the original formulation? Lacan never provides an explanation. But my best guess has the double benefit of making sense of Lacan's reticence to talk about *das Ding* after introducing it, while also revealing something essential about what he was trying to theorize in the first place. A primary danger in speaking of *das Ding*, a risk I fear may be raised by my own discussions in this book, is the way it inclines us toward reifying or oversubstantializing what is involved. The issue concerns the baseline ontology of psychoanalysis for Lacan. The key point is that the Thing is not a *thing* at all. As Lacan says of it, "The Thing is also the Non-Thing."[10] *Das Ding* has no objective existence whatsoever. If it is not an object, neither is it any sort of prehistorical perceptual givenness. It is rather a locus of pure lack, a zone of something unknown. To use the term from Lacan's own lexicon most appropriate for the purpose, *das Ding* is something purely *supposed* by the subject.

The Thing about a Psychoanalyst

"It is through the intermediary of the *Nebenmensch* as speaking subject that everything that has to do with the thought processes is able to take shape in the subjectivity of the subject."[11] Given such sweeping pronouncements, it seems almost unthinkable that Lacan appears never to have added any specific comment about the place and function of the Thing in the clinical process of psychoanalysis. This absence seems all the more strange when we pause to ask ourselves whether the transformative power of analysis doesn't reside in the capacity of the psychoanalyst to somehow represent, to embody, even to impersonate *das Ding*. Just imagine the basic situation. You have contracted to meet repeatedly with a complete stranger to whom you will speak with absolute candor about your most intimate secrets. It is an arrangement that is arguably unique in the history of the human race. As a possible candidate for something similar, one might think of meeting a prostitute, though of course that relation is pointedly *not* centered on talking about oneself. Meanwhile, this stranger is seated behind you, out of sight. She scrupulously refuses to indulge in all reassuring small talk. She intentionally leaves you in the dark with respect to her personal life. And she is everywhere willing to allow awkward silences to hang painfully in the air. The silent, unseen presence of the analyst must very potently raise the specter of *das Ding*.

Or perhaps Lacan did address the Thing in the analyst after all, *avant la lettre*. "If you reread the text [from 1955 titled 'The Freudian Thing']," he says, "you will see that I am essentially speaking of the Thing."[12] In that essay Lacan rejects the ego-to-ego conception of analysis championed by some object-relations theorists in favor of a "game of four players" composed of "two subjects each of whom is provided with two objects, the ego and the other."[13] Lacan compares this fourfold structure to a bridge game in which the analyst occupies the position of the "dummy." He then describes this "dead" position in terms that are strikingly resonant with his later discussions of *das Ding*. "The analyst concretely intervenes in the dialectic of analysis by playing dead—by 'cadaverizing' his position, as the Chinese say—either by his silence where he is the Other with a capital O, or by canceling out his own resistance where he is the other with a lowercase o. In both cases, and via symbolic and imaginary effects, respectively, he makes death present."[14]

Associating the position of the analyst with the anxiety-provoking character of *das Ding* makes new sense of Freud's famous remark about analysis producing in the patient a "controlled paranoia." The encounter with the invisible person of the psychoanalyst is unavoidably unnerving. We could further support the identification of the analyst with the Thing by referring to Lacan's theory of the four discourses, developed in Seminar XVII—those of the master, the university, the hysteric, and the analyst. In the structure of discourse appropriate to psychoanalysis, the analyst occupies the position of the *objet a*.[15]

But immediately another question arises. Precisely if the linkage between the analyst and the Thing is suggested in these ways, how are we to make sense of Lacan's other, ubiquitous characterization of the position of the analyst as the "subject supposed to know"? According to that formula, one of the most conspicuous constants of Lacan's teaching, what the analyst embodies is not the enigma of the little Other, but the big Other of the symbolic code, the ultimate know-it-all. Isn't that the real meaning of the analogy to the dummy hand in bridge? The analyst is supposed to hold a full hand of cards before a single trick is played. And doesn't that explain the patient's inclination toward paranoia? The analyst *already knows* everything. The analyst possesses all the subject's dirty little secrets in advance.

It might seem that we are getting unproductively dragged down into the weeds of Lacanian minutiae. But what is at stake is in fact a crucial issue, one that is pivotal for clarifying the internal relation between the little and big Others. We've already touched on the key orienting idea: the subject's defense against *das Ding*. If this defensive function is served by the most primitive launching of the signifier, the vocal object that is "ceded" into the space between the subject and the Other, the objective is to establish a defensive cordon, secured and consolidated by the elaboration of a *system* of signifiers, the establishment of a symbolic *code*. That consolidation effects the regulation of speech and language in accordance with fixed rules of meaning. The general name in Lacanian theory for such a regulatory regime is "the big Other."

The upshot is that the analyst embodies *both* the little and big

Others, though at different levels of the analytic encounter. To the extent that the patient regards the analyst as the subject supposed to know, the analyst incarnates the big Other, the guarantor of the symbolic code. And yet, however much anxiety *that* supposition might invite, arising from the way the analyst may readily appear in the role of an all-knowing judge, identifying the analyst with the symbolic big Other serves to stave off an even more intolerably anxious prospect. The "proof" of this view is that the progress of analysis as Lacan conceives of it proceeds toward the conclusion that the big Other *does not know*. In fact, analysis aims at the realization that the big Other *does not exist*. The ultimate objective of psychoanalysis is to encourage a relaxation of the subject's investment in the symbolic law, a prime result of which is to return the subject to the most primitive sources of anxiety, rooted beneath the level of the symbolic law in the abyss of *das Ding*.

Among other things, this point provides an answer to Michel Foucault's critique of psychoanalysis. We earlier posed the analytic relationship as virtually unique in human history. Foucault disagrees. The psychoanalyst, Foucault claims, is essentially a secular update of the medieval priest-confessor.[16] But from the Lacanian point of view we are adopting here, Foucault completely misses the deeper point. True, as a representative of the big Other, the analyst as subject supposed to know is in fact akin to the priest, who serves as an avatar of an entire social, cultural, moral order and the symbolic code that stabilizes it. If accommodation to the symbolic Law were the only goal, Freud's discovery would indeed be merely a means for better adapting oneself to societal norms, policed by the analyst herself. But for Lacan the essential movement of analysis proceeds in a completely different direction. The action of analysis aims at shifting the subject *beyond the law* in order to engage the archaic relation to the Thing that forms the very core of the unconscious. The role and function of the analyst must extend beyond even the analyst's famous "neutrality" toward something that outstrips the domain of the ego altogether, something "beyond the pleasure principle" that transcends the world of our everyday comings and goings. Analysis aims to evoke something radically *Other*.

Behind the Wall of the Law

The big Other names the regularization of the symbolic function that defends against the unknown Thing. The goal of this chapter is to lay out more precisely how that defense operates and how it is overcome. Its most archaic level is that of the primally ceded objects, among which are the first inarticulate cries of the infant. Lacan analyzes the monosyllabic sounding of the second-person pronoun as itself a primitive defensive gesture, the emission of a kind of sonic object that functions to put the Other at a safer distance.

> What does the emission, the articulation, the sudden emergence from out of our voice of that "You!" (*Toi!*) mean? A "You" that may appear on our lips at a moment of utter helplessness, distress or surprise in the presence of something that I will not right off call death, but that is certainly for us an especially privileged other—one around which our principal concerns gravitate, and which for all that still manages to embarrass us. . . . I believe that one finds in that word the temptation to tame the Other, that prehistoric, that unforgettable Other, which suddenly threatens to surprise us and to cast us down from the height of its appearance. "You" contains a form of defense, and I would say that at the moment when it is spoken, it is entirely in this "You," and nowhere else, that one finds what I have evoked today concerning *das Ding.*[17]

A whole second layer of the defense enabled by the signifier is constituted by the web of everyday routines and the banter of chitchat that lubricates it, plus the normalizing expectations attached to social roles and conventions. This web, the basic architecture of social performativity, provides the guardrails of everyday life that protect us from too challenging a confrontation with the Other. As Žižek puts this point:

> We need to resort to performativity, to symbolic engagement, precisely and only insofar as the other whom we encounter is not only the imaginary semblable but also the elusive absolute Other of the Real Thing with whom no reciprocal exchange is possible. In order to render our coexistence with the Thing minimally bearable, the symbolic order qua Third, the pacifying mediator, has to intervene: the "gentrification" of the homely Other-Thing into a "normal fellow human" cannot occur through our direct interaction but presupposes the third agency to which we both submit—there is no intersubjectivity (no symmetrical, shared, relation between humans) without the impersonal symbolic Order.[18]

Both of these first two "levels" of symbolic defense are ultimately grounded on the laws that govern the semantic and syntactical functioning of language that Lacan calls the law of the symbolic order. Here, too, Žižek puts the matter forcefully. "What if the ultimate function of the

Law," he asks, "is not to . . . retain our proximity to the neighbor, but, on the contrary, to keep the neighbor at a proper distance, to serve as a kind of protective wall against the monstrosity of the neighbor?"[19] From this perspective, the enigma of the Other's *jouissance* becomes the undetectable "dark matter," by definition invisible, that underlies the edifice of the social-symbolic world.

As many thinkers have claimed in various ways, the social world is built on the division of property. Indeed, the Greek word for "law"— *nomos*—originally meant something like a "feeding place" or "pasture," later coming to designate any kind of assigned space or district, and finally referring to all ordered division, including usage, custom, and law. The most elemental function of the law is to separate. Such partitioning establishes the material space of property. Good fences make good neighbors. But for Lacan, the baseline of the division concerns relations not to things but to *persons*, the division of the I from the you, the subject from the Other.[20]

Separation from the neighbor-Thing is also served by the most basic rules of grammar, including the separation of subject and predicate that allows for the transitivity of verbs. An actor is separated from what is acted upon. Grammar grants each subject an illusion of independence. Nietzsche was well aware of the way grammatical structure helps secure our sense of being a discrete and stable individual, a sense that is ultimately a fiction. In a passage from *Beyond Good and Evil* relevant to the act of thinking itself, he makes the key point:

> With regard to the superstitions of logicians, I shall never tire of emphasizing a small terse fact, which these superstitious minds hate to concede—namely, that a thought comes when "it" wishes, and not when "I" wish, so that it is falsification of the facts of the case to say that the subject "I" is the condition of the predicate "think." *It* thinks; but that this "it" is precisely the famous old "ego" is, to put it mildly, only a supposition, an assertion, and assuredly not an "immediate certainty." After all, one has even gone too far with the "it thinks"—even the "it" contains an *interpretation* of the process and does not belong to the process itself. One infers here according to the grammatical habit: "Thinking is an activity; every activity requires an agent; consequently—."[21]

The guiding structures of the symbolic order deliver us from our raw vulnerability to the neighbor-Thing. As Lacan says of it, the signifier places a "magic circle" around the Thing, leaving it in a kind of suspense that "suffers from the signifier." Ultimately, the discourses of both science or religion tend to spare us a direct encounter with the abyss of the Thing.

"Neither science nor religion is of a kind to save the Thing or to give it to us, because the magic circle that separates us from it is imposed by our relation to the signifier. As I have told you, the Thing is that which in the real suffers from this fundamental, initial relation, which commits man to the ways of the signifier."[22]

This line of argument returns us to a key point: to identify the elementary defensive function of the signifier with respect to the enigmatic Thing in the maternal Other is to retrace Lacan's notion of the paternal metaphor.[23] In the paternal metaphor, the Name of the Father is substituted for the unknown desire of the mother. There can be no subject without establishing a certain distance from the maternal Thing.[24] What makes psychoanalysis distinct from everyday discourse, however, is the way analysis expressly aims at reaccessing the abyssal dimension that is occluded by the paternal metaphor. Analysis seeks to bypass the defenses of the ego in the direction of the subject's unknown desire. How, then, is that bypass possible?

The Signifier in Question—the Question in the Signifier

In what way does psychoanalysis succeed in breaching the defensive hedge of the symbolic big Other to reaccess the unconscious Thing? Lacan's response is unwavering: analysis works by being a *talking* cure—by means, that is, of analysts specially positioning themselves with respect to the subject's speech, the play of the signifier.

But that only reshapes the question: How is the signifier capable of allowing a reversal of its own defensive function? How, as Lacan put it early in his career, is the signifier able "to recover the debt that it engenders"?[25] The answer is that the defensive function is only half of the signifier's double-sided nature. If the ceded object of the infant's cry opens up a space of separation between the subject and the Other, it also indispensably offers various possibilities of a future link.

That potential is present already in the infant's inaugural vocalizations insofar as they constitute not only a defensive putting-at-a-distance but also the most primitive attempt to *name* the Other. Here, however, it is crucial not to miss the distinctiveness of Lacan's conception of naming. Is it a matter of merely denoting an object? Not at all. On the contrary, the primary temptation to be resisted is thinking of naming as the one-to-one correspondence of a word to a thing, as if the signifier were merely a kind of tag attached to an object. The breakthrough of Saussurean linguistics was precisely to reject the tempting illusion of any simple binarism of word and object. Saussure insisted instead on a conception of the sign that located meaning less in simple correspondence to things than in the diacritical relation of every sign to the network of other signs.

Lacan accepts the main thrust of that structuralist corrective. But he also expands upon it. First, Lacan inverts Saussure's famous diagram of signifier and signified by putting the signifier on top, thereby signaling what he calls "the primacy of the signifier over the signified." Lacan then especially stresses the bar that separates the two. The vector of meaning that connects signifier to signified is finally less important than the subtler reverberation of meaning within the larger signifying system. The most fertile contribution of the signifier consists in the way it opens *a horizon of semantic indeterminacy*. Every entry into speech unleashes an unavoidable *excess* of the signifier over the signified. Ultimately less important than any specific signification is the way the "resistance" of the bar between signifier and signified has the effect of holding open the possibility of "something more." Aswim in the ocean of language, the speaking subject is continually exposed to the possibility of *something other*.

Lacan illustrates this productive resistance to signification with the playful example of two children who misinterpret the signs they see appearing as their train enters a station. "Look," says the brother, "we're at Ladies!" "Imbecile!" replies his sister, "Don't you see we're at Gentlemen." Lacan remarks that "the rails in this story materialize the bar in the Saussurean algorithm in a form designed to suggest . . . its resistance."[26] The comedy of the situation is obviously related to the children's mistaking bathrooms for towns, a category mistake concerning what is signified. But the larger stakes of the story are connected to the power of the signifiers themselves, in particular the way that the signifiers of gender difference, far from calling up discrete objective realities, trail off into subtleties and complexities that lie well beyond the capacity of even a reasonably sophisticated adult to fully fathom. The value of the example thus consists, as Lacan continues, in suggesting how "the signifier reflects its light into the darkness of incomplete significations."[27] Lacan contends that the energizing of such a penumbra of incomplete tendrils of meaning, including even subtler reverberations that border on contradiction or pure nonsense, is in fact the signifier's most important function.

In Lacan's view, the "resistance" of the bar separating signifier and signified is what makes possible the metaphoric conjunction between two distinctly different terms. It provides the wiggle room across which the poetic spark can fly. The point might be compared to the resistance in a complicated electrical circuitry. With sufficient resistance inhibiting passage along the primary wire that conducts the charge toward its intended destination, the energy will naturally seek to move along secondary circuits. Under those circumstances, who knows what wholly unintended bulbs might light up?

This point illuminates one of Lacan's earliest and best-known discussions of metaphor, focused on an example he takes from Victor Hugo's poem "Booz endormi": "His sheaf was neither miserly nor spiteful." The ostensible purpose of the metaphor, what is obliquely being said about Booz, concerns his generosity. The implication is that the harvest he has gathered into sheaves, specified as "neither miserly nor spiteful," might be shared out with those in need. Yet Lacan is careful to point to a more subtle consequence of the metaphoric conjunction. Just as the very binding together of the grain stalks into sheaves implies by negation the very opposite of scattering or handing out, the metaphor that speaks for Booz's magnanimity also subtly hints at its negation. By means of the metaphor, Booz is linked to the very greed and spitefulness the metaphor would seem to deny. As Lacan says, when the metaphoric sheaf stands in for Booz himself, "it has replaced him in the signifying chain at the very place where he was to be exalted by the sweeping away of greed and spite. But now Booz himself has been swept away by the sheaf, and hurled into the outer darkness where greed and spite harbor him in the hollow of their negation."[28] Every enunciation of the signifier, as if inevitably casting a kind of negative shadow of the very thing it signifies, tacitly calls up its very opposite. The articulation of the signifier is thus tied to an essentially contradictory function. It partly erases the very thing it signifies, leaving behind an essential vacancy that invites being filled by the reverse of what it signifies.

Taking these considerations together, we are led to the following assertion: even as the signifier provides a margin of separation from the Other-Thing, it also provides a potential stand-in for its unknown dimension. If the first inchoate eruptions of the voice, inflected with anxiety, begin to shape the emerging interval of distance between the subject and the Other, they are also destined to become the means by which the question of the Other, the enigma of *das Ding*, will be ceaselessly reposed. In this way, the signifier inaugurates a defensive separation from the Thing but also offers never-ending resources that will open new pathways toward it. As Lacan says, "The world of our experience, the Freudian world, assumes that it is this object, *das Ding*, as the absolute Other of the subject, that one is supposed to find again."[29] "Here we're touching on the very thing that makes the relation to the Other possible, that is, on that whence emerges the fact that there is such a thing as a signifier. This site whence emerges the fact that there is such a thing as the signifier is, in one sense, the site that cannot be signified. It is what I call the site of the lack-of-signifier."[30]

This discussion touches on the most elemental implication of Lacan's theory of the signifier, perhaps precisely what he had in mind by claiming that he had "defined the signifier as no one else had dared." In every entry into language, in every iteration of signifying material, there resounds some echo of the unanswered and unanswerable question of the Other. Here, too, the Lacanian conception of the signifier departs from a common assumption among students of language, in this case the idea that the elemental function of signification is *indicative*. If we allow that the primal "name" does not merely point to an object-referent but also refers to something unknown, the beyond of the Other-Thing, the conclusion to be drawn is that the original function of language is not merely indicative but *also interrogative*. At the most elementary level, every utterance implicitly poses a *question*.

This way of appreciating the double function of the signifier finds an oblique but suggestive confirmation when we turn to the example of parental names—ma-ma, pa-pa—remarkably similar versions of which can be found across many languages. Why this repetition of phonemes: ma-ma, pa-pa? Roman Jakobson famously suggested that the second iteration of the phoneme functions to indicate that the first is to be taken as no mere sound but rather *as a signifier*.[31] The Lacanian view fully endorses Jakobson's point, though it also enables us to expand upon it. We are accustomed to thinking of this elementary *Nachträglichkeit* of meaning as a retroactive specification of the intention, buttoning it down in the way that the last word of a sentence so often establishes *après coup* the meaning of the opening phrase. But what if we are also to recognize in the infant's phonemic repetition—"ma-ma"—a posing of the question of what is unknown in the Other? When the second sounding of the phoneme indicates that the first is a signifier, the effect is also to open a potential question about what exactly it means. In this way, the doubling of the phoneme rehearses the originary partition of the Other, the division in the *Nebenmensch* remarked by Freud that posits one portion that corresponds to imaginary recognition and another portion that escapes registration in the specular image and remains wholly enigmatic, an open question.

Perhaps it is not wholly a coincidence that in Chinese, a language that shares the "ma-ma" of English and many other tongues, the morpheme "ma," with appropriate alteration of the tonal pronunciation, has two significations. In the first case, it functions to signify "mother." In the second instance, however, sounded with a different tone and available for being appended to most any phrase, the same morpheme functions to announce the interrogative mood. Echoing the function identified by Jakobson in which the second phoneme of the parental name retroactively alters the status of the first, this second usage of "ma" becomes the most common indicator of a question in Chinese. Added at the end of an otherwise indicative sentence —"Blah, blah, blah, blah, ma?"—it retroactively transforms what had been said up to that point into a question. There is a similar use of "no?" in some Western languages. As in: "This is an interesting point, no?"

The Signifying Matrix

What most distinguishes Lacan's view from a host of other theories of language is his insistence that meaning can never be fully stabilized, that a question not only can be but always implicitly *is* posed by every entry into language. Attending only to the way the signifier calls up a definite signified, we risk losing sight of the way the signifier rolls along in front of itself a kind of sliding void, the space of a pure potential-for-meaning. As Lacan puts this point: "The signifier, by its very nature, always anticipates meaning by deploying its dimensions in some sense before it. As is seen at the level of the sentence when the latter is interrupted before the significant term: 'I'll never . . . ,' 'The fact remains . . . ,' 'Still perhaps . . . ,' Such sentences nevertheless make sense, and that sense is all the more oppressive in that it is content to make us wait for it."[32]

What is emerging from this discussion is what we might call the "elementary matrix of the signifier." The aim of the phrase is to point to the twofold function we glimpsed in the example of the "ceded object," which introduces a distance between the subject and the Other but also locates or marks the very otherness of the Other, thereby opening the space of a question about what remains unknown. In his twentieth seminar, Lacan uses the term *signifiance* to refer to this tropism toward a open potentiality of meaning.[33] Unlike *signification*, which indicates the more specific semantic cargo of the signifier, *signifiance* names the power of the signifier (or, more accurately, of the network of relations in which every signifier is located) to hold open a horizon of meaning-as-yet-to-be-determined.

With respect to the first aspect of the signifying function, that of separating and distancing, we can say with fresh literalness that "the word is the murder of the Thing." This phrase, quoted more than once by Lacan, recalls the philosophy of Hegel.[34] The "murder" has to do with the way the word substitutes itself for the thing and to that extent displaces or even negates it. Yet once we allow that the signifier also holds open a more indeterminate dimension of meaning, another Hegelian concept, one far more central to Hegel's entire theoretical edifice, becomes even more relevant. The double function of the signifier with respect to the unknown Thing constitutes an exemplary instance of Hegel's concept of *Aufhebung*, the very heartbeat of his famous dialectic. In accord with the twofold meaning of the German word, something that undergoes *Aufhebung* is simultaneously canceled *and* preserved, both negated *and*, in some sense, affirmed.

At the most elementary level, the linguistic signifier serves to accomplish a primordial *Aufhebung*. The signifier cancels *das Ding*, distancing the subject from the object, but it also preserves precisely what is canceled, marking it for further cognizing sometime in the future. The signifier establishes a locus suspended between the subject and the Other, putting what remains unknown and potentially threatening about the Other at a safe distance, yet thereby repositioning it and allowing it to return as a question.

The result is that discourse is never fully transparent. It always regenerates a dimension of the questionable. "Every discourse presents itself as heavy with consequences," Lacan says, "but ones that are obscure. Nothing of what we say, in principle, fails to imply some. Nevertheless we do not know which."[35] Discourse never fails to bear within itself something of the dimension of *das Ding* and to reproduce its consequences for the unfolding of thought.[36]

But Hegel is not the only source for conceptualizing the twofold function of the signifier. The other source is Freud. The double action of the signifier that we have identified, simultaneously distancing and disclosive, defensive and expressive, is strikingly parallel to Freud's theory of the compromise formation of the symptom. Like the symptom that effects a "compromise between the warring forces of the mind," the relation of the signifier to what it signifies effects both a kind of negation or suspension, the substitution of a mere sound for the thing itself, *and also* a promise of new access, a portal through which the exploration of the Other-Thing can unfold.

My contention is that this way of conjoining the Lacanian signifier with the Freudian symptom brings into high relief one of the most fundamental and far-reaching consequences of Lacan's rewriting of psychoanalytic theory. The implication is that the paradoxes of symptomatic behavior are not confined to exceptional moments in which human nature is bent under the pressure of traumatic contingency. *Human nature is symptomatic through and through.* Something deeply akin to the bifold dynamic that Freud discovered in the symptom, simultaneously repressive and expressive, defensive and discharging, expunging and explorative, is operative even at the level of the micro-increments of language. In the human psyche, we might say, it's symptomatic compromise "all the way down."[37]

It Speaks

The bifold function of the signifier that I'm calling its "elementary matrix" can be further illuminated by briefly returning to Nietzsche's remark about how a thought comes "when 'it' wishes, and not when 'I' wish."[38] Nietzsche here points to a phenomenon as totally ubiquitous as it is exceedingly strange, something to which we generally remain completely oblivious. My own speech stream generally proceeds out of my mouth— the paradox is striking—without my say-so. The words appear to come by themselves, as if they were flowing forth less *from* me than *through* me, as if the words were forming themselves. In beginning a sentence, even a sentence about the most banal and quotidian topic, I myself don't know precisely how the sentence will end. I don't exactly foresee which words will emerge, even just several words down the line. On reflection, we might readily conclude that it is not "I" who is choosing the words at all. They seem to come into my mouth unbidden, by a kind of automatism. And yet my speech is almost always accompanied by a sense that, yes, this is what I want to say. It is *I* who am speaking. These considerations point toward the operation of a fundamental self-delusion at the heart of the apparently simple phenomenon of saying something.

Nietzsche's appeal to the idea that a thought comes when "it" wishes can be drawn upon to explain what Lacan early on called "empty speech." I typically feel most comfortably "me" when I'm seamlessly caught up in the blah-blah-blah of idle chatter in the most trivial, virtually prescripted exchanges. Yet such empty speech is not only the most vacuous discourse; it also most resembles the speech of everybody else. Paradoxically, then, it is possible to feel like "myself," most seamlessly "in my own skin," precisely when I am most indistinguishable from other people.

Yet Nietzsche's suggestion that "it thinks" also resonates powerfully with Lacan's very similar play on the "it" of the Freudian id: *le ça*. "*Ça parle*," claims Lacan. *It speaks*. If the free flow of the speech stream usually spills banalities, it also passes important traces of something unconscious. That both functions are involved is illustrated by the slip of the tongue. In the motivated slip of the tongue—the classic case cited by Freud is that of the chairman of the convention who gavels the opening of the meeting by declaring "I hereby call this meeting adjourned!"—my actual speech sometimes flatly contradicts my conscious purpose, revealing the influence of some other impulse that I have repressed. I accidentally speak—*it speaks*—what I truly want to say.

"But," protests the critic, "don't both of the phenomena you've just described—mouthing everyday blah-blah and the slip in which something unintended slips out—amount to the same thing? In both cases, you point to the way the speech stream 'comes to me,' as when we sometimes say, 'It occurred to me to say . . .' or 'I found myself saying. . . .' The point you're making echoes Heidegger's claim about how man doesn't speak language; rather language speaks man."

Not so fast! There are two levels here. Stirring them together too quickly is a mistake. Lacan makes sense of the difference between two modes of experiencing oneself "spoken by language" by distinguishing between the ego and the subject. Ego identity is founded upon the paradox of the first level: my ego is most secure when I am most mirrored by other speakers, when I am most firmly buoyed up by the flow of the most superficial exchanges. By contrast, the subject is at issue at a second level of linguistic functioning, when what comes out of my mouth unexpectedly jars my well-worn sense of myself. The slip of the tongue introduces a gap or hiccup of speech in which my ego is brought up short. The collision with conscious intent signals the force of unconscious desire.

The psychoanalytic situation seeks to invite such slippages of speech and to maximize their disorienting effects. When the analyst plays "the dummy" by stubbornly remaining silent, she submits the speech of the analysand to a measured pressure of depersonalization and also provides the resonant echo chamber in which the glitches and unexpectedly loaded stumbles of speech cause me to hear myself with a new ear. What is at stake is an attempt to invite ruptures in the discourse of the ego in the space of which the desire of the subject, what Lacan calls "the discourse of the Other," becomes audible.

The two gradients of speech at issue here reflect the two sides of the elementary matrix of the signifier. The discourse of the ego remains flat-footedly on the well-trod terrain of meaning. The result is the sense of saying what I mean and meaning what I say, a sense that is ultimately deceptive. In the slip of the tongue, by contrast, the rule of meaning is interrupted by something incongruous, unintended, even nonsensical, in which the trace of an unconscious impulse announces itself.

The matrix of the signifier therefore presents two potentialities. On one side, we have the attachment of the signifier to a well-established signified. Call it the signifier's primary *semantic* force. It grounds a stable *meaning*. It accounts for the fact that when we hear the word "hippopotamus" it is almost impossible to avoid thinking of a hippopotamus. But there is a second, essentially elusive dimension of every utterance of the signifier that opens out toward a more indeterminate horizon. This second dimension is linked to *das Ding* and its status as an unknown. It's tempting, in contrast with the determinate meaning of the *semantic*, to call this other, more slippery and indistinct dimension simply *mantic*. In fact, what is at stake is well reflected in the sense of the Greek word *mantikos*, which referred to prophecy and divination. What is *mantic* reaches out into something beyond our ken. Intimately related to *mantikos* is the word *mania*, which in Greek implies a kind of inspired madness. In its mantic dimension, the spoken word always reaches beyond a definite assignment of meaning toward an ecstatic horizon of indeterminacy, a meaning-as-yet-unknown.

This twofold dimensionality of the signifier, semantic versus mantic, is reflected in (though by no means exhausted by) the common distinction between denotation and connotation. Denotation involves reference to some definite object or state of affairs, whereas connotation spreads out in various directions as incomplete tendrils, mere hints or shades of meaning. We owe this potentially more fertile and far-reaching dimension to the way every signifier is bound up with the larger system of other signifiers.

Lacan is intensely interested in such an allusive penumbra of meaning, particularly in his analyses of metaphor and metonymy. But there is clearly, and crucially, something more in the Lacanian conception of the signifier. We touched on it earlier in discussing Lacan's notion of the bar that separates signifier and signified. Lacan posits a kind of positive resistance to definite signification. The result is the symbolic projection of a gap or void. As he puts it, "The fashioning of the signifier and the introduction of a gap or a hole in the real is identical."[39] There is an excess of all semantic import that is borne by every signifier and that passes beyond even the most vaguely connotative resonance of meaning. One is tempted to make a reference here, as Lacan himself does more than once, to the pre-Socratic notion of non-being. Every signifier harbors within itself an appeal to pure lack, to a Thing that is a No-thing.

This open horizon of the signifier, the dimension that Lacan variously calls *manque à être* or *béance*, is on display at the heart of the psychoanalytic method. For how else are we to account for free association? In free association, I give myself over to a pure openness to apparently unrelated ideas. A subjective posturing toward an unfettered readiness to receive whatever comes to mind is the heart of the psychoanalytic method—the means by which dreams, slips, and fantasies will be opened toward a larger horizon of connections to other things—but also a key *goal* to be achieved by analysis. To have passed through a successful psychoanalysis is to feel oneself more readily called by what doesn't make sense from the standpoint of conscious calculation. The "well-analyzed" person has become more open to the fertile, potentially transformative influence of thoughts that hover on the border of complete nonsense. The positive outcome of analysis is to become a little more comfortable with the unknowable Thing.[40]

Lacan connects the indeterminate, Thingly horizon of the signifier to the domain of the religious in his reading of Heidegger's well-known meditation on the clay jug or vase. Fittingly enough for our purposes, Heidegger put forward his theory in an essay titled "The Thing," an essay that Lacan clearly had in mind when he articulated his own conception of *das Ding*.[41] For both thinkers, the focus on the vase has the advantage of centering the discussion on an object that virtually defines the human being. For the paleoarcheologist, pottery fragments at the site of an excavation are the surest clues to the past existence of human beings. Heidegger brings out its sublime dimension by inviting us to recognize that the vase is essentially a skin of clay wrapped around a void. The vase materially captures the Nothing and renders it serviceable.

Lacan augments Heidegger's conception by insisting that the simple gesture of molding clay around a central void effects, at least implicitly, a leap of virtually infinite abstraction. The vase is the material embodiment of an openness to some as yet indeterminate meaning. The void becomes the locus of content yet to come. Precisely in order to understand Heidegger's own example it is therefore necessary to pass completely beyond the materiality of the container toward its own being as a signifier. Lacan asserts, as if he were offering a kind of Zen koan, that Heidegger's vase is the signifier that signifies signifying itself.

> If it really is a signifier, and the first of such signifiers fashioned by the human hand, it is in its signifying essence a signifier of nothing other than of signifying as such or, in other words, of no particular signified. . . . This nothing in particular that characterizes it in its incarnated form characterizes the vase as such. It creates the void and thereby introduces the possibility of filling it. Emptiness and fullness are introduced into the world that by itself knows not of them. It is on the basis of this fabricated signifier, this vase, that emptiness and fullness as such enter the world.[42]

The relevance of this Lacanian point about the "pure" signifying power of the vase becomes even clearer when we allow ourselves to imagine the vase taken up into the religious ritual, transcending completely its promise of containing worldly goods of one sort of another. In such a context, the object in question becomes a container of absolute sublimity. No longer a pot, bowl, or jug, we might say, but a *chalice*. Yet such a religious deployment of the pot is less an addition to some merely practical function than a mode of making explicit its original potential of ontological indeterminacy.

Lacan further expands upon the religious resonances of the power to evoke the void that resides at the heart of language, the power that makes possible the fashioning of the vase, by claiming that it is the signifier that is the true creator *ex nihilo*:

> Now if you consider the vase from the point of view I first proposed, as an object made to represent the existence of the emptiness at the center of the real that is called the Thing, this emptiness as represented in the representation presents itself as a *nihil*, as nothing. And that is why the potter, just like you to whom I am speaking, creates the vase with his hand around this emptiness, creates it, just like the mythical creator, *ex nihilo*, starting with a hole.[43]

Rethinking Religion
(or, What Is the Sacred?)

Having acquainted ourselves with the key Lacanian concept of *das Ding* as the abyssally unknowable dimension of the Other, the task now is to draw on that background to pose a new psychoanalytic theory of religion. Lacan clearly indicates that the Thing is somehow intimately connected with the religious. "Freud left us with the problem of a gap once again at the level of *das Ding*," he says, "which is that of religious men and mystics."[1] We can now anticipate the main point. When Lacan ventures that "the true formula for atheism is that God is unconscious," his claim is that the awe in the face of the divine arises from the locus of the Other-Thing.

How, then, to further unfold that point?

At the outset, it is appropriate to mark the challenge before us. One of the interpretive principles Lacan most insists upon when it comes to the problem of sacred is the difficulty of lumping all religions together. A single conceptual frame risks blinding us to essential differences. In his 1974 interview, published as *The Triumph of Religion*, Lacan insists that "to try to put all religions in the same basket and do what is called 'the history of religions' is truly awful."[2] If, in what follows, we seek to interpret a range of religious formations by relating them to the overarching notion of *das Ding*, we will need to highlight what is distinctive in each of the traditions we examine.

Yet even as we remain mindful of a range of differences, the elementary example of prayer helps point the way forward. Isn't the prayerful petition always addressed in some way to the unknown Thing in the Other? Doesn't even the most heartfelt prayer, even the prayer most deeply confident of its addressee, hang in some mixed suspense of hope and fear, never fully sure of being granted a response, or even of being received? The prayer is an appeal, a supplication—essentially a question—that knows it may go unanswered. Even prayers of thanks or praise beg to be heard with no guarantee that they will be. Simone Weil was correct: *even for the most fervent believer, every prayer is inevitably an echo in a Void.*[3] Otherwise said, every prayer resonates in the hollow of the Other-Thing.

What we need to examine is the way different religious formations offer varying relationships to that abyss of the unknown.

In chapters 4, 5, and 6 we examine in turn the three religious formations that most inform the unfolding of the sacred in European history— Greek polytheism, Judaism, and Christianity. In chapter 7, we'll broaden the scope to include some much briefer notes about non-Western traditions and Islam, along with an examination of the religious dimensions of capitalism. In each of these accounts, I venture a number of sweeping claims, sketched in extreme compression. I can well imagine scholars of religion at virtually every turn protesting against my characterizations as oversimplified and readily debatable. No doubt many will find it irritating, even scandalous, that I rarely pause even to mark the directions alternative readings might take.

In anticipation of such objections, let me emphasize at the outset that the point of the following analyses is *definitely not* to provide a fully adequate or comprehensive accounting of any religion. The aim is rather to offer some bare-bones sketches of several key traditions developed along a very particular interpretive line of Lacanian theory. The goal is to imagine in crude outline what religion looks like viewed through the lens of Lacan's conception of the unconscious. To that qualification, it must be added that Lacan himself never puts forward any fully formed elucidation, either of the traditions I address or of the religious in general. He does, however, repeatedly offer very provocative commentaries on religion, a bread-crumb path of highly suggestive quotations scattered throughout his writings and seminars. My treatments rely on those key references the way a rock climber depends on a few well-driven pitons to traverse a broad cliff face. My hope is that the interest and illumination sparked by the resulting perspective will repay the reader's willingness to follow that bread-crumb trail.

4

Greek Polytheism

The Worship of Force

The gods are a mode by which the real is revealed.
—Jacques Lacan

For the modern reader of Homer or Hesiod, the mythic pantheon of ancient Greek gods can easily seem like a cartoon litany of colorful but zany characters. We can't help forming for ourselves the question posed by the title of Paul Veyne's book *Did the Greeks Believe in Their Myths?* What could it possibly have meant to *believe* in such stories? Such, after all, is the meaning of the Greek word *mythoi*: stories. Some scholars have even maintained that the myths cannot be taken to constitute a religion at all. In this chapter, my aim is to shed some light on the meaning and function of the archaic Greek gods and the tales of their exploits, indeed on the meaning of the archaic Greek ethos altogether.

In getting started, it is crucial to again note some limits of my argument. It should be admitted up front, for example, that among the following three chapters on the primary religions of the West—Greek paganism, Judaism, and Christianity—reliance on Lacan's commentary is by far the slimmest in my treatment of the Greeks. The reason, quite simply, is that Lacan devoted far more attention to the history and dynamics of monotheism than of polytheism. While I take the following account of the archaic Greek sense of the sacred to be deeply consonant with Lacan's outlook, it is an account that is adumbrated only piecemeal by Lacan himself. Moreover, the crucial guiding thread for my entire effort is provided by a single, enigmatic quote. Referring to ancient Greek religion, Lacan claims that "the gods are a mode by which the real is revealed."[1]

The challenge is deciding what this sentence could possibly mean. The problem isn't with the basic thesis. It's not hard to imagine that the pagan gods were somehow stand-ins for the unthinkable real. The catch is the last bit: the real as *revealed*. Isn't the Lacanian real precisely what *cannot* be revealed? The answer to this question will require sketching the basic outline of the archaic Greek *Weltanschauung*.

The Void of the Temple, the Drama of Sacrifice

Freud's account remains useful for establishing a baseline. The proliferation of Greek gods and demigods, myths and legends, nymphs and satyrs, soothsayers, seers, and oracles, cultic and ritual practices provided a sprawling apparatus for reckoning the distribution of favors from the greater powers on which human life depended. The resulting regime of worship was oriented toward the unknown in two interrelated senses: the unknown of the gods' intentions for human beings and the unknown prospects for their future dispensations. These dimensions of unknowing haunted the entire phantasmagoria of Greek religious life, and it is there that we already find a global reverberation of the Lacanian Other-Thing.

In one of his most famous writings, *The Origin of the Work of Art*, Heidegger analyzes the ancient temple in terms that echo his discussion of the vase.[2] In both the vase and the temple, we have an envelope of stone that encloses a primal vacancy. For Heidegger, the shelter of the temple's open space enabled the intersection of the "Fourfold" of earth and sky, mortals and divinities. One could equally say that the yawning void of the temple provided a spatial analogue for *Dasein*'s exposure to the presencing event of Being. The sacred space conjured the empty clearing in which *Dasein* is confronted by its own being-in-question.

Lacan offers a parallel account. He poses the temple as a cardinal example of his definition of sublimation, in which "a work of art always involves encircling the Thing."[3] The temple, Lacan says, is "a construction around emptiness that designates the place of the Thing."[4] By means of suspending the worshipper in a hollow vacancy of space, the temple evokes "the character of a beyond of the sacred—something that we are precisely trying to identify in its most general form by the term, the Thing."[5] In the most literal sense, the temple interior makes room for the divine. "God's power," Lacan says, "resides in the capacity to advance into emptiness."[6]

Rituals of sacrifice, the everyday heartbeat of ancient Greek religion, required such a preliminary consecration of sacred space, itself a kind of void. Outside a proper temple, the circumference of that space

was most commonly marked by strewing barley grains, already in itself
an act of sacrifice. Grains that might otherwise have been eaten were
intentionally scattered. But the larger question is about the meaning of
ancient sacrifice. How to conceive it?

Walter Burkert provides a classic account of Greek sacrifice in *Homo
Necans*.[7] Once the consecrated zone was marked and the altar prepared,
the space could not be entered by menstruating women, who were
thought to be sources of pollution. It was also expected that priests con-
ducting the sacrifice would practice sexual abstinence for a period before
the ceremony. Once the congregants were assembled, the sacrificial
animal—typically a goat, lamb, or calf—was introduced into the circle,
preferably led by virgins. The animal was often raised specifically for the
purpose, and was preferably a specimen without scar or blemish. It was
particularly auspicious for the victim to show no signs of panic or resistance, appearing to carry itself willingly to its own death. Perhaps for that
reason, the sacrificial knife remained hidden in a special basket and was
taken out only at the last moment. The officiant then used it to sever a
tuft of fur from the forelock of the beast's head, tossing it onto the fire
atop the altar. The women in the assembled throng would heighten the
tension by sounding the sacrificial scream, the *ologylé*. Only then, after the
first, symbolic violation accompanied by the scream, would the animal be
killed, its throat cut with a single stroke. The jetting blood, pulsing from
the victim's neck in convulsive spurts like a dreadful crimson ejaculation,
would be carefully caught in a special bowl.

Once dead, the animal would be cut open and its innards inspected
for irregularities that might signal evil portents. The victim's body thus
became a kind of book in which congregants sought to read the secrets
of their future. Only after this consultation would the carcass be dismem-
bered and the various parts roasted on the fire and served around to be
eaten. At the conclusion of the rite, the bare bones and skin were sometimes reassembled to create a deathly facsimile of the living creature,
then reduced to ashes on the flaming altar.

In keeping with the general premises of his reworking of Freudian
theory, Lacan's interpretation is not thematic but structural. The fundamental purpose of sacrifice is to reenact the birth of the signifier. The
ritual of sacrifice aims to reposition the human subject in relation to lack,
and thus to desire and its regulation. Indeed, signification itself, as the
act of substitution in which "the word is the murder of the thing," is essentially a kind of sacrifice. Lacan even invites us to discern the dynamics
of sacrifice as the hidden meaning of our lives, regardless of our religious
belief or lack of it. "We don't live our lives," Lacan says, "whoever we are,

without tirelessly offering to goodness knows what unknown divinity the sacrifice of some little mutilation, whether valid or not, that we impose upon ourselves in the field of our desires."[8]

In the ritual of Greek sacrifice recounted by Burkert, it is possible to trace the whole trajectory of emerging signification as Lacan conceives it. The ritual commences with the wholeness of the body imago, modeled by an animal without blemish, an animal that has never been submitted to the cut. So far, there appears to be nothing unknown or withheld from the celebrants. But at the pivotal moment of the ritual, the sounding of the chilling shriek of the *ologylé* signals an anticipation of something unimaginable. Indeed, the communal scream can readily be interpreted as being in itself a kind of uncanny, primal signifier, instigating a horrifying suspense, the meaning of which is completely indeterminate. The climatic death stroke then effects the evental moment, the pivot between life and death, known and unknown. What follows are various cuts of the body, the vivisected limbs and organs of the victim recalling Lacan's notion of part objects, the most primitive embodiments of the *objet a*, the harbingers of inchoate desire.

The larger function of this sacrificial drama was to establish the possibility of exchange between mortals and divinities. The logic of the procedure was well spoken for by the later Latin formula *do ut des*, "I give so that you will give." Of course, there was a certain amount of "cheating" on the part of the mortals, who got to feast on the choice loins while the gods had to content themselves with the fragrant smoke wafting upward to the heavens.[9] But the larger aim was to stabilize an economy of exchange. In its ultimate meaning and function, Lacan suggests, "sacrifice is not at all intended to be an offering, nor a gift, both of which are propagated in a quite different dimension, but the capture of the Other in the web of desire."[10]

The Agon of Forces

How, then, are we to enter more deeply into the ancient Greek relation to the divine? One way is simply to accompany them to dinner. In the first book of the *Iliad*, Homer recalls Odysseus's band gathering on the beach for the evening meal:

> When prayers were said and grains of barley strewn,
> they held the bullocks for the knife, and flayed them,
> cutting out joints and wrapping these in fat,

two layers, folded, with raw strips of flesh,
for the old man to burn on cloven faggots,
wetting it all with wine.

Around him stood
young men with five-tined forks in hand, and when
the vitals had been tasted, joints consumed,
they sliced the chines and quarters for the spits,
roasted them evenly and drew them off.
Their meal being now prepared and all work done,
they feasted to their hearts' content and made
desire for meat and drink recede again,
then young men filled their winebowls to the brim,
ladling drops for the god in every cup.
Propitiatory songs rose clear and strong
until day's end, to praise the god, Apollo,
as One Who Keeps the Plague Afar; and listening
the god took joy.

After the sun went down
and darkness came, at last Odysseus' men
lay down to rest under the stern hawsers.

When Dawn spread out her finger tips of rose
they put to sea for the main camp of Akhaians,
and the Archer God sent them a following wind.
Stepping the mast they shook their canvas out,
and wind caught, bellying the sail. A foaming
dark blue wave sang backward from the bow
as the running ship made way against the sea,
until they came offshore of the encampment.
Here they put in and hauled the black ship high,
far up on the sand, braced her with shoring timbers,
and then disbanded, each to his own hut.

Meanwhile unstirring and with smoldering heart,
the godlike athlete, son of Pêleus, Prince
Akhilleus waited by his racing ships.
He would not enter the assembly
of emulous men, nor ever go to war,
but felt his valor staling in his breast
with idleness, and missed the cries of battle.[11]

From the very outset, we are unmistakably in a world profoundly foreign to our own. For the ancients, the meal was itself a ritual of sacrifice. Before the eating must come the killing. The living beast is ushered into the midst, its eyes skittishly darting. Then its throat is slit, the hide is stripped, and the limbs carved away and spitted for the open fire. For the denizen of a modern household, such a scene, far from offering the welcome pleasures of feasting and fellowship, would border on the traumatic. And no wonder. The organization of modern life appears dedicated to concealing the cardinal fact of existence around which the lives of the ancients turned, a fact reinforced on a daily basis: nothing lives but something else must die. It is a lesson both about the interconnectedness and interdependence of all things, and about the way in which all things have their place in a hierarchy of being that indispensably requires conflict and violence. In this respect, Heraclitus still had one foot firmly planted in the archaic world that he and his fellow *philosophoi* were otherwise busy dismantling. As he reminds us, the word *bios* is appropriately ambiguous: "The name of the bow (*biós*) is life (*bíos*), but its work is death."[12]

A significant trace of this archaic sensibility survives in the writings of the premier Greek novelist of the twentieth century, Nikos Kazantzakis, who, among other things, penned his own sequel to Homer's *Odyssey*. Kazantzakis's most memorable character, Zorba the Greek, is forever reminding his more modern-minded boss of the inexorable cycle of death and life that underlies all existence. Zorba insists that we fully savor this cycle, even in its gruesome moments. We need to recognize how the lamb consumed at the evening meal enables the transformation of flesh into love and joy. When we dance in the firelight after dinner, the lamb lives again. And it doesn't merely live. The lamb, too, now dances.

If the feast scene of *Iliad* book 1 confronts us with the cycle of life and death, it also displays another crucial feature of the Homeric world, a fact that is even more foreign to the modern reader. It was a world in which there were no *things*, only *forces*. The archaic Greeks had no conception of the inert and lifeless objects that compose the entire landscape of our modern experience. The notion of a mere *thing* did not exist, at least not in any sense that we would recognize. On the contrary, the Greeks imagined only forces of varying kinds and magnitudes. The implicit ontology of the Homeric world was thus akin to the primitive animism of virtually all aboriginal cultures. The elements among which the ancients dwelled—wood, fire, meat, wine, wind, and water—all possessed their own vitalizing (or mortifying) force. The metal of the spear tip, for example, was to be feared as a virtual incarnation of lethality. It radiated death. Homer repeatedly calls it "death-dealing bronze." Or, again, only an idiot or a madman would doubt the active, daunting force of stone. Hefting it in your hand, it pushes back. No wonder that, when his bronze spear point is bent or broken by the blow of an axe, the suddenly defenseless warrior grabs a good-size rock. With his own strength now joined with the of power of stone, the pair will again be a formidable adversary.

Homer's verses present a whole series of such animations. Even in the English translation, we hear of the phenomena of the natural world not merely occurring but *acting*. Dawn "spreads her finger tips of rose." A foaming wave "sings." The wind is "caught" by the sail, like a wild animal in a net. Even now, many centuries after the extinction of the archaic experience, our language still harbors vestiges of that world composed only of competing forces. We still say that night "falls," that dawn "comes," that snow "buries" the field.

Even hunger and thirst are presented by Homer as fundamental forces with which human beings have to contend. The evening meal, we are told, "made desire for meat and drink recede again." Those desires will be back, of course, like the tides of the sea. We do not control such forces. The best we can do is to temporarily fend them off. Akhilleus is said to feel "his valor staling in his breast." Here, the prowess of courage is treated as a force at least partly independent even of the man who is most famous for it, a kind of power that may burst forth with great fury or, at another moment, flag and fail. It is not for nothing that the first word of the *Iliad* is "rage"—"The rage of Akhilleus, doomed and ruinous."[13] Rage is a force all its own, at times arising as an overmastering storm of ferocity. In this sense, the great Italian tenor Luciano Pavarotti spoke like a Homeric Greek when he referred to his marvelous capacity of voice as a kind of foreign presence alive in his body, a power of its own over which he himself had limited control. He regarded it as an independent, gifting force that would someday, like it or not, abandon him.

The same can be said even more emphatically of sexual desire. Eros is taken to be a great cosmic force that deploys itself in dizzying variety— homosexual, heterosexual, pederastic. In the grip of its bewitching power, human beings are mere pawns. Even the most moralistic among the speeches in Plato's *Symposium*, that of Pausanias, allows that there can be no shame in the urge itself, however crazy the objects of its hunger. Eros is an incorrigible imp who threatens to make a fool of even the most upright and stalwart man. Unlike the later Christian judgment, which damned concupiscence of the flesh as an intrinsic moral taint, the Greeks appear to have made no moral judgment of the erotic impulse itself. No man *chooses* the objects of such urges; Eros arranges them before us, decked out in all their mesmerizing allure. There is nothing disgraceful in the force itself, says Pausanias; we become culpable only in the degree to which we degrade ourselves as pathetic slaves of the erotic itch. We debase ourselves only when we become mere playthings of Eros's power.

My first thesis, then, is that the archaic Greek experience cannot be understood apart from an implicit but definitive ontology: no "things," only forces. The world described by Homer is a world of contending agencies, arranged in a broad hierarchy of varying powers, between which there unfolds a great, unceasing contest, or agon. Human beings wield power over a range of lesser forces, of course, but they are no match for gods. And here we find the key for understanding the entire Greek pantheon. For what were the gods but wielders of more-than-human force, powers greater than those of mortal men? The mightiness of storm and thunderbolt belonged to Zeus. The overwhelming force of the tidal currents and waves, as well as that of earthquake, was the province of Poseidon. The power of fertility belonged to Demeter, and that of sexual desire to Aphrodite. Who could doubt the enormity of those forces, capable, should the gods and goddesses desire it, of starving men to death or of driving them mad with desire? Light and the emotive power of music belonged to Apollo. And how great was the power of Dionysos! The potency of wine, sufficient to rouse the wildest spasms of dancing as well as all manner of mad, self-destructive passions, was obviously divine. War, too, was identified with a god—Ares. The Greeks would have stared uncomprehendingly at Clausewitz's definition of war as politics carried on by other means. War was a great and terrible force, an all-consuming fury that laid waste to cities, a great rolling catastrophe of destruction that feasted on blood.

Defining the gods as more-than-human forces immediately explains the three most basic features of ancient Greek divinity.

1. If each of the gods represents a natural force of some sort, the resulting religion is inevitably *polytheistic*. The concrete experience of everyday life in antiquity, a world completely alien to the push-button regime of "modern conveniences," taught the fundamental lesson that existence is a matter of sustaining oneself in the cross fire of multiple, often conflicting forces, some apparently lending a hand in the task of survival, others making things more difficult, if not downright fatal. One is always surrounded by god forces and subject to their influence.

2. The gods are powerful, but all power has its limits. In the Greek pantheon of divine forces, there was *no unlimited power*. No god was omnipotent. Not only did the idea of an infinite force not exist for the Greeks, but they would almost certainly have considered it to be nonsensical, a kind of contradiction in terms. The very concept of a force implies limits in various dimensions: directionality, degree of intensity, duration of influence, and so forth. Even Zeus had his limits. Powerful though he

was, he could not prevent the destruction of the Trojans, clearly his favorites in their battle against the Akhaians.

3. The Greek gods are *immortal*. Gods in virtually every culture are eternal. But if divinities basically represent forces of nature, the link with immortality is especially well evidenced. The influence of the gods in human affairs comes and goes, rises and falls, but never fails to return.

This first stage of my argument is by no means original. To identify the Greek gods with natural forces repeats one of Freud's central theses in *The Future of an Illusion*. And as it did for Freud, the core thesis illuminates the central purpose of the archaic Greek religion of sacrifice. Sacrifices were made in hopes of inviting the larger forces into concert with one's own purposes, or at least of evading their vengeful opposition. The magnitude of sacrifice, measured either by the sheer number of victims or by their intrinsic value, was crucial to the success of the sacrificial gesture. The quantity of victims is spoken for in the Greek word *hecatomb*, which referred to the sacrifice of a hundred cattle, the scale of ritual required, say, for the launching of an army. As to value, one outstanding example is Agamemnon's sacrifice of his daughter, Iphigenia, in an effort to persuade the gods to release the winds that would blow the Argive ships to Troy.

The ancient ontology of contending forces seems indirectly confirmed by a distinctive feature of the Greek language. Linguists tell us that it is the most verb-rich language known, set apart not only by the sheer percentage of verbs in the basic lexicon but also by the immense complexity and subtlety of tenses, voices, and moods. The Greek language is emphatically, perhaps even uniquely, a language of action and force. At the opposite end of the spectrum is modern English, the most noun-heavy language to have ever existed. English, we might say, is the language par excellence of property over action, fact over force, status over striving.

How, one might now ask, can such an implicit ontology of contending forces support the Lacanian notion of a big Other? It is by no means obvious. Perhaps the closest approximation would be the deep pagan sense of "everything in its place," the sense of a pyramid of greater and lesser forces, to each its own. The archaic universe was ordered by precincts of power. Zeus ruled the sky, Poseidon the sea, Demeter the earth, and Hades the underworld.[14] And in human society, too, there was an order: kings were meant to act as kings, slaves as slaves. The order of the cosmos implied an ordered hierarchy of domains. Then, too, everything was subject to the lordship of time. By eventually delivering all things to their death, time judged everything.[15] The ultimate name for such lethal judgment in the pagan Greek world was *moira*, or fate. As testified to by the death of Hektor, Zeus's favorite, even the father of gods had to bow before the dictates of fate. Yet the all-encompassing power of fate itself remained shrouded in darkness. *Moira*, from which nothing escapes, was the archaic face of the unknown par excellence.

What Appears Is Real, What Is Real Appears

We now turn to the second, absolutely fundamental feature of the archaic worldview: *the primacy of appearances*. When, in book 2 of the *Iliad*, Priam sits with his counselors high above the horde of Akhaian troops, he needs to ask exactly who's who, but even at a great distance he can easily pick out the great ones: Agamemnon, Odysseus, Aias, Diomêdês. Unlike powerful men of our own epoch—the novelist, the scientific genius, the great painter, even the senator, many of whom might easily be mistaken on the street for any ordinary fellow—the Homeric heroes looked the part from a mile away. The truth could be read off the skin of things.

This principle of truth-telling appearances undergirds the ancient culture of augury and soothsaying. Also in book 2 of the *Iliad*, a tale is told of the day the Argive ships arrived at Troy. On that day, in the precincts of the sacred altars, a "blood-red serpent . . . twined and spiraled up the tree," only to hideously wrap itself around a nest of sparrows and devour the clutch of baby birds, "all cheeping pitifully, while their mother fluttered and shrilled in her distress."[16] In the ancient world, no one seeing such a scene would have hesitated to accept it as a telling omen. Of course, to arrive at its precise interpretation would have required the offices of priests and seers. But the underlying truth—that nothing appears but what is real, and nothing that is real fails to announce itself in appearance—would have been doubted by no one.

Most of my students have never for a moment entertained this ancient verity. The modern cast of mind, well accustomed to all manner of invisible realities from atoms to hormones to inflation, doesn't hesitate to dismiss episodes like that of the snake and the sparrows as "mere coincidence." Which is one reason why my students find reading a text like Hesiod's *Theogony* so difficult. The poem inevitably feels to them like an interminable and arbitrary list of names. Not so for its original audience. What the students fail to grasp is that Hesiod's tale of the origin of gods and men is everywhere undergirded by the way reality simply *appears*.

Why is Earth female and Sky male? Because it *looks* that way. "Broad-bosomed" Earth lies passively, with hills like mounded flesh, beneath the overarching embrace of a moody Father Sky, who showers her with impregnating ejaculate (rain, of course). The class shifts uncomfortably in their seats when I clue them in that the "furrows" of Earth in which the seeds of Sky are planted recall one of most ancient of metaphors: that of the moist fold of the feminine genitalia, plowed by the fertilizing phallus. I can't resist adding that the budding sprouts that poke out of that same smooth fold are a perfect visual analogue of birthing babies. Students also stare blankly at Hesiod's description of the children of Earth and Sky: giants with a hundred arms and fifty heads. But you only need to look, I tell them. The children of Earth and Sky are just where you'd expect to find them; precisely at the horizon, at the meeting place of the two primal parents, and they look exactly as they are described. They are *trees*.

It goes on. What sense does it make that Sky buries his children in the bowels of Earth, so that Mother Earth is eventually groaning with the bloat of unborn offspring? And what does it mean—here things get really wild—that the son of Sky, Cronos, in cahoots with his groaning mother, overthrows the power of Sky by *castrating* him? Again, just *look*. Sky buries Earth's children, sealing them in her womb under the blanket of . . . snow. And castration isn't an arbitrary mode of attack. Cronos must strike Sky in the seat of his power: the vitality of procreation. But it gets even better. The sickle with which Cronos lops off his father's member reappears once every month, and where else but in the sky? It is the crescent sliver of the moon. It's an added bonus that the waxing of the moon was for the Greeks an obvious visual metaphor of the swelling belly of pregnancy. And how lovely is the resulting myth: the power of Sky, momentous though it is, obeys an even greater power. Storms and droughts finally pass, as do seasons. The power of Sky bends to the ultimately superior rule of Time.

The final proof of the veracity of appearances is to be found in Hesiod's myth of Prometheus. Once he has escaped from being chained to the rock, prey to having his liver chewed out day after day, Prometheus steals fire and gives it back to man. When Zeus discovers this crowning deceit, his justice is swift and terrible. With the blessing of fire must come a curse: woman. In the Hesiodic universe, femininity had existed from the first (witness Mother Earth) but not for human beings. The interesting thing, however, is the precise manner in which woman functions as a punitive scourge.

> At the orders of the son of Cronus, the famous lame smith-god [Hephaestus] shaped some clay in the image of a tender girl. The bright-eyed daughter Athena dressed and decked her in silvery clothes. A marvelous embroidered veil fell from her head and was held in her hands. Round

her head the goddess tied a golden diadem on which the smith-god himself had exercised his skill, to please his father Zeus. When Zeus had completed this beautiful curse to go with the blessing of fire, he displayed the girl in an assembly of gods and men, all decked out in the finery supplied by the bright-eyed daughter of the lord of hosts. Gods and men were speechless when they saw how deadly and how irresistible was the trick with which Zeus was going to catch mankind.[17]

Woman is a terrible bane precisely because she violates the most basic tenet of all existence: things should appear as they actually are. Woman is a maliciously intentional exception. She was fashioned as a living lie. Her alluring beauty is nothing but a cruel ruse. As soon as she has seduced a man to fall in love with her deceptive beauty and marry her, she reveals her true nature. Women, says Hesiod, are "a plague which men must live with. They have no place where the curse of poverty is; they belong with luxury."[18] What is perhaps most amazing about this primal narrative of sexism is its stubbornly long shelf life. We have only very recently graduated from the mid-twentieth-century American stereotype of the gum-chewing, coffee-drinking wife, gossiping on the phone all morning with her catty girlfriends while maxing out the credit cards in the afternoon.

The Unknown God in the Real

Having sketched the archaic Greek ontology of force and the primacy of appearance that accompanies it, the crucial step remains: to fill in the relation between the two. The key point can be simply put. While force was always assumed to produce appearances, *the force itself, its own inner substance and meaning, remained an unknown.* And the intentions of the gods, the most profound and powerful forces, remained more unknown than anything else. Here, we finally arrive at the meaning of Lacan's obscure dictum that the gods are a mode by which the "real is revealed." For the Greeks, pure force always gave rise to effects in the appearances of things but was never revealed in itself.[19] "Appearances," said Anaxagoras, "are a glimpse of the unseen."[20] In the pagan world, one saw things happen, but behind those appearances lay a noumenal unknown that remained impenetrable. Force in and of itself was unthinkable, something *numinous.*[21] As Lacan puts this point:

> In that pagan ambiance at the time when it was flourishing, the *numen* rises up at every step, at the corner of every road, in grottoes, at cross-

roads; it weaves human experience together, and we can still see traces of it in a great many fields. That is something that contrasts greatly with the monotheistic profession of faith. The numinous rises up at every step and, conversely, every step of the numinous leaves a trace, engenders a memorial. It didn't take much for a new temple to be erected, for a new religion to be established.[22]

What called for the erection of a new temple was precisely the spectacular character of some readily visible occurrence, something no one could miss. But concerning what exactly caused the spectacle, what god or gods might have been behind it and what their intentions were, mere mortals could only speculate. The temple thus became the house in which an impenetrable mystery was preserved and honored. The ways of the gods remained inscrutable. In fact, it was often not possible to tell exactly which god may have acted in a particular case. In addition to temples dedicated to specific divinities, the Athenians therefore sought to cover all the bases by erecting an all-purpose altar to "the Unknown God." The Greek world was populated by a throng of powerful divinities whose motive intentions remained mostly inaccessible to human beings. Struggling mortals were surrounded by multiple embodiments of what Lacan called the unknowable Other-Thing.

My critic once again vents a protest. "Casting the gods in the role of a noumenal unknown strikes me as a deeply suspect claim. You seem to grant to the prephilosophical ancients an epistemological savvy that they couldn't have possessed. Do we need to remind ourselves that Homer was not a Kantian? Aren't you committing a gross fallacy of anachronism?"

On the contrary, I'm convinced that my argument, precisely with its focus on the human relation to the unknown, is the best way to *avoid* anachronism. To get started, let's at least agree on this: one of the most conspicuous features of the Homeric sense of the world, repeated in many texts with great emphasis, was its conviction about the severe limits of human knowledge, particularly about the intentions of the gods. The point is eloquently made in a famous quotation from Semonides: "Zeus controls the fulfillment of all that is, and disposes as he will. But insight does not belong to men; we live like beasts, always at the mercy of what the day may bring, knowing nothing of the outcome that God will impose upon our acts."[23]

In book 2 of the *Iliad*, Homer appeals to the Muses to grace him with a knowledge that is lacking to human beings. "Tell me now, Muses, dwelling on Olympos, as you are heavenly, and are everywhere, and everything is known to you—while we can only hear the tales and never know."[24] Indeed, such was the fundamental role of the Muses: to provide rare, narrow, and fleeting windows on the realities known only to the gods, realities about which mortal human beings generally know nothing.

Nowhere in Greek literature is the theme of human unknowing more powerfully dramatized than in Sophocles's *Oedipus Rex*. The tragic heroism of Oedipus was to take upon himself the horrifying burden of his own unknowing, made all the more excruciatingly ironic, first, by the fact that he so prided himself on guessing the riddle of the Sphinx, and second, that it was Oedipus himself who so aggressively insisted upon learning the identity of Laius's murderer. The key to the deepest tragic tension is not merely that Oedipus eventually comes to an unbearable knowledge, but that even his demand to know was utterly blind. To acknowledge that ultimate irony, in a gesture that highlights the limits of human knowing, Oedipus gouges out his eyes with the brooch pins from Jocasta's robe.

If we can take it as agreed upon that the archaic worldview saddled human beings with an almost complete ignorance of fate and the intentions of the gods, we can and should still ask why that was the dominant view and what exactly was at stake. In his indispensable study, *The Greeks and the Irrational*, E. R. Dodds supplies a powerfully compelling answer. Dodds theorizes, contrary to what one might be tempted to suppose about the intellectual faculties of "primitive" peoples, that the Greeks of the Homeric age were extraordinarily sensitive, not only to abrupt shifts in the appearances of things in the world, but also and especially to their own shifting states of mind. They focused with particular acuteness on those moments when one's thinking or judgment underwent a sudden change. Their explanation of such changes appealed to the intervention of one or another god. As Dodds explains:

> The most characteristic feature of the *Odyssey* is the way in which its personages ascribe all sorts of mental (as well as physical) events to the intervention of a nameless and indeterminate daemon or "god" or "gods." . . . The recognition, the insight, the memory, the brilliant or perverse idea, have this in common, that they come suddenly, as we say, "into a man's head." Often he is conscious of no observation or reasoning which has led up to them. But in that case, how can he call them "his"? A moment ago they were not in his mind; now they are there. Something has put them there, and that something is other than himself.[25]

The full consequences of this argument beg highlighting. Prime among its implications is that the archaic Greek sense of self lacked any firm boundaries. As Dodds puts it, "Homeric man has no unified concept of what we call "soul" or "personality."[26] In the archaic conception, psychic life is subject to frequent incursions of unknown, foreign influences. The Greeks attributed such apparently arbitrary eruptions of ideas and attitudes to divine interventions. "I suggest," Dodds goes on, that "the inward monition, or the sudden unaccountable feeling of power, or the sudden unaccountable loss of judgement, is the germ out of which the divine machinery developed."[27] Dodds even ventures the following challenging observation: "I doubt if the early literature of any other European people—even my own superstitious countrymen, the Irish—postulates supernatural interference in human behavior with such frequency or over so wide a field."[28]

Along this line of argument, one might reasonably assert that the prephilosophical Greeks anticipated Freud by isolating the essential problem of the unconscious. It's just that where Freud traced anomalies of human feeling and behavior to the unseen, symptom-ridden dynamics of libido, the Greek answer was to attribute unexpected spasms of impulse, thought, and feeling to the interference of gods. Confronted with an interruption in the smooth flow of one's thoughts and judgments, just as with an anomaly in the expected course of outward events, the Greeks would erect a road sign that said: "Here, a god acted. Accept it as it is, because you can know nothing more about it." As Lacan makes this point: "The gods of antiquity . . . could reveal themselves to men only in the guise of something that would cause a ruckus, in the *ágalma* of something that breaks all the rules, as a pure manifestation of an essence that remained completely hidden, whose enigma was entirely below the surface."[29]

We now ask: *What if that's exactly the way they wanted and needed it? What if the real function of the whole tapestry of myth was not to solve a mystery, but to provide a screen behind which it could remain one?*

Myth Was Not Proto-Science

The real fallacy of anachronism is to treat the Greek myths as if they were an early, naive attempt to do what modern science does: explain things. Any such account of myth as proto-science supposes that, in the absence of any more rational approach, the best the ancients could offer was inventive narratives, typically stories of origins. It is not difficult to discern this mistake underlying Paul Veyne's approach in *Did the Greeks Believe in Their Myths?*[30] The problem is that *belief* is the wrong category with respect to the whole problem of myth. What was at stake for the culture of myth was not giving a credible account of reality, nor even a best guess. True, Veyne cites a long lineup of ancient authors who express carefully considered doubts about the reliability of the myths. But all of those authors—Pausanias, Philostratus, Livy, Dionysius of Halicarnassus, Plutarch, Polybius, and so on—were writing centuries after the Homeric period. They were all inheritors of the philosophical revolution of the sixth and fifth centuries B.C.E. The living era of myth thrived centuries before that.

As Veyne sees it, the problem is how the ancients could have reconciled themselves to the multiple variants and internal inconsistencies of the mythic narratives. My contention is that this approach frames the entire problem incorrectly, misunderstanding the true function of myth in the archaic mind. Veyne imposes on the Homeric period the epistemological demands of late antiquity. In the Homeric epoch itself, no one worried about the inconsistencies and contradictions of myth for the simple reason that no one understood myth as an attempt to give a rationally consistent account of the nature and history of the gods.

The real function of myth was more nearly the very opposite of explanation. Myth was the serious play of the poets. Not only was it perfectly acceptable that myth presented a multifarious and jumbled series of stories about the divine beings; *it was preferable that way*. True, such stories typically helped imagine relationships between various gods, and between gods and mortals. They also frequently contained nuggets of folk wisdom and tradition. But the Greek myths also played another role. Behind the bright screen of colorful characters was a subtler but far more important purpose: that of underscoring the ultimately unknowable status of the gods. Myth was intentionally meant to leave open a dimension of reality beyond understanding. Lacan clearly perceived this other function of *mythos*: "Every myth," he says, "is related to the inexplicable nature of reality [*réel*]."[31] Myth engagingly presented a fanciful version of reality but also served to call up something of the real in the Lacanian sense, something about which reliable knowledge simply isn't possible. To vary Hegel's famous quip about the mysteries of the Egyptians that were mysteries to the Egyptians themselves, what seems to us unbelievable in the myths of the Greeks was unbelievable to the Greeks themselves.[32]

The fact is that we don't have any commentators on myth from the period of their most vitalizing cultural function. But that very absence is itself telling. No one bothered to write a critique of the mythic poets in their own time because no one had any qualms about their inconsistencies or contradictions. Providing a correct accounting of reality was not the point.

But we are still left to make sense of how ancient Greek myth actually functioned. An indispensable clue is provided by Nietzsche, one of the first and most radical students of the ancient world to insist on a strong distinction between the culture of the archaic, Homeric period and the classical period that took shape with the rise of philosophical questioning two or three centuries later. Holding fast to that distinction, Nietzsche claims that the purpose of myth was not epistemological but aesthetic and ethical. On the side of its aesthetic function, myth achieved an effect of sublimation exactly as Lacan defines it: elevating the object to the dignity of the Thing. For Nietzsche, the gods of the Greek myths constituted "a beautiful dream image."[33]

Along the way, of course, the mythic dream offered valuable lessons about the ways of the world. There was often a sort of "moral" to the story. But what was most deeply potent about the mythic dream image was its capacity, as Freud might have put it, to evoke an unimageable "other scene." The pure form of the resulting situation was thus a precise analogue of the original situation of *das Ding* described by Freud: what can be known from the imaginary form of the body gives way to something uncognizable, something about which it is only possible to say, "Something is there, I know not what." Myth was fully intended to leave the question of the gods *open*. Myth might in this precise sense be said to be a form of genuine piety. It did not even *presume* to know. The way myth multiplied stories about the gods, many of which were incompatible, was completely consistent with the archaic sense of the divine as finally inscrutable. In myth, the amusing and even comical were also capable of evoking awe.

Myth's capacity to evoke wonder in the face of the unknown, which we here call its aesthetic dimension, served to frame its more decisive function, which was ethical. As we have no contemporary commentators to guide us, we can only return to the texts of the poets themselves and seek their larger meaning. In book 5 of the *Iliad*, in the midst of the blood-heat of battle, Aeneas begs Pandaros, the finest Trojan archer, to take down Diomêdês, who had been mowing a mighty swath through the Trojans. "Here, lift up your hands to Zeus," says Aeneas, "let fly at that one, whoever he is: an overwhelming fighter, he has already hurt the Trojans badly, cutting down many of our best." Pandaros hesitates, however, wondering if the mighty oncoming killer might not be a god. "I cannot swear he is no god," he says. Or if it is Diomêdês, then surely he has the aid of a god. Some god is acting through him. Pandaros goes on:

> If it be Diomêdês,
> never could he have made this crazy charge
> without some god behind him. No, some god

is near him wrapped in cloud, and bent aside
that arrowhead that reached him—for I shot him
once before, I hit him, too, and squarely
on the right shoulder through his cuirass joint
over the armpit. Down to the ditch of Death
I thought I had dispatched him. Not at all:
my arrow could not bring him down.
Some angry god is in this.[34]

This passage well exemplifies Dodds's point about the way the Homeric Greeks attributed anomalies in character, behavior, or events to the work of the gods. Pandaros doesn't hesitate to chalk up Diomêdês's outsize prowess to the intervention of a divinity. But also notable is that he continues to waver in his judgment about it. Is this really a god? In all probability, yes—all the evidence points that way. But one can never know for sure. "Some angry god is in this," he says. But he doesn't specify which god, nor does he guess at the divine intentions. The archaic Greek gods always remained in some sense "wrapped in cloud."

The Archaic Ethos

The key to understanding the larger function of myth in the archaic period lies in seeing that its aesthetic dimension—its framing of something unknown—ultimately set the stage for an ethical drama. The core of that ethic was the value placed on a resolute and honorable stance in the face of the unknown and dreadful. As an imaginative play of stories about divinities that were ultimately shrouded in darkness, myth invited mortals to nobly and courageously take their own stand in the midst of the terrifying unknowing of existence.

To get a better grip on that linkage, consider the Gorgon. An extremely ancient image, the most common representation of the Gorgon presents a frontal view of a horrifying face, eyes bulging wildly, mouth wide in a demonic grin, fangs projecting menacingly, topped by a tangled mop of wriggling snakes. The Medusa slain by Perseus was a Gorgon, whose power to horrify was so great that to gaze upon her literally turned men to stone. If any image could be offered as an embodiment of *das Ding*, this is it.

It might seem strange, then, that this grimacing face adorned an astonishing range of ancient Greek household objects, everything from krater handles to bowls and even dinner plates. The Gorgon was almost unquestionably a representation of the ultimate abyss at the bottom of existence—and of death, that final horror on the one-way train of life. The Gorgon's dreadful grin seemed to say, "It's all for nothing. In the end, there is only darkness. Into that darkness, I will swallow you." The Gorgon's frequent depiction on household goods may therefore have functioned as an apotropaic, fending off the very darkness that it otherwise represented. One is reminded of the way the Evil Eye, to this day and in precisely the same part of the world, is guarded against by hanging one or another image of it over one's doorway. But even as a talisman that might keep the horror of the Gorgon at bay, its image reminds us of the void at the base of existence.

Given this view of its meaning, it's not surprising that the Gorgon head was a common embellishment of weaponry and armor. It was often emblazoned on an armored breastplate and was therefore the first thing an opponent would see when engaging in combat. Or maybe the last. This symbol of the ultimate void at the bottom of things must have presented a dreadful prospect. But that was also exactly the point. The Gorgon's cold reminder of mortality wasn't merely a cheap means of buckling the knees of the enemy with fear. It also functioned as the very thing that gave the deepest meaning to the ethical significance of battle. Mindfulness of the darker, unknown aspects of reality was the measure by which noble conduct was reckoned.

True courage was gauged by the directness of one's physical proximity to danger. War, Agamemnon said, was "the battle test that brings honor to men."[35] It was for this reason that the lowest man on the ladder of battlefield respectability was the archer. It is not for nothing that Homer styled the hapless Paris, the thief of Helen, as an archer. By striking at a distance, the archer spares himself any direct exposure to the deadly fray. Paris's flight from Argos to Troy with his trophy wife redoubles our sense of his base and cowardly behavior, conducted at a safe distance from reprisal. The archer's arrow was the original "cheap shot."[36]

To cite a modern echo of the Homeric ethic of courage, one could do worse than to consider bullfighting, an art that originated in the same region of the ancient world. In the classic tradition of bullfighting, the one Ernest Hemingway fell in love with, the idea of an "old matador" was an oxymoron.[37] Almost by definition, the consummate *torero* didn't live long. But risking life and limb was a key part of his prestige and absolutely the key to the breathtaking impact of his art. The point, after all, was not merely to slay a potentially deadly animal but to posture oneself commandingly and artfully in the face of death. The electrifying aspect of the masterful *torero* was the way he allowed the bull's horns, lowered into the killing position by the picador's precise severing of the neck muscles, to pass within inches of his guts. The truly sublime moment, the moment at which the crowd responds by madly waving white handkerchiefs, was when the matador, rather than suddenly jumping to one side to avoid being gored, jerking out of position with an awkward lurch in order to save himself, accomplished the same end by a deft, almost nonchalant swivel of his hips. To all appearances, he was not facing a deadly bull at all, but dancing with the village beauty.[38]

The crowd at a bullfight is for the same reasons very sensitive to the timing of the kill. The most thrilling and impressive finish involves the *torero* inviting a final charge while standing his ground, his sword poised at the oncoming beast in a final gesture of perfectly self-controlled and stylish poise. Just as the bull gets to him, the *torero* thrusts the slightly curved tip of the sword into an extremely precise spot on the back of the bull's neck, the only spot at which it is possible to sever the spinal cord. When it is done perfectly, the bull uncannily drops to the ground at his master's feet, stone dead. The effect is completely shocking, as if the most extreme and deadly violence had been accomplished with the artful precision of a tango dance.

In the context of the *Iliad*, it is Akhilleus who most embodies this virtue, though only with the addition of a crucial twist. Unlike the bullfighter, who is facing an immensely larger and more powerful beast while armed only with his light épée and a scarlet cape, Akhilleus knows very well that he, the son of a goddess, is the most formidable warrior of all those assembled at Troy. The truly Homeric stage of noble behavior, for which risking imminent death was the indispensable pivot, had therefore to be set up with an artificial device. Homer provides it when Akhilleus's goddess-mother Thetis tells him that only two courses lie before him. The first is that he returns to Argos and lives a life that is long and comfortable but lacking honor. The second is that he avenges the loss of Patróklos but only at the price of his own death. Long life in shameful comfort or short life with lasting glory.

Everything that occurs in the poem from that moment is inflected by the reader's knowledge that Akhilleus is deliberately embracing the void, willingly throwing himself into the jaws of the Gorgon. Homer consistently portrays death as a cold, empty, and meaningless existence in the underworld. It is Akhilleus himself who, midway through the *Odyssey*, momentarily rises from his permanent exile in Hades to answer Odysseus's question about the afterlife. Akhilleus's reply is pitiless: "Better to be a starving farmhand on earth, slaving for some poor farmer, than to lord it over all the exhausted dead."[39] When he chooses to redress the death of Patróklos, he consigns himself to unending twilight as a miserable shade.

Perhaps the most dramatic window on Akhilleus's towering courage occurs as he stands over Prince Lykaon, one of Hektor's brothers whom he has wounded, and who now cringes with fear and begs to be spared. Akhilleus's brief speech leaves no doubt about his awareness regarding his own impending death.

> Come, friend, face your death, you too.
> And why are you so piteous about it?
> Patróklos died, and he was a finer man
> by far than you. You see, don't you, how large
> I am, and how well-made? My father is noble,
> a goddess bore me. Yet death waits for me,
> for me as well, in all the power of fate.[40]

The Homeric ethic positioned the hero in relation to the darkness of the unknown and the abyssal character of existence. Virtue and nobility consisted in comporting oneself courageously in the face of that darkness. The resulting picture might be compared to a jeweler's diamond that shines forth even more dazzlingly when laid on a jet-black pillow. Courage elevated the hero to a kind of godlike status of his own.[41]

We say "godlike" and not actually "godly" because, of course, the human hero could not escape his mortality. The best he could do was to skirt the darkness, having struck a pose of unflappable courage and nobility. In the end, the Greek hero, as the dying Cyrano said of himself, had only his panache.[42] But—and here we come to what is perhaps the most important point of all—this "inferiority" of the mortal hero was precisely the source of his ultimate superiority, even to the gods. No god could possibly attain such glory, if only because the gods could not die. In the moral compass of Homer's universe, the gods were by definition excluded from true nobility. It is no accident that Homer so often presents them as acting like spoiled brats with superpowers. Without being able to prove themselves in the face of death, the gods could not rise to the heights of virtue and dignity attainable by mortals. In this way, the inner secret of Homer's world was that the inferior being, inferior at least by the measure of sheer power and force, was the only one capable of the most sublimely elevated ethical heroism. Paradoxically, it was the very power of the gods, and especially their being exempt from death, that excluded them forever from attaining the lofty status of a noble hero.

The Ideal of the Redoubtable

As we move toward summing up the archaic ethos sketched here, let us begin by contrasting the Homeric ideal with the outlook of Kantian morality. The ethic of nobility and honor was in no way an ethic of rule following. Submission to a universalized imperative would never have occurred to any Homeric hero. The entire mindset associated with "Thou shalt not . . ." had no place in the archaic Greek sensibility. An incident midway through the *Iliad* well illustrates the point. In book 10, "Night in the Camp: A Foray," Diomêdês and Odysseus sneak behind enemy lines, capture a Trojan soldier named Dolon, and then appear to propose a deal.[43] They will spare Dolon only if he tells what he knows about the Trojan numbers and positions. But as soon as Dolon has told them all, Diomêdês decapitates him with a single blow and Odysseus triumphantly lifts the bleeding head as an offering to Athena.

For a modern reader, even one who's never heard of Kant, this betrayal feels scandalous. How can we respect any "hero" who cuts a man down immediately after giving his word that he wouldn't? Yet my contention is that the contemporary audience of Homer's poem would not have flinched in the slightest at what we would judge as a lousy double cross. What Homer's listener would have most expected from a great man, far from submitting himself to obeying a rule, any rule, was rather acting in a manner that answers to the circumstances while maintaining his own aplomb. Had the fortunes of the Akhaians not darkened so much over the preceding weeks, had Dolon not so quickly and pathetically spilled the beans, had Odysseus and Diomêdês felt for whatever reason a passing twinge of compassion—for any number of reasons, they might well have spared him. On another night, things might have gone differently. The crucial thing is that the hero acts in a manner consistent with maintaining his own sense of composure and self-control.

We might call this rough and ready, even rogue, ethics "the ideal of the *redoubtable*." The dictionary gives a range of synonyms: fearful, formidable, eminent, worthy of respect and admiration, awe-inspiring, daunting, impressive, imposing, commanding, indomitable, invincible, mighty. The unifying theme is one of *self-controlled and self-determined power*. The Homeric ethic, appropriate to clans ruled by warrior chieftains, was one of self-respect and self-mastery. The hero doesn't hesitate to act extravagantly, even violently. If the hero's action implies mastery over others and things, his behavior also and above all implies mastery over himself. The primary desideratum is to be able to say, "I'm the one in control, and if I'm not, it's because some massively greater force, acting upon me from the outside, has temporarily knocked me off my feet. But I'll be back!"

The Homeric ethic valued the individual who is "his own man." Every man of substance must prove that *some* things, many things in fact, are simply beneath his dignity. The redoubtable man is fearsome, but not as a wild beast is fearsome. The fearsomeness of the great *torero* is utterly different from that of the bull. It is his very self-control, his commanding nature, and his willingness to risk himself that is impressive. He is intimidating less for the expectations he has of others than for those he has of himself. He retains self-respect and self-composure, even in the face of the ultimately unmasterable force of death.

All of which might be chalked up on the positive side of the ledger for the redoubtable hero. But there is another side of the heroic ethic that points to a decisive weakness. Even when the great man shows the most sublime heroism in overcoming himself—and we have to admit that such moments of truly self-directed control were less common than spectacular displays of power over objects and enemies—it remains the case that the stature of the Homeric hero resided in proving himself as an autonomous ego. In the end, the archaic ideal was founded upon the assertion of *self*. If the courage and nobility of the hero were measured in relation to an abyssal unknown, that relation remained for the most part a wholly external one. The heroic subject never substantively engaged the abyssal Thing but merely drew himself up into a posture of impressive resistance against it, a refusal to be mastered by it. *Or at least he needed to be seen that way.* Akhilleus's choice of a short life with honor was inseparable from courting the approval of others around him, and perhaps even more importantly, the approval of posterity, of admirers in the future who would hear of his legend long after his death. His ethical life was essentially played out on a stage. He was a star whose stature unavoidably depended on a circle of adoring fans.

The weakness of the redoubtable hero was that his pose of self-possession arguably required certification by the admiring crowd. Aristotle acknowledges this defect in his *Nicomachean Ethics* when he rejects honor as a candidate for the highest good. Honor cannot be the highest good because it depends upon something external to the one who is honored. All of which means that the Homeric ideal was always worryingly close to crass narcissism. Homeric honor was caught up in the paradoxes and self-defeating dynamics that Hegel analyzed in the master-slave dialectic. The master is ultimately undone by the fact that his status as master depends on the awed regard of the slave. He is only a master in the mirror.

The Homeric hero never escaped the merely reactive project of investing himself in a quasi-imaginary posture. In this sense, the stance of the hero quite conspicuously assumed the aspect of a symptomatic compromise, at once obsessed with the anxiety-producing void, almost compulsively needing to exaggerate its threatening aspects, while also defensively distancing itself and seeking consolation in the reassuring approval of the tribe. The fundamental structure embodied by the archaic ethos thus emerges as precisely homologous with the bifold structure of the "perceptual complex" of the Freudian Thing. The hero invested himself in a commanding imago in order to steel himself in the face of the anxious unknown of the Thing. The pagan cult of worshipful devotion to the redoubtable hero can thus be interpreted as a defensive formation. The pose of epic courage was in fact a symptomatic compromise, divided between courageous exposure to an abyssal darkness and an essentially imaginary investment in a shining, compensatory persona.

If the hero's stature was a reflection of his self-possession in the eyes of others, he also functioned as an inspiring model for that very crowd, thereby allowing them to stabilize their *own* relation to the abyssal character of existence. The Everyman, too, could in his own humbler way seek to *imitate* the redoubtable. The heroes of legend were thus the ethical models by means of which everyday life stabilized itself in the face of anxiety, pain, loss, deprivation, and death.[44] Perhaps it is from this point of view that we can recognize in a more complete way how and why the pagan Greek culture invented theater. To live even an ordinary life was to play a role for which the model was larger than life. The very basis of the archaic ethos was a kind of *drama*. Quite literally, life imitated art.

The larger point at stake here rejoins the beginning of our discussion, focused on the offering of sacrifices in the sacred void. We have only to imaginatively put ourselves in the place of the ordinary people who performed such sacrifices, then waited in the anxious hope that they would be smiled upon by greater, godly forces. Imitation of the hero's pose sufficed as a means of maintaining one's courage in the face of the sacrificial gamble. The example of Akhilleus's single-minded battle for honor or Odysseus's tenacious endurance held out inspiring models for those who fearfully understood their fate to hang in the balance of dark forces ultimately beyond their control.

From Odysseus to Oedipus

"Translated into your Lacanian terms," says the critic, "the redoubtable man invests himself in the imaginary identity of the ego. But isn't this account much more applicable to the heroes of epic than to the later protagonists of tragedy? As you yourself remarked, Nietzsche insisted that the archaic and classical periods are worlds apart."

While a fully adequate response would take us too far afield from our larger trajectory, the critic's question is a crucial one. Lacan provides the first clue to an answer when he says of the story of Oedipus that "all of the heroes of Greek mythology have some sort of connection with this myth."[45] The reason is precisely the relation of the hero to the void of unknowing. As Lacan says in a later seminar, "The reason Freud found his fundamental figure in the tragedy of Oedipus lies in the fact that 'he did not know.'"[46] But allowing for this thread of continuity, Lacan also accentuates the distance that separates the figures of tragedy from the heroes of epic. For the heroes, the challenge was to retain self-possession in the face of an overwhelming counterforce. The epic hero transcended death and destruction by achieving honor and glory that could not be erased. What is new in a figure like Oedipus is the way he is his own adversary, his own obstacle. His destruction is brought about through a conflict with something internal to himself. It involves what Lacan calls "the transition from myth to existence," where "existence" is inseparable from a transforming catastrophe brought about by the unknown in oneself. "Oedipus does exist," Lacan says, "and he fully realized his destiny. He realized it to that final point which is nothing more than something strictly identical to a striking down, a tearing apart, a laceration of himself."[47] For Lacan, the crucial question is posed by Oedipus himself: "Am I made man in the hour when I cease to be?"

The context of Lacan's remarks is crucial. They occur toward the conclusion of his second seminar, devoted to the theory of the ego. The upshot of the relevant section, titled "Desire, Life, and Death," asserts the necessity for the subject to undergo a mortifying rupture of imaginary identity in order to access its desire. It is at this point that we come upon something foreign to the epic hero. The reason is that the tensions that give rise to the moment of tragic self-realization are in the context of tragedy *internal* to the protagonist. True, Oedipus is clearly caught up in the iron grip of fate. But even more crucial is his overweening pride about his own claims to knowledge, his insistence on solving the riddle of the sphinx "not by birds and omens" but by his own wits. The most devastating thing about Oedipus's undoing is the extent to which it is brought about by his own actions. The result, as we see so poignantly in *Oedipus at Colonus*, is the "subjective destitution" that Lacan associates with the passage through psychoanalysis.[48]

The epochal reorientation at stake here correlates with a shift in the ways the gods were thought to intervene in human affairs. As C. Fred Alford observes,

> In the *Iliad* and the *Odyssey*, gods generally intervene as physical presences, jerking warriors' hair, throwing rocks, breaking chin straps, misdirecting spears, and so forth. When they penetrate the psyche it is generally to enthuse (*entheos*) a warrior. In the tragedies, on the other

hand, the intervention of the gods is more abstract and profound—
they inflict madness, hubris, and self-destructive desire. This requires
that the gods dip more deeply into the psyche. . . . [T]he more the
gods act like psychic, rather than physical forces, the more they must
penetrate and dominate the psyche to do so. . . . Tragic psychology
appears more sophisticated precisely because it captures the fact that
men are driven, compelled, and rendered unfree by forces operating
internally as well as externally. The tragedies show man as even less free,
autonomous, and in control than in the epics, for the forces that render
him thus operate within the self: not on the self, as in the epics, but
through it.[49]

This tendency toward internalization in the figures of tragedy forms the
implicit spine of Nietzsche's argument in *The Birth of Tragedy*. The epic
conflict between the forces of Apollo and Dionysos with which the Homeric heroes contended is later reposed in tragedy as conflicting currents
internal to the protagonists themselves. Such a process of internalization
enabled the traditional satyr plays to give way to dramas energized by tensions arising from inside individuals and families.

For Nietzsche, the emergence of tragedy poses an implicit challenge to the heroic ethos to the extent that the Apollonian stature of the
epic hero was destabilized by the effects of Dionysian frenzy, embodied
in "the spirit of music." Nietzsche goes so far as to say that the "mystery
doctrine" of the Dionysian principle centers on the dark notion of "in-
dividuation as the primal cause of evil."[50] But for precisely those reasons,
the tragic outlook is only a transitional moment on the path to the philosophical age and its relentless investigations into the internal complexities of the soul. It is the second theme that is the real heart of Nietzsche's
book, which aims less at distinguishing tragedy from epic than at exhibit-
ing the antithesis between tragedy and the revolution of Socratic philosophy that eventually eclipses it. On that score, the book might better have
been titled "The Death of Tragedy."

All of which may be taken as an introduction to some brief discussion of philosophy itself against the backdrop of the archaic age and its
ethico-religious stance toward the unknown.

The Madness of the Philosophers

One often hears it said that where the mythopoetic tradition simply accepted appearances for reality, the revolution of early Greek philosophy

rejected appearances in favor of identifying a very different reality concealed behind or beyond what appears. The preceding account of the Homeric ethos suggests a partial revision: where the mythic mind assumed the impossibility of penetrating behind appearances to reliably know anything, the philosophers proposed not only that one *could* know the invisible depths but that one could know those hidden truths with even greater certainty than the appearances themselves. For anyone attuned to the traditional mythopoetic culture, such a proposal was tantamount to madness, or sacrilege, or both.

Thales is often credited with being the first to pioneer the intelligibility of a reality behind appearances. Rejecting the evidence of the senses, he proposed that all things are composed of a single, fundamental element: water. Stone, wood, bronze, wine, flesh, even fire—for Thales, they all became nothing but different forms of the same substance. Wrong as he was in specifics, Thales had for the first time conceived the idea of matter, the primal stuff out of which everything is composed. Intellectually, he stands closer to us than he was to Homer.

Other philosophers followed, all of them attempting in different ways to define the First Principle, or *arché*—what all things have in common and what remains the same through change. Anaximenes continued in the materialist vein, proposing air, not water, as the primal substance. Pythagoras then changed the paradigm from the material to the purely formal, asserting number and mathematical ratio as the prime, invisible reality. The mysterious reality behind appearances became identifiable with calculable abstractions. The unthinkability of sheer force was replaced by the intelligibility of pure ideas. Such was the inspiration for Plato's famous theory of forms. Legend has it that there was a sign over the door of Plato's Academy that nodded approvingly toward Pythagoras: "He who does not know mathematics, do not enter here."

The early philosophers exploited the very separation that the mythopoetic culture assumed between appearance and unknowable reality. They simply replaced the unknowable with some version of the knowable. Of course, this titanic battle between perspectives is somewhat challenging to describe neatly because the two sides were asymmetrical. The Homeric ethos was not an argument. No one in the epoch of myth ever bothered to conceptually distinguish between appearance and reality. For them, the entire category of knowledge, at least in the metaphysical sense of an insight into the very fabric of existence, simply did not exist. They merely assumed that whatever appeared was the offspring of cosmic forces that remained beyond human capacity to fathom. But where the mythical mind was content to leave the ultimate sources of things in darkness, the philosophical mind demanded that everything be accounted for in the full light of day. Along the way to fulfilling that demand they had to make fully explicit the chasm between images and pure ideas, between the senses and the intellect, the body and the mind. The worldview of metaphysical dualism was born.

This picture of the break from the mythic culture initiated by the philosophical revolution roughly parallels the analysis offered by Heidegger. In Heidegger's interpretation, the emergence of philosophy triggered a massive disenchantment of the world. At stake was the essential mysteriousness of the world, captured in the originary meaning of the Greek sense of *physis* as an emerging-into-presence of something incalculable and unknown, something that in itself remains forever hidden.[51] The philosophers audaciously colonized this dark source of all presencing by offering a range of conceptual schemas to account for it. Over the centuries that followed Thales, the original enigma of *physis* finally became the realm of mere "nature." The path was open for the elemental mysteries to be eventually reduced to the workings of a clocklike mechanism. The result, in Heidegger's view, was an epochal impoverishment of experience, an event that he characterizes as the "oblivion" of the question of Being.[52] The pith of Heidegger's analysis is well captured in a remark by Susan Sontag: "Interpretation is the revenge of the intellect upon art. Even more. It is the revenge of the intellect upon the world. To interpret is to impoverish, to deplete the world—in order to set up a shadow world of meanings."[53]

This perspective sheds new light on the condemnation of Socrates. Certainly for any newcomer to ancient history, it is not obvious why the Athenians demanded the death of this elder eccentric who threw over his vocation as a stone mason to pester people in the marketplace with questions about the true meaning of things like courage, friendship, justice, love, and beauty. What exactly was his crime and why was it sufficiently serious to deserve the death penalty? The ostensible charge was twofold: impiety (not believing in the gods of the state) and corrupting the youth (intellectually contributing to the delinquency of minors). History has preserved several versions of Socrates's defense before the Athenian jury, but not a single document has survived that gives us any insight into the argument made by the prosecution.

In the view we have taken, Socrates's guilt becomes clear. In late fifth-century Athens, Socrates had become the poster child for what the inherited culture regarded as a sacrilegious act of hubris. His crime was desecrating the sacred zone of the unknown in which the inscrutable intentions of the gods resided. Socrates assumed, even demanded, that those sacred groves should be accessible to anyone, even a slave boy, provided that he was prepared to devote a little focused effort to the craft of abstract thinking.[54] For the guardians of the old school who defended the Homeric sensibility, men who still revered the silent testimony of the myths to an unknowable reality both sublime and terrible, Socrates represented the pillaging of the divine void of the temple, someone who wanted to light up the sacred darkness that framed everything noble and virtuous.

Of course, this picture of the litigants' case against Socrates omits any consideration of Socrates's own profession of ignorance. In the most famous part of his defense as Plato paints it for us, Socrates claims that his wisdom, if he has any, consists merely in knowing how little he knows. It is at this point that a more perspicacious auditor of Socrates's argument to the jury might have detected a new and distinctively Socratic form of piety, one that would have quite interestingly resonated with the archaic outlook that insisted on reverence in the face of our fundamental ignorance about the foundations of existence. Had a greater proportion of the jury been impressed by that Socratic piety of questioning, Socrates might well have been acquitted. Plato's *Apology* gives more than one hint that Socrates himself appreciated that irony even as it sent him to his death.

Woman as Symptom

We cannot leave the polytheistic world of the Aegean without acknowledging that the Greeks had a woman problem. Throughout the archaic epoch and long into the later period informed by philosophy, Hellenic civilization remained profoundly misogynist. Thales claimed to have been grateful to have been born a human being and not an animal, a Greek and not a barbarian, and—he seems to have saved the most important for last—a man and not a woman. Pythagoras listed the feminine on the inferior side of his table of cosmic opposites. The male was included with the one, the straight, the unchanging, the limited, the right, and the good. The female was lumped with the many, the curved, the changing, the unlimited, the left, and the bad. Women are fickle, fuzzy minded, and shifty. As such, the feminine is essentially tied to the false and deceitful, the crooked and perverse.[55] The Pythagorean judgment that woman is a lie aligned almost perfectly with that of Hesiod. The only difference between their accounts was that where for Pythagoras the dangerous feminine merely took its place in a universal dualism, Hesiod's account depicted woman as specifically invented to be a curse.

Antipathy toward women was deeply enmeshed with the archaic

Greek relation to the unknown and abyssal dimension of existence. We have already seen how the Gorgon face functioned as a kind of generalized emblem of horror for the Greeks. It is no wonder that the Gorgon was distinctly female. In fact, Greek culture had an abundance of female terrors, from the man-eating Sphinx, to the vengeful Furies, or Erinyes, to the infamous Pandora. It was love of a woman that unleased the cataclysm at Troy.

Mindful of the account we have given of the Greek ethical ideal of the redoubtable man, it is not difficult to understand why the Greek attitude toward women was charged with such a potent mixture of fear and loathing. Once you have accepted that the cosmos is a great agon of contending forces, many of which wield powers immensely greater than any mortal man possesses, and when you have also committed yourself to heroically maintaining self-control and self-determination in the midst of that play of forces, you are bound to have female trouble. In the first place, and perhaps most profoundly disturbing, woman is herself not a bounded whole. In the natural course of things, her body comes to house an uncanny intruder, a kind of slow-growing parasite, in the form of the gestating child. All the more disturbing is the way the wriggling stranger will be pushed out of her in a rush of bloodied fluids, accompanied by terrifying screams.

The spectacle of a body inhabited by a foreign object is made infinitely more unnerving by the fact that the same body appears to be deeply attuned to the forces that twirl the celestial orbs. Woman bleeds from the great wound between her legs in rhythm with the phases of the moon and the flowing of the tides. No veneer of cultivated manners and polite restraint can fully allay the fear that woman's very body links her to the terrifying, unknown powers that twist the gyre of life and death. Simone de Beauvoir offers a particularly elegant summary of this view in *The Second Sex*: "The periodic hemorrhage of woman is strangely timed with the lunar cycle, and the moon also is thought to have her dangerous caprices. Woman is a part of that fearsome machinery which turns the planets and the sun in their courses, she is the prey of cosmic energies that rule the destiny of the stars and the tides, and of which men must undergo the disturbing radiations."[56] Above all else, woman appeared to the archaic male mind as representing both the origin of life and also the inevitability of death. Menstrual blood was a source of pollution for precisely this reason, simultaneously the very sap of life and also the horrid index of death. Again de Beauvoir:

> What man cherishes and detests first of all in women—loved one or
> mother—is the fixed image of his animal destiny; it is the life that is

necessary to his existence but that condemns him to the finite and to
death. . . . Although he endeavors to distinguish mother and wife, he
gets from both a witness to one thing only: his mortal state. He wishes
to venerate his mother and love his mistress, at the same time he rebels
against them in disgust and fear.[57]

The final insult, of course, is that men, who seek above all the nobility of
self-determination and self-control, cannot resist being caught up in lust
for the folds of female flesh. Woman thus becomes the ultimate index of
masculine failure.

In the opening pages of *Civilization and Its Discontents*, Freud responds to a letter from his friend Romain Rolland, in which Rolland criti-
cizes Freud's treatment of the religious in his recently published *Future
of an Illusion*. Rolland contends that Freud misses the meaning of the
deepest religious impulse, which is to be traced back to what Rolland calls
the "oceanic feeling," a sense of deep oneness with the universe. Freud
confesses that he can't judge the matter as he has never experienced such
a feeling. The Greeks would unquestionably have responded the same
way. In this respect, the archaic Greeks were the near polar opposite of
the "back to nature" sensibility that animates a broad slice of our contemporary culture. Nature for the Greeks was a murk of dark and deadly
powers. The idea of trying to draw closer to nature would have struck
most Greeks as the equivalent of crawling into a barrel filled with scor-
pions. The feminine itself, as inextricably bound up with the forces and
cycles of nature, was something to be conquered by heroic resolve. To
quote Katharine Hepburn's line in *African Queen*, reminding Humphrey
Bogart to behave himself: "Nature, Mr. Allnut, is what we were put here
to rise above."

What Women Know

There remains, however, a key part of the puzzle to be filled in. So far,
our characterization of women's challenge to archaic Greek masculin-
ity seems little different from what we have generally characterized as
the threatening unknowns of existence itself, the foil of heroic resolve.
Why did women pose such a special threat? One intriguing hypothesis
is to suppose that women's proximity to the dark forces that drove the
cosmos hinted at their possession of an occult knowledge unavailable
to men. If that were the case, men's investment in heroically facing the
unknown would be compromised by women's possession of a kind of in-

sider's knowledge. Not only are men excluded from such a secret knowledge, but its being the special prerogative of women threatened to cut the legs out from under the pose of the redoubtable man.

The everyday division of labor between men and women in virtually every early society we know of aligns with very different kinds of knowledge. Hannah Arendt offers a particularly compelling picture of that split in the chapter "The Public and the Private Realm" in *The Human Condition*. Greek women were almost completely confined to the domestic space, a domain ruled by unforgiving necessity, and charged primarily with the maintenance of the body: delivering it at birth, cleaning and clothing it, nourishing and watering it, binding its periodic wounds and tending it in sickness, washing and wrapping it in death. This regimen naturally gave rise to a whole range of special forms of knowledge that were more or less completely beyond the ken of males. We can readily imagine that the result was a complicated mix of fear, disgust, envy, and resentment. The ministrations of women were inserted between a man and his own body, a reminder that his body was in some inescapable sense not his own. Such an ancient suspicion of women's abyssal knowledge appears to have percolated down through the centuries, informing the recurrent paranoid fantasy about witch-women who are in league with the darker forces, have had sex with the devil, have animal "familiars," and so on. Is not the whole bloody history of the "hammer of witches" a response to a deeply held male suspicion concerning the nefarious ends of "women's wiles"?

But there's one more crucial point. Women's secret knowledge would have been anathema, for different reasons, for *both* the archaic worldview and the philosophical outlook that replaced it. For the Homeric sensibility, any claim to knowledge in the domain of the ultimate things—fate, the gods, and the powers of life and death—would have threatened to undermine the heroic project of self-assertion in the face of the unknown foundations of existence. Indeed, it is readily tempting to suppose that the archaic preference for maintaining a kind of sacred ignorance about the darker things amounted in itself to a mode of defense against them.[58] But with the rise of philosophical speculation, a whole new objection to such secret "female" knowledge had to be mobilized. Such feminine secrets represented the antithesis of conceptual understanding and rational calculation. If the archaic objection was that women know too much, the philosophical complaint was that they know in aberrant, nonrational ways that must be forcefully rejected.

These two completely contrary posturings in relation to what is threatening about feminine knowledge intersect in Jocasta, the mother of Oedipus. If both the archaic and philosophical eras found women's knowledge impossible to tolerate, Jocasta is the ultimate representative of that impossibility. For all of the libraries of commentary about Sophocles's play, very much including the commentary of Freud himself, it is astonishing that so little attention has been paid to Jocasta. It is as if all of the interpretive oxygen was consumed by the effort—admittedly a challenging one—of facing up to the dreadful fate of the man who murders his father and copulates with his mother. But in her own way, Jocasta poses an even more deeply disturbing and traumatic prospect. In fact, it is possible to wonder whether, for the fifth-century audience, it wasn't the figure of Jocasta that evoked the most deeply unsettling horror.

The question is not so much *what* Jocasta knew, as *when* she knew it. One thing seems indisputable: she realizes Oedipus's true identity well before he does. Just prior to the moment when she reenters the house and commits suicide, she includes among her parting words to her son: "I pray you may never find out who you are."[59] Yet multiple indications throughout the play point to the dreadful possibility that she knew from the moment Oedipus appeared in Thebes. How did she know? One might, of course, suspect a "mother's intuition." But there is another, much more suggestive factor. Having heard the dreadful prophecy about his growing up to murder his father and marry his mother, Jocasta had given her infant son, his feet skewered, into the hands of a herdsman to be left to die on a mountainside. How likely was it that she might fail to notice that the new king, her husband-to-be, was dragging a deformed foot?[60]

That she must almost certainly have known Oedipus's real identity upon meeting him as an adult is further suggested by the fact that the herdsman who exposed the child was also the man who had witnessed Laius's murder on the road from Corinth. It was he who had testified, falsely, that it was not a single man but a gang that had attacked the royal cart. Jocasta herself suggested that the herdsman be summoned to clarify the pivotal question of whether the attack was conducted by one assailant or a group.

To these circumstantial suspicions, which we can only assume Sophocles fully intended to arouse, the playwright adds an astonishing speech in which Jocasta argues that, after all, it isn't so strange for a son to dream of bedding his mother. With this speech, music to Freud's ears centuries later, she tries to calm the increasingly agitated and anxious Oedipus, who becomes only more insistent on knowing the truth.

> What has a man to fear, when life is ruled
> By chance, and the future is unknowable?
> The best way tis to take life as it comes.
> So have no fear of marriage with your mother,

> Many men before this time have dreamt that they
> Have shared their mother's bed. The man to whom
> These things are nothing lives the easiest life.[61]

Putting together this train of suggestive evidence, it becomes difficult to assume that Jocasta did *not* know Oedipus's true identity from the start. And yet casting an eye over the secondary literature about Sophocles's play, few commentators have lingered to consider the question. Little wonder, perhaps. The thought that Jocasta might have acquiesced in knowing silence to her own son joining her bed to conceive four children over two decades is a truly dizzying idea, even for a modern audience. And yet the chorus leaves us with precisely that thought at the end of the play: "How could the furrows your father sowed have endured you so long in silence?"[62]

Whether in the form of the heroic culture of the Homeric period, or in the age of philosophical reflection that followed and extinguished it, Greek culture was focused overwhelmingly on what Lacan defined as *das Ding*, the unrepresented abyss of the real. When we realize this fact, the figure of Jocasta steps forward as its ultimate confirmation. In Jocasta, the enigma of the Thing walks and talks, precisely as what remains hidden and unknown, the traumatic confrontation with the uncognized void of the Other's desire.

5

Judaism

The Worship of Law

> There is never anything else at stake under the name of spirit
> than the signifier itself.
> —Jacques Lacan

My central claim in this book is that religion can be defined as a cultur-
ally mediated relation to the unknown beyond that Lacan called *das Ding*.
In archaic Greece, a relation to the Thing was stabilized by the veil of
myth. That veil functioned to partially domesticate the force of the real
by means of situating it behind a dazzling theater of images. Yet precisely
by withholding something from view, the veil also never allows us to forget
it. The deeper unknowability of divine intentions remained the religious
preoccupation of the ancients. And that abyssal unknown was also the
dance partner of the heroic ideal. The adoration of heroes, elevated by
their ennobling proximity to the primal darkness of existence, thus became deeply akin to the worship of deities.

Viewed in this way, archaic Greek polytheism can be mapped onto
the most primitive schema identified by Freud in his initial sketch of the
Thing, involving a more or less polar division between the imaginary
and the real. The Greek experience was divided between appearances,
embroidered by myth, and an unknown beyond that never showed itself
directly. The heroic ethos located itself on the limen between the two
realms. The hero was defined by his capacity to courageously skirt the
abyssal darkness of death while striking the pose of an admirably autonomous ego. Greek virtue in the Homeric Age was an imaginary answer to
the abyssal question of the real.

"I have to confess to some confusion about the role of the symbolic
function in all of this," interrupts the critic. "Aside from linking Greek

sacrifice with the primal emergence of the signifier, the bulk of your analysis of the archaic ethos is almost exclusively aligned along the axis of the imaginary and the real. The symbolic seems mostly left out. Yet you make a great deal of the way the Thing is intimately linked with language. In fact, I was getting ready to hear you claim that the relation of the Lacanian subject to the signifier can ultimately be taken to imply that every human being, precisely as a speaking being, is implicitly religious."

The critic is exactly right about the direction of my argument. To the extent that the signifier opens upon an indeterminate dimension and thereby always implicitly invokes the dimension of *das Ding*, the relation of the human being to language might be said to be already an opening upon the sacred. But what is implicit in the function of the signifier doesn't appear in the same way or to the same degree in every formation of custom, cult, or credo. Here, we can rely on Hegel's distinction between *an sich* and *für sich*, or what is "in itself" versus what is "for itself." His purpose was to distinguish what remains implicit or latent from what may later become explicit, directly and definitely symbolized. If religious life is always mediated by the signifier, it nevertheless remains a question of more or less, and of how that mediation works in different contexts.

Despite its heights of poetic achievement, and despite the premium placed by the Homeric Greeks on eloquence in speech, the archaic age appears to have been more conspicuously bound up with the axis between the imaginary and the real than with any explicit interest in the operations of the signifier. In fact, one might even venture the hypothesis that it was the failure of the archaic culture to thematize the problem of language that eventually gave rise to the philosophical revolution among the Greeks, the very thing that led Heraclitus to meditate on the universal Logos and Plato to propose his theory of pure forms (*eidé*). The emergence of philosophy, stimulated by the appearance of writing, may have arisen as an attempt to fill in the gap.

Be any of that as it may, the critic is perfectly correct that Lacan traces the origin of the religious to the functioning of language. "The symbolic," as he says, "is the basis of what was made into God."[1] This way of looking at the matter provides the perfect point of entrée to a discussion of Judaism. Interpreted in Lacanian terms, Judaism is the religion of the signifier par excellence. It is Judaism that most expressly and consistently devotes itself to the pure functioning of the signifier, and particularly to the incompleteness of its power of signification, its opening toward something unknown.

The Jewish Covenant

Toward the end of *Anxiety*, not long after offering a discussion of the sub-lime effect of the nearly closed eyelids of Buddha statues, Lacan invites his auditors to "imagine that you are dealing with the most restful *desir-able*, in its most soothing form, a divine statue which is just divine—what would be more *Unheimlich* than to see it come to life, that is, to show itself as a *desirer*?"[2] But isn't such a uncannily direct encounter with the divinity precisely what occurs in Abram's experience of the alarming approach of Yahweh? In the founding story of the Jewish faith, the future father of the Hebrew nation finds himself directly confronted by *das Ding*, the unknown and completely unnerving desire of the Other.

The pagan Greeks were no strangers to the idea of direct inter-course with the gods. When a sudden rush of inexplicable power coursed into their limbs, when they found themselves puppeted by an explosion of extraordinary rage or felt themselves suddenly and irresistibly struck by some idea or vision as by the force of a physical impact, they would not hesitate to say that they had been touched, even momentarily inhabited, by a god.[3] But Yahweh is something completely different. The Hebrew god is not content with episodic sparks that momentarily narrow the gap between mortals and divinities. He insists on the establishment of a per-manent and unlimited bond. Where the pagan gods came into occasional *contact* with humans, Yahweh insists on a binding *contract*. He demands a *covenant*. Even if they could have for a moment suspended their disbelief that any deity would behave in this way, the pagan Greeks would have found the proposal of such a pact to be not only infinitely terrifying but also infinitely undesirable.

Yahweh is also unlike the pagan gods because his primary relation-ship is not with his fellow divinities but with the human world below him. This is the meaning of his famous "jealousy." Like the poker player who bets his whole wad on the last card, Yahweh is all in with his proposal to Abram, and he demands the same in return. If the very multitude of the Greek gods helped to blunt their potentially traumatic impact, the Jew-ish covenant, requiring an unlimited and interminable commitment to a single, infinitely powerful being, allows no escape. Yahweh is adamant that Abram and all of his descendants forswear all other gods and ad-here exclusively to him. Abram thus not only is brought into an abyssal confrontation with *das Ding* but is asked to remain suspended over that abyss indefinitely. The result is that Abram's own status as a subject is radi-cally altered. No wonder that, henceforth, he will be no longer Abram but Abraham.

What is most shatteringly uncanny in Yahweh's extending the covenant to Abraham, what makes it most comparable to the Lacanian notion of *das Ding*, is the way it makes Abraham infinitely answerable to the desire of an unknown Other. What is new in this encounter with divinity is that the god definitely wants something from him. But what exactly is wanted? A covenant, yes, the terms of which specify an exchange in which each party gives something to the other. But why enter into that exchange at all? Or better: What exactly is it that this god wants? Lacan evokes the ultimate unanswerability of this question in an aside on the story of Ruth.

> In its root and essence, desire is the Other's desire, and this is strictly speaking the mainspring of the birth of love, if love is what occurs in the object toward which we extend our hand owing to our own desire, and which, when our desire makes it burst into flames, allows a response to appear for a moment: the other hand that reaches toward us as its desire. This desire always manifests itself inasmuch as we do not know. "And Ruth did not know what God wanted from her." But in order not to know what God wanted of her, it must still have been clear that God wanted *something* of her.[4]

The enigma of the Other's desire is the enigma of love. Lacan lays out a two-stage process. An initiating gesture, the signal of one's own desire (the reaching out of one's hand), motivates a return gesture ("the other hand that reaches toward us"). What is crucial in this drama, what prevents it from collapsing into a banality, is the role of the unknown. As Lacan says of it, "Desire always manifests itself inasmuch as we do not know." Even if the Other takes my proffered hand as a signaling of desire, the Other doesn't know what precisely that desire consists of. But then again, of course, neither do I. I don't know the source and meaning of my own desire, if only because my desire reaches out to touch what is unknown in the Other. I reach out to the *Other's* desire. The encounter of love is the flirtation between something unknown in the Other and what is unknown in oneself.

For precisely that reason, the Jewish religion inaugurates a religion of love. The contrast with the Greek experience could hardly be more striking. The whole notion of a "love of God" was completely foreign to the world of the archaic Greeks. As E. R. Dodds reminds us, the Homeric culture had no word for "love of God." "The love of god . . . is missing from the older Greek vocabulary: *philotheos* appears first in Aristotle."[5] But there is nothing sappy or sentimental in the Jewish love of God, and Lacan's stress on the rootedness of love in the unknown helps us understand why. The very approach of Yahweh to Abraham, prompting the question of what may have motivated that uncanny initiative, plunges him into the unknown. It is in this sense that we should read the *fear of God* that characterizes the relation to the divine evinced in the Torah. The fear of God is not to be opposed to the love of God, as if we are confronted with two opposing attitudes. Because love is ineluctably and constitutively bound up with unknowing, fear and love are at the most basic level inseparable.

It is worth pausing a moment over this conjunction of love and fear. Commonsensically speaking, it is by no means obvious why they go together, and the question of their juncture becomes only more puzzling when we acknowledge the link between the fearful and the unknown. Human beings generally regard the unknown as one of the most painful and loathsome things we have to deal with. Yet one of the most invaluable features of the Lacanian concept of *das Ding* is its capacity to supply an answer to the question of the profound linkage between desire and dread. If the psychoanalytic theory is correct, the unknown is capable of assuming the prospect of something alluring only because it was originally associated with the inner secret of the fellow human being to whom we were in the past intimately attached. The consequence, as we have seen, is that the subject's relation to *das Ding* is the very ground and heartbeat of ambivalence. In agreeing to worship the daunting figure of Yahweh, Judaism centers religious life on the paradox of a loving fearfulness and a fearful loving.

Gimme Shelter

That there remains something truly fearsome about the Hebrew God is attested by the role of veiling in Judaism. We have already noted the function of the veil in the archaic Greek experience. We identified it with the role of myth itself. Myth served to buffer mortals from the abyssal character of divinity by concealing it behind a screen. But with Judaism, the massively more intimate and imposing approach of divinity called for more targeted measures. Among them were coverings of various sorts, arranged not to conceal the god but to enshroud and protect the worshipper. Before entering the temple of God, the devout Jewish man dons the prayer shawl called the tallith. Only after praying for a moment beneath the sheltering canopy of the tallith, as if gathering himself before venturing a more direct contact with the awful majesty of the divinity, does the Jewish worshipper make bold to enter the sanctuary. The *kippah* or yarmulke performs the same covering function in a discreet and compact form. For many Jewish communities, the *kippah* is a near constant of masculine costume, presenting an appearance of modesty and devotion beneath the watchful eye of a potentially wrathful deity.[6]

In the pagan world, it was divinity itself that required veiling. As Nietzsche is fond of reminding us, the goddess of truth in the ancient world was cloaked by a veil, sparing mortals too direct a confrontation with an overwhelming reality. For the pagans, however, the truly abyssal character of that reality derived from the fact that there is ultimately nothing there. The only true seeing was therefore an acceptance of blindness, which is why the archetypical soothsayer of the pagan world, Tiresias, was *blind.* True wisdom knew that *there is ultimately nothing to see. There is only the Void.*

In the pagan context, veiling was also closely associated with the feminine, a practice that is still echoed by contemporary norms of women's dress. The most common, of course, is the bridal veil. Recalling the entrance of the sacrificial animal into the ritual precinct of ritual bloodletting, the wife-to-be enters the sacred space of the marriage vows shrouded by a veil. The implication, rooted in the archaic linkage between the feminine and the dark, autochthonous powers of nature, is that the veil discreetly conceals and renders publicly acceptable, even charming, what might otherwise be scandalous, obscene, or downright threatening.

In the Judaic context, by contrast, the male is submitted to veiling. In the case of Moses, who veils himself after his forty days and nights with God, it is tempting to assume that we are dealing with something akin to the archaic Greek function of the veil. It is as if Moses had absorbed into himself something of the awesome power of God and needed to be veiled to protect his fellow mortals from too direct an exposure.[7] But the main purpose of Jewish religious veiling is a matter of ensuring the properly modest and reverential posture of the worshipper who presents himself before the deity. "Cover your head in order that the fear of heaven may be upon you," instructs the Talmud.[8] While the specific rules concerning the wearing of the yarmulke vary across different Jewish traditions, there is broad agreement that a head covering is appropriate for prayer or religious study, for the performance of rituals, and for eating. Covering oneself is generally associated with piety, modesty, shame, or mourning. Among the pagans, what most called for veiling was the outbreak of passion, the visible evidence of divine intervention. Among the Jews, what needs covering are the potentially problematic consequences of action. A long tradition of commentators has taken this difference to mark a shift from a culture of shame to a culture of guilt.[9]

The difference between the archaic Greek polytheism and Abrahamic monotheism is here interpreted in terms of a more intimate and correspondingly more intense encounter of the worshipper with *das Ding*. In the frame of Greek myth, the unthinkable real of the Thing was given anthropomorphic shape as an active subject—one or another god—whose intentions and disposition remained largely unknown. But the divine Thing of paganism was rendered immensely more tolerable by being posed not as a single subject but as a positive throng of divinities. The Greek gods were in this way a mitigated embodiment of *das Ding*. Its potentially threatening character was thankfully qualified by the very plurality of gods. Yahweh, by contrast, appears to Abraham in traumatizing singularity. From now on, Yahweh tells Abraham, there will be only one God for you.

If Yahweh marks a decisive advance toward the primal *Nebenmensch* in its essential singularity, he also reflects the internal division of Freud's construction, distributed between a cognizable portion, configured in the imaginary, and a noncognized remainder, present only by absence, maintained as a blank, unknowable "Thing." Greek polytheism kept apart these two facets of the primal Other, constructing a religious culture that remained conspicuously divided between a theater of imaginary forms—the tapestry of myth—and an unknowable beyond of the abyssal real. Yahweh directly engages the human being as another subject.

A last, crucial point: Yahweh is distinguished by the fact that he directly and intimately *addresses* Abraham. Yahweh is above all the God who *speaks* to man. He makes himself known only as a voice. The pagan gods, too, are sometimes depicted as speaking to mortals, as when Akhilleus is tempted to draw his sword on Agamemnon at the opening of the *Iliad* and Athena restrains his hand. But such pagan "counsels" of the gods tend typically to be ventriloquized by other, mortal speakers. Or else the pagan gods "speak" through the anomalous events of portents and omens. In one way or another, communication between mortals and pagan divinities tended to be oblique. The speaking of Yahweh is disarmingly direct. In this way, the covenant with Yahweh properly inaugurates what Lacan calls the big Other.

The order of powers and the laws of fate were as close as one might come to something like the big Other in the pagan context. With Yahweh, we are in a new game altogether. Yahweh trumps both time and fate, effectively taking them up into himself. Yahweh is not merely another, far more powerful subject; he announces himself as the only such subject. Yahweh embodies the *subject itself*. Where the archaic Greek strove to act nobly in the face of a subjectless void at the bottom of the world, the Jewish subject of the covenant finds itself uncomfortably answerable to the unlimited desire of the ultimate Other-Subject.

The Terms of the Deal

The terms of Yahweh's covenant with Abraham would no doubt strike a Martian visitor to Earth as risibly absurd. For his part, Yahweh vows to make Abraham the "father of many nations." Yahweh will see to it that the multitudes of Abraham's descendants are protected from calamity and blessed with enduring fruitfulness. When Abraham's ninety-nine-year-old wife, Sarah, hears of this part of the deal, she understandably bursts out laughing. Stranger still, however, is the massive asymmetry with Abraham's part of the bargain. By cleaving to the covenant, he will become the most mighty and venerable man in the land. And what must he do to obtain such a magnificent reward? Merely snip off the useless flap of skin on the tip of his penis.

A lot might be (and has been) said about this exceedingly strange demand.[10] But Yahweh's insistence on circumcision becomes readily explicable from a Lacanian point of view. For Lacan, the most distinctive and decisive feature of the founding story of Jewish monotheism, aside from the most obvious fact of proposing a *single* deity, resides in the fact that Abraham's interaction with Yahweh confronts him not with a mere quantum of force but with *a subject of desire*. The very strangeness of the demand for circumcision, along with its near-infinite disproportionality as a stake in the covenantal contract, suggests the exigency of a desire the underlying motive of which remains obscure.

The apparent bizarreness of the covenant's stipulation of circumcision becomes less baffling when we remember Hesiod's story about Cronos's castration of his father, Sky (Ouranos). In that case, Cronos's assault was aimed at the organ-source of Sky's procreative power. The result was a reordering of the hierarchy of powers, with the mighty fertility of Sky giving way to the even greater supremacy of Time. Perhaps the best way to interpret the meaning of the gesture of circumcision is that it attests to a voluntary submission to a greater power. The children who will come into the world from this organ are begotten not by Abraham but by God. As Lacan would put it, Abraham takes upon his organ of generation the "mark of the cut," thereby symbolically submitting himself to the law of desire, which passes by necessity through the locus of the Other.

The Abrahamic covenant also transforms the history of blood sacrifice. Where other deities of the ancient Middle East demanded the ritual slaughter of sheep, goats, and cattle, and the capacity of sacrifice to appease the gods was directly proportionate with the sheer number and quality of the animals slaughtered, Yahweh insists on a bloodletting that is mostly symbolic. The object of Abraham's sacrifice, the "victim" put to the knife, is nothing of any real consequence. In the covenantal "sacrifice" of the foreskin, what is given up to the god is ultimately a trivial object, in purely anatomical terms probably the most readily expendable piece of flesh offered by the human form.

But the relative worthlessness of the object of sacrifice only serves to highlight the true meaning of the ritual. What Yahweh demands is less a particular object of sacrifice than the pure willingness to give it up. Yahweh is ultimately interested in Abraham's devotion and obedience. His test of Abraham forsakes the value of mere objects in favor of pure intentions. Abraham's willingness to undergo circumcision symbolizes his posture of pious submission, a testament to his recognition that all true paternity henceforth belongs not to him but to God. By this route, the Jewish covenant marks an epoch-making shift away from a life in thrall to externalities in the direction of a purely inward life of the spirit.

The culture of paganism placed no such value on any internal disposition. Quite literally, going through the motions was sufficient for the pagan mind to ensure the effectiveness of religious ritual. It was for this reason that the Roman parents of young converts to Christianity were baffled that their children would sooner be torn apart by lions than agree to pantomime the traditional pagan sacrifices. Visiting her in prison shortly before her martyrdom, Perpetua's father makes the argument especially clearly. You needn't depart from your new beliefs, he pleads. All you need to do is perform the outward motions required by the traditional rite. Perpetua refuses and goes to her death in the arena.[11]

The most important fruit of Abraham's encounter with Yahweh is the birth of the invisible soul. It is entirely appropriate, then, that the "sacrifice" of Abraham that seals the covenant is centered on a wound to oneself. This gesture inaugurates a religion based on the way the institution of the law imposes upon the subject a relentless requirement of questioning itself.

. . . and Offer Him There as a Sacrifice

If the opening drama between Abraham and Yahweh confronts us with a series of perplexing questions, this is even more true of the second chapter of the story: the moment when Yahweh demands the sacrifice of Isaac. The first challenge is the way it appears to enact an obscene return to the regime of pagan sacrifice. In apparent conformity to the polytheistic rules of sacrifice that required the slaughter of objects of obvious value, Abraham is here asked to give up what is unquestionably the most valuable object of all. The story of Abraham and Isaac suddenly seems to align itself with that of Agamemnon and Iphigenia. Judged on its external particulars, we can only think that Yahweh has completely abandoned his own radical redefinition of sacrifice, that of putting aside the value of the object in favor of an inward disposition of sheer willingness to give something up.

Or has he? Yahweh's demand that Abraham drag his son up Mount Moriah and offer him there as a sacrifice puts Abraham to the ultimate test of faith and obedience. If the original novelty of the "sacrifice" of the covenant was to test pure willingness to relinquish something, made more palpable by the worthlessness of the object, the command to sacrifice the most valuable possible object only radicalizes the original purpose. If Abraham accedes to this most horrifying of demands, he will have proved his inward obedience in the course of the most strenuous possible test. Kierkegaard's *Fear and Trembling* offers an extended reflection on the unthinkable complexity of Abraham's willingness to carry out Yahweh's call to sacrifice his son. Indeed, according to Kierkegaard, the whole point of the story is to introduce us to the abyssal space of spiritual inwardness, to reveal how the heart of the monotheistic believer is tensed by a dizzying range of undecidables. In that vertiginous inner space, the knotted dynamics of love and sacrifice become impossible to disentangle.

But there is another problem. For how are we to understand that the second chapter of the story of Abraham appears simply to undo the first? Sarah's improbable pregnancy provided the indispensable means by which Yahweh's covenant to Abraham could be fulfilled. In then demanding the sacrifice of Isaac, Yahweh appears to take back precisely what he promised.

Perhaps the best answer to this riddle comes into view when we take note of the weakness inherent in the original covenant. In purely formal terms, it remains a quid pro quo. Despite the discrepancy in value between the two sides of the exchange, Yahweh is prepared to give something to Abraham only if Abraham is willing to give something back. The exchange is formally identical to the Roman dictum of sacrifice: *do ut des*, I give so that you will give. Precisely as such, it risks descending to the level of a mere market transaction, utterly lacking in the spiritual commitment that is the primary motivation of Yahweh's entire proposal. The contracting of the covenant therefore requires a kind of double inscription, the second portion of which is accomplished only when Yahweh demands the sacrifice of Isaac and Abraham accedes to that demand. The opening gambit of the covenant clarifies that what is wanted from Abraham is the adoption of a wholly spiritual posture, the demonstration of an absolutely uncompromising and willing obedience. The second, indispensable supplement restages that demonstration of a willingness to sacrifice, and does so on an infinitely greater scale, by means of demanding that Abraham abandon all expectation of compensation. When the Jewish worshipper gives himself fully to the will of God in accepting circumcision—or, for that matter, in any participation in sacred ritual—he must also give up all certainty of actually getting something in return for his trouble. If the story of Isaac were not enough, the ultimate confirmation of this suspension of expectation as a central feature of Jewish faith is, of course, the book of Job.

"But surely the pious Jew is not unique in this respect," objects the critic. "Pagan sacrifice, too, left those who performed the ritual in ignorance of whether any possible benefit might be forthcoming. One never knows if or when or how the gods might be swayed by the offerings of sacrifice."

The critic's point is only half valid. It is true that neither pagan nor Jew could be sure that the performances of sacrifice would have the desired effects. But to take the Isaac episode fully seriously is to realize how radically the Jewish faith breaks with the pagan position.[12] To the extent that Abraham provides the cardinal model for Jewish piety, the Jewish worshipper must give up in advance all expectation of reward for sacrifice. The worship of Yahweh becomes an end in itself.

To this first point a second, subtler but ultimately more important one must be added. It is a point deeply significant for the continuing thread of our argument about the role of *das Ding* in the constitution of the religious posture. If both pagan and Jew remain suspended in an essential unknowing about the possible rewards of worshipful observance, the unknowing of the Jew is significantly different from that of the pagan. The reason is rooted in the singularity of the Jewish relation to the one true God. Here we encounter the consequences of having inaugurated a more decisive relation to the Lacanian big Other. Abraham's relation to Yahweh, and by extension that of every Jew who follows in the Abrahamic tradition, is bookended by unknowing. One knows neither why God approaches with the proposal of the covenant nor what exactly will come of it. Yahweh is an unfathomable mystery, both in the very inception of his relation with his chosen people and in the terms of its fulfillment.

The absolutely key point remains, however, that the moment of unknowing in the Jewish relation to God is focused on a *single* Other. The confrontation with the unknown ceases to be dispersed across an unspecified range of unpredictable forces personified as deities. On the contrary, it emanates from a single locus of subjectivity. With the possible exception of Akhenaton's brief, ill-fated foray into monotheism, the Jewish covenant is the first time that the entire horizon of the unknown comes into focus as coincident with the secret interior of another subjectivity.[13]

It is the first time that religious experience explicitly touches upon its primordial source in the relation to the enigmatic desire of the Other.[14]

The Voice from the Burning Bush

Casting an eye over the Torah, one is struck by the number of double inscriptions. Abram is renamed Abraham. The covenant with Yahweh is tested by two dramas of sacrifice. Indeed, the covenant itself seems doubly inscribed, as Yahweh's appearance to Abraham is repeated by his later appearance to Moses. And Moses's transmission of the law is also doubled, as it first appears in Exodus, when Moses returns from the desert with the tablets of the law, and then again in Deuteronomy. The very name *Deuteronomy* means "the second law." But perhaps the ultimate double inscription occurs in the name of God himself. When Yahweh answers from out of the burning bush Moses's question about his name, he answers "Eyeh asher eyeh"—"I am what I am." Lacan seizes upon this last double inscription in particular to argue that the Jewish religion should be recognized as pivoting in the most profound way upon the function of the linguistic signifier in the speaking subject.

Lacan's first move in making this point is to emphatically reject the most familiar interpretations of what is spoken from the burning bush, interpretations that have traditionally taken their cue from Greek metaphysics. God does not here assert his substantial self-identity, the A = A of Aristotelean logic. In saying, "I am what I am," God does not say, "I am the One who truly is (the completed fullness of Being)." Nor is he announcing an unchanging essence (e.g., "What I am will remain the same for eternity"). On the contrary, Lacan insists, the true significance of *Eyeh asher eyeh* is more nearly the opposite. The voice from the flames puts forward less an answer than a question. It is a voice that problematizes itself in its own sounding. As some scholars of Hebrew had already argued well before Lacan's arrival on the scene, the phrase *Eyeh asher eyeh* may be less well rendered in the present indicative—"I am what I am"— than in the future conditional—"I will be what I will be." But Lacan offers his own distinctive twist. We should read the words from out of the fire as "I am what I is"—"Je suis ce que je est."[15]

For Lacan, the voice from the burning bush, precisely as the utterance of a *subject*, is to be heard as a declaration of noncoincidence, of discrepancy between *what* is asserted and the position *from which* it is asserted. The position of the subject is altered in the very act of stating it. What is at stake could readily be Lacan's most fundamental contribution: the notion of *the divided subject*. The ultimate horizon of that dividedness is, of course, the cleavage between the conscious and the unconscious. It is the divide that resonates in Freud's famous dictum, a saying whose profundity, Lacan repeatedly suggests, is on a par with the most elemental teachings of the pre-Socratics: "Wo Es war, soll Ich werden"—"Where It was, there shall I come to be." Lacan's innovation is to ground that division in the dynamics of speech itself. One of his preferred glosses for it is the distinction between the *sujet énoncé* and the *sujet de l'énonciation*."[16] To cite a simple example, as soon as I say, "I am getting frustrated with this situation," I have already, by virtue of my own statement about myself, moved by some increment to a new position. My frustration has been modified in some degree by having been put into words. I am already in some measure beyond the very situation that has been frustrating me.

Lacan's most radical statement of what is at stake in the divided subject is his definition of the subject as "what is represented by a signifier for another signifier." The movement of the speech stream, the very heartbeat of discourse, is constantly re-creating double inscription—double inscription that makes a difference. Speech can only specify the meaning of anything that has been said by resort to . . . more words. Taking into account this inexorable semiotic self-reflexivity, continually both ahead of itself (in the inchoate anticipation of meaning) and retroactively determining what has been said (as each articulation folds back on what preceded it and qualifies its import), it becomes deeply problematic to speak of the "being" of the speaking subject at all. The subject is less something spoken for by any particular signifier than it is a function of the gap between signifiers, tensed by multiple prospective and retrospective vectors. The subject is less an entity in its own right than an inherently unstable effect of a process that is ceaselessly to be determined in some future formulation. If we can speak of the "being" of the subject at all, it is a form of "being" that is infinitely deferred.

Toward the end of the *Anxiety* seminar, Lacan cites a paper by Theodor Reik on the Jewish shofar, a long, primitive, cork-screwed trumpet made from a ram's horn. The shofar is typically sounded only on the High Holidays of Rosh Hashanah, the Jewish New Year, and Yom Kippur, the Day of Atonement. Lacan offers the following account of the uncanny sound it makes.

> Those who've treated themselves to this experience, or who are going to, will bear witness, I think . . . to the deeply moving, stirring character of these sounds. Independently of the atmosphere of reverence, of faith, even of repentance, in which these sounds blast out and resound, an unusual emotion emerges along the mysterious paths of a specially auricular affect that cannot fail to touch, to a truly uncommon degree, all those who come within earshot of it.[17]

Lacan doesn't accept all of Reik's analysis, but he agrees with Reik's most basic thesis: the shofar, deeply associated with the renewal of the covenant, offers a soul-shuddering stand-in "for the voice of Yahweh, the voice of God himself."[18] Reik compares the sound, both fascinating and terrifying, to the bellowing of a bull. There is some basis for the comparison in scripture, which refers to "the roar of God."[19] Moreover, the fact that the instrument is taken from a ram's horn recalls the ram that is substituted at the last moment for the sacrifice of Isaac. The "trumpeting" of something like the shofar is also crucially mentioned twice in the context of Moses's confrontation with Yahweh on Mount Sinai.[20] In both cases, the people are struck with fear by its sounding.

Fear of what exactly? According to Lacan, the shofar serves to evoke the pure voice, the voice stripped of its function of locution and reduced to its bare sounding. It is the voice from which *what* is spoken has been subtracted, leaving only the sheer fact that something has been said. For Lacan, this elemental resonating of the voice, devoid of all articulation of structures of signification, is an embodiment of the *objet a*. Mladen Dolar offers a marvelously evocative treatment of the pure sonority of the voice in *A Voice and Nothing More*.[21] The truly uncanny fact is that it is almost impossible not to feel *addressed* by this sound. It announces a demand to be heard. What exactly it is saying remains completely unspecified. It is for this reason that the strangely disturbing sound of the shofar, like the bleating of a dying animal, is such an effective stand-in for the voice in the whirlwind. It reaches out to us, closing the distance that separates us from it, and yet remains impossible to comprehend.

It is this quality of unlocatable presence that makes it possible to compare the wail of the shofar to the voice of God. It is a pure sounding of *das Ding*.[22] "It leads us," says Lacan, "onto the ground where, in Freud's mind, in its most searing form, the function of repetition was traced out."[23] What we have here, as Lacan puts it, is the voice of the lost object that was never possessed. Its most profound and uncanny feature resides in harboring a deep ambiguity. We inevitably feel called by this raw, uninterpretable voice. It is inevitably a voice sounded *for us*, that calls *to us*. And yet, it also strangely anticipates our own cry, our own reaching out toward the Other. Lacan thus concludes his discussion by remarking that "this dimension is what gives the interrogation borne by the locus of the Other its meaning. To spell it right out, isn't the one whose memory is to be awakened, the one who is to be made to remember, God himself?"[24] The deepest secret of the sounding of the shofar is that it is at once the unnerving sound of the voice of the ultimate Other, and yet also the sound of our own voice, the howl of our cry to the Other that will bring him (or her) to us.

Lacan's analysis of the shofar points toward the linguistically mediated being-beyond-itself of the subject that constitutes the heart of the Jewish religion. In paganism, the subject wholly allocates the unknown to the Other; the question is only how one comports oneself in relation to it. In Judaism, the unknown is taken into the subject itself. The question becomes what it is that the Other wants of me, and how I am to respond to it. It is a question that cannot be settled once and for all, and whose internal ambiguities guarantee its power over the subject. By this route, Judaism becomes the quintessential religion of the law, and of the submission of the worshipper to its rule. And all law, Lacan insists, is finally reducible to the law of language.

The Ten Commandments as the Laws of Speech

Lacan's analysis of the Ten Commandments builds upon his interpretation of the name of God spoken out of the burning bush. At the deepest level, the commandments enjoin the submission of the subject to the laws of speech and language: "The list of the Ten Commandments," Lacan says, " . . . announce the laws of 'I speak.' If it is true, as I stated, that the truth speaks 'I,' it appears to be self-evident that: 'You will adore the one who has said: 'I am what I is.'"[25]

The first clue to this linguistic interpretation is contained in the very opening of the first commandment. As many commentators from the rabbinic tradition have observed, the Decalogue opens with a triple reference to the *speaking* of God: "God spoke all these words, saying, I am the Lord your God who brought you out of the Land of Egypt, out of the house of bondage: You shall have no other gods besides Me."[26] As Kenneth Reinhard and Julia Lupton point out in their superb study "Lacan and the Ten Commandments," the repeated references to speech in the opening line ("God spoke [*v'y'daber*] all these words [*kol ha-davarim*], saying [*limor*]") led commentators "in two directions at once: toward the radical singularity of God's expression on the one hand, and the equally sublime multiplicity of his speech on the other."[27] Here, we once again encounter the problem of double inscription, though with this difference: the first iteration cannot be understood by human beings. The initial word spoken by Yahweh is humanly unintelligible. A long line of rabbinic interpreters struggled to grasp this twofold character of the divine law, knowable and unknowable. "The medieval French commentator Rashi argued that God spoke the entire set of commandments in a single incomprehensible and terrifying utterance [2:102]; Maimonides adds that God's speech lacked distinct phonemes [Agnon 260]; another commentary reinforces this image of radical condensation by suggesting that God's voice had no echo [Midrash Rabbah 3:336]. Yet Rashi goes on to write that after speaking the commandments all at once, God began to repeat them one by one."[28] This ambiguity of the simultaneous and the successive reflects the divide between the real and the symbolic, between a traumatic core that cannot be psychically metabolized and a series of attempted substitutes. Yahweh appears impossibly to be both at once. What, then, does this "both at once" mean for his worshippers? It means first and foremost that there remains something unknown and unknowable about the Jewish God. He passes down a tablet of laws that can be written down and talked about, but he himself, the source of those commandments, remains inscrutable. Retaining and honoring Yahweh's ultimate unknowability then becomes in itself a sacred duty for the Jewish people.

It is for this reason that the code of laws laid down by the Jewish God, the very laws that Lacan claims are ultimately identifiable with the laws of language, are themselves anchored in a law concerning the use of language: the prohibition of all attempts to directly name him. He can only be referred to indirectly, typically as Lord (*Adonai*). His name can be rendered in script by the tetragrammaton, YHWH. Most tellingly for our purposes, one of the most common means of avoiding directly naming him seizes upon the word "Name" itself. God is thus referred to as *haShem*—"the Name." In saying *haShem*, one literally keeps to the first stage of signification, that of a signifier without any definite signified. As *haShem*, the nature of YHWH himself remains unspoken for, shrouded in enigma.

The Jewish religion is quite literally centered on the mystery of *naming*. Lacan highlights this point by locating Yahweh in his shorthand for the chaining of signifiers: S1→ S2 [S3 . . .]. The Hebrew God instantiates S1, the signifier without a signified, the signifier that stands outside the rest of the network of signifiers. It can be approached only by resort to some other signifier, S2, S3, and so on, but can never be adequately compassed. Said otherwise, S1 marks the place of a lack that cannot be filled in, a gap that sets the rest of the signifying machinery in motion. As Reinhard and Lupton say of it, "The name of God is the exception that proves the rule, the signifier that transcends any meaning it might attract, and in the process inaugurates the signifying chain. Through its exclusion from that chain, the S1 maintains the S2 in their plurality, their lack of totality."[29]

S1 stands for an inexhaustibility of meaning that echoes throughout the whole train of signifiers. In this view, S1 is not so much a particular signifier as a stand-in for the function of pure *signifiance*, the pure-expectation-of-meaning-as-yet-unspecified that accompanies every signifier. The very distinction between S1 and S2 (and on to S3, S4, etc.) arises from the fact that no signifier is capable of defining itself. As Lacan himself came to realize after coining the phrase early in the development of his thought, there is no such thing as "full speech." Every iteration of the signifier leaves open not only a margin of possible misunderstanding (what exactly did he mean by saying that?) but also a slippage or indeterminacy of meaning (insofar as no signifier univocally speaks its meaning without generating an undecided remainder).

This remainder is precisely what Lacan claimed to have discovered, his most valuable contribution not just to psychoanalysis but to the intellectual history of humanity altogether: the *objet petit a*. The inestimable gift of the Jewish people to that history was to have created a religion centered upon precisely that remainder, the locus of something as-yet-unknown that is at least potentially called up by every signifier. Judaism represents the sacral institutionalization of the fact that the Thing in the Other remains forever beyond our capacities to adequately symbolize it. The Jewish religion dedicates itself to honoring its unspeakable and fearsome dignity. As Lacan says at one point, "The burning bush was Moses' Thing."[30]

With this point we recognize one of the most characteristic features of Jewish life: the value placed on articulate contestation. For the Jewish community, open-hearted debate, informed by the scriptural tradition yet still uncertain of its precise meaning, is in itself the posture of true devotion. This embrace of faithful dispute only underscores the ultimately unknown status of divine will. Judaism is the religion of perpetual worry over the law and its meaning. To be Jewish, one is tempted to say, is to endlessly disagree with one's fellow Jews about what it means to be Jewish—and to fully tolerate the consequences of that disagreement.

Whereas the archaic Greek outlook remained on the axis between the real and the imaginary, Judaic culture invested itself in the dichotomy between the real and the symbolic. In both instances, the primary task was that of coping with the enigma of the real, both defending against its traumatic potential and honoring its terrible dignity. The two cultural formations offered radically different solutions to the same problem: that of the unknown that is divinity itself. Between the two, the nature of divinity was construed in vastly different ways. The Greek option allowed divinity to remain associated with brute force, itself unknowable but inevitably giving rise to readily apparent effects in the world. It was a solution that allowed the power of the divine to remain palpable in physical phenomena. It was this feature of the Greek *Weltanschauung* that preserved the enchantment of the world. For the Jews, by contrast, the divine dimension is wholly taken up into the symbolic function, which opened the way for the worship not of mere force but of symbolic law. The price paid was arguably a greater alienation from the sensuous surround of the world, particularly the natural world, but the gain was the potential for an uncommon degree of social and cultural solidarity, a closing of ranks with one's fellows that remained out of reach in the Greek context. "Love thy neighbor" became for the first time a possible tenet of religious life.

The Letters of the Law

The second commandment, too, is deeply relevant to the question of language and naming. The commonplace understanding of the commandment to make "no graven images" is by no means entirely wrongheaded. The Jewish God must not be identified with any idol or icon, as he remains forever invisible, even unthinkable. To allow the divine to be debased by association with a mere image is to reduce the infinite to the level of the finite. Divinity is ineluctably beyond sensuous representation. But the underlying point is arguably even better made by reference to the function of linguistic signification. The prohibition of idolatry refers to an insistence on the way all meaning transcends the register of images. The resources of the symbolic must not be reduced to the imaginary. Indeed, for Lacan the second commandment demands nothing less than "the elimination of the function of the imaginary."[31]

Yet the everyday meaning of words tends to be trimmed to the mold of imaginary embodiment. The meaning of the word "home" is thoughtlessly drawn into orbit around the image of a cozy house with a welcoming walkway to the front door and a wispy trail of smoke curling reassuringly from the chimney. The tenderness of "love" becomes incompatible with anger or pitched argument. The meaning of "politics" is associated with impressive, columned buildings. Such images contract the polyvalence of the signifier to banalities.

The second commandment's prohibition of images insists on what makes language possible. The paradox discovered by Saussure is that the signifier is capable of representing an absent object or situation only because it is situated in a sprawling network of differences with other signifiers that cannot itself be an object of representation. The diacritical system that makes language possible is itself unimageable. The power of language that mobilizes thought derives from a structure that remains in itself unthinkable.

The commandment about keeping the Sabbath also begs to be related to the sanctity of the signifier. In fact, the fourth commandment seems especially relevant to the question of language, at least as Lacan conceives it.[32] The reason is that Lacan is less interested in the practical, everyday uses of language, the priorities of mere communication, than in the quirks and even failures of language. Lacan is most focused on the products of language that are spun off precisely when language, as Wittgenstein put it, is "on idle."

The fourth commandment is virtually unique in the history of human culture. It is a direct order—binding not only for the master of the house but for slaves, servants, and guests as well—to take the day off. The wording of the commandment attributes the necessity of Shabbat to the fact that God himself rested on the seventh day of creation. Indeed, the Hebrew word *Shabbat* means "rest." Yet the mysteriousness of the commandment already announces itself at that point, inasmuch as rest would hardly be necessary for an omnipotent creator. The implication would therefore appear to be that the value of the day of rest consists not in a need for relief from work, but rather in some more positive end, a rest *for* something, something that cannot happen without resting.[33] For Lacan, that more positive function concerns the opening of a void or gap, in which the service of mere utility gives way to something over and beyond the regime of practical necessity. "I believe that that extraordinary commandment, according to which, in a land of masters, we observe one day out of seven without work . . . that suspension, that emptiness, clearly introduces into human life the sign of a gap, a beyond relative to every law of utility."[34]

That the gap opened by Shabbat especially concerns the register of words is indicated by the fact that the "work" of reading and study, particularly of Torah, far from being prohibited, is the most valued form of "rest." The implication would appear to be that we are called by the Sabbath above all to listen in a new way to language. The rabbinic tradition specifies that the day of rest is for "observing" and "remembering." Only in such a posture of renewed openness might we hear new resonances of words, the unheard-of dimensions of the signifier. The Sabbath suspends routine *signification* in order to devote oneself to pure *signifiance*. In disconnecting ourselves from practical activity, we become open to the fact, as Lacan puts it, that "what this structure of the signifying chain discloses is the possibility I have—precisely insofar as I share its language [*langue*] with other subjects, that is, insofar as this language [*langue*] exists—to use it to signify *something altogether different* from what is says."[35] On the day of rest, we savor the void as an opening, a new beginning. The aim is to emerge from such rest larger, more encompassing, having absorbed something that the bustle of the work week might have prevented us from noticing.[36]

The Jewish coming-of-age rituals of bar and bat mitzvah display the deep Jewish commitment not just to the study of Torah but also to the way in which the essential message of the sacred text remains open to interpretation. Candidates for the ritual are expected to read from the Torah to the assembled congregation, a task typically requiring many months of Hebrew study. But the young are also in some traditions expected to *teach* in a *d'var Torah*, providing a commentary of their own that explores, expands, or applies the lessons of the passage they read.

The Jewish respect for the power of the word of God is strikingly represented in the Orthodox tradition by the tefillin, small black leather boxes containing tiny scrolls on which passages from the Torah are inscribed. One such box, the *shel rosh*, is strapped to the middle of the forehead. Another, the *shel yad*, is affixed to the upper arm with leather straps that entwine down the forearm and onto the hand and fingers. After completing his bar mitzvah, a young man becomes eligible to wear the tefillin during prayer. The clear implication is that the power borne by the words themselves will be communicated to the eyes with which the prayerful worshipper perceives the world and to the arms with which he will act upon it.

The first four commandments deal with the relation to Yahweh, the fifth with care and respect for one's parents. Yet here, too, there is a ready interpretation that turns the meaning of the commandment toward the subject's relation to the signifier. The issue becomes less a matter of what we owe to our parents for their labors in sustaining our growing bodies than for the way in which they bathed us from birth in a river of signifiers. To honor one's parents can be taken in this sense to be a matter of becoming more aware of the extent to which every subject is, as Lacan puts it, "the slave of a discourse in the universal movement of which his place is already inscribed at this birth, if only in the form of his proper name."[37] Only in recovering and being transformed by the fuller meaning of that subjective inscription laid down by one's parents, only by somehow living up to one's own name, does the slave have any possibility of liberation.

In sum, the first tablet of the Decalogue, beginning with the ineffable name of God, indicates in multiple ways the centrality of naming and signification, and also emphasizes the ways the usages of language pose perpetually open questions. The result for Jewish identity and tradition is the formation of a culture deeply devoted to ceaseless contestation in the medium of words. Judaism is the very antithesis of a rigid fundamentalism that cleaves unwaveringly to one or another literal meaning of scripture. It is hardly an exaggeration to say that there is no point of religious belief in Judaism that has not been complicated by multiple interpretations.

The great monument to such contestation is the Talmud, which is less a statement of doctrine than a history of contending interpretations thereof. The Talmud might easily appear to be merely a giant compendium of devout disagreement were it not for the fact that the discord between views is counterbalanced by tolerance for different perspectives. The Jewish intellect well fulfills F. Scott Fitzgerald's definition of a first-rate intelligence as "the ability to hold two opposed ideas in the mind at the same time, and still retain the ability to function." It is a fascinating testimony to the Jewish embrace of such contestation that more than one Jewish tradition identifies the Talmud as coequal with Torah. Indeed, some orthodox Jews maintain that both texts should be included in what was spoken by Yahweh on Mount Sinai.

Jewish devotion to the sanctity of the signifier, and especially to the zone of indeterminacy that attaches to its penumbra of meaning, might be invoked to explain two of the most striking facts concerning the Jewish contribution to world culture. The first is Jewish humor. Noted already by Freud in his book on jokes but increasingly recognized by others in the twentieth century, the Jewish community has spawned an inordinate number of comedians. Even limiting ourselves to American comics—from Sid Caesar to Groucho Marx, Jack Benny to Amy Schumer, Woody Allen to Joan Rivers, Jerry Lewis to Jerry Seinfeld—the list can easily be extended to an astonishing length. The second fact is the extraordinary record of Jewish achievement in literature and science. To take just one index: though the Jewish people constitute only 0.2 percent of the world's population, Jewish artists, scholars, and scientists account for more than 20 percent of all Nobel prizes ever awarded.[38] It is tempting to connect both of these areas of extraordinary Jewish achievement to the way the Hebrew spirit intensely embraces the complexities of the linguistic signifier.

Laws of the Neighbor

Whereas the first five commandments concern the relation to God, the last five from the second tablet enumerate duties toward one's fellow human beings.[39] For Lacan, however, the underlying issue behind the two tablets remains the same. The unifying focus, the real topic of the

Decalogue, is nothing other than the subject's relation to *das Ding* as it is reflected in the problematic of naming. In the first five commandments, that relation is centered on the figure of Yahweh himself, as the unnamable power that orients the subject toward the rule of the law. The first tablet thus lays down the essentials of the subject's relation to the signifier. Put in Kantian terms, what is commanded is an infinite respect (*Achtung*) for the open-endedness of signification, the ineluctably transcendent dimension of language.

The commandments of the second tablet then turn to the neighbor with whom and about whom I speak. This "doubling" between the tablets, perhaps most obviously indicated by the likeness of the second and seventh commandments—the one about "no other gods before me" and the prohibition against adultery—already hints that the two tablets address some common underlying issue. Lacan makes it explicit. At the most fundamental level, the Decalogue addresses the subject's bondage to the Thing in language, first in relation to the words spoken by the (big) Other and second in relation to the respect that must be shown to the (little) Other.

On the surface, all five of the commandments on the second tablet (aiming at murder, adultery, theft, lying, and covetousness) create an impression of merely negative limits on behavior, devoid of any recommendations for positively enhancing engagement. The law here appears to keep scrupulously to its Greek meaning of partitioning (*nomos*). Its function seems limited to merely separating subjects. To each its own. The upshot appears to fall conspicuously short of promoting positive love or affirmation for the neighbor in favor of mere nonencroachment. Yet this very negative character can be understood in a positive way insofar as the result is to hold open the place of the Other, to establish the precinct of the Other as worthy of respect. Commandments 6 through 10 have the effect of mandating the sacral character of the Other's being, to be maintained in its very otherness, to be accorded its own claim to inviolate integrity. The last five commandments, we can say, all aim to make room for the neighbor-Thing.

Precisely if something like "making room for the Thing in the neighbor" is discernible in the laws of the second tablet, we have to expect an internal contradiction to arise in and among those commandments insofar as maintaining a complete and consistent relation to *das Ding* is in principle impossible. For that very reason, Lacan maintains that the final two commandments, the one prohibiting bearing false witness and the one against coveting one's neighbor's property, form an especially important couplet. Taken together, they sum up the impossible consequences of the earlier commandments for the subject's relation to *das Ding*. Here is his characterization of the ninth commandment:

> I want to take up the prohibition on lying insofar as it is related to what presented itself to us as that essential relationship of man to the Thing, insofar as it is commanded by the pleasure principle, namely the lie that we have to deal with every day in our unconscious. "Thou shalt not lie" is the commandment in which the intimate link between desire, in its structuring function, with the law is felt most tangibly. In truth, this commandment exists to make us feel the true function of the law. . . . "Thou shalt not lie" as a negative precept has as its function to withdraw the subject of the enunciation from that which is enunciated. Remember the graph. It is there that I can say "Thou shalt not lie"— there where I lie, where I repress, where I, the liar, speak. In "Thou shalt not lie" as law is included the possibility of the lie as the most fundamental desire.[40]

The intention of this passage is to point to a double bind that is not only unavoidable but absolutely constitutive for the speaking subject. The ninth commandment prohibits us from lying, and yet, at least with respect to the Thing in the Other, every entry into language inevitably falls short. Every word about the Thing is inevitably a lie. The pronouncement of every signifier marks the space of the unknown Other as a question but also inevitably oversteps itself in some measure by providing an answer. Subjectivity itself is founded, as Freud put it, on a *proton pseudos*, an originary falsehood, by means of which the Other-Thing is located by the signifier yet also distorted by it. What is most imperative to name is precisely what cannot be named. Every signifier calls upon it but ends up offering a false substitute.

Lacan compares the double bind involved with the famous paradox of Epimenides, who affirmed that "all men are liars." If he is being honest, Epimenides undoes the truth of his own statement. In stating the truth that all men are liars, he proves himself to be the exception to the rule. If, on the other hand, he is lying, then there must exist at least one honest man. Therefore, not all men are liars. "The point," Lacan goes on to say, "is that speech doesn't itself know what it is saying when it lies, and that, on the other hand, in lying it also speaks some truth."[41] In being commanded to tell only the truth about the neighbor, the subject is beset by an impossible task, as nothing that can be said of the neighbor-Thing can do justice to the task. In obeying the injunction against bearing false witness, I must inevitably lie. I am unavoidably caught up in a contradiction.

The underlying issue here is precisely parallel to Yahweh's prohibition of all attempts to speak his name. It might also be worth observing that Lacan's claim here that the subject has always already lied in some way, that the very being of the subject is founded on some *proton pseudos*, recapitulates the biblical notion of an original fall. It could just as well be taken as the ultimate ground of classical theological arguments about original sin. But that is to put the matter in its "objective" framing. In the remark quoted above, Lacan also addresses the way a similar impossibility afflicts every subject in the form of the unavoidable division that occurs whenever an attempt is made to say something true about oneself. The subject can never close the gap between what it has enunciated and the position from which it enunciates. The Other cannot be spoken, but neither can the subject. Already when I predicate something of myself (I am angry, I am impatient, I am incapable), I have already inadvertently "lied." I am already in some minimal degree beyond the very predicate to which I have attached myself.

Lacan reads the force of the commandment against lying against the backdrop of the unavoidability of lying. A closely related contradictory tension inhabits the tenth commandment, which bars coveting thy neighbor's goods. The last commandment calls up the way we cannot resist supposing something about the neighbor's experience of enjoyment, while also admitting that it is an enjoyment that we can only suppose. We cannot know. In an important sense, this commandment, which can easily seem to be a relatively minor add-on to the other nine, is the most important of all, as it points most clearly to the Thing in the Other. It calls up not merely the objects the Other possesses—his ass, his cattle, his house, his wife, his children and servants, and so on—but rather the way(s) he enjoys them.

At this point we again encounter the essential ambiguity that inhabits the Lacanian concept of *jouissance*. The term refers not only to the subject's enjoyment but also to the legal right to take that enjoyment. The term *jouissance* thus harbors a link with the whole problematic of the legal status of property. The English word "enjoyment" reflects a parallel double meaning, referring both the actual gratification taken in something but also, in a legal context, the right to that gratification. The owner of a vacation house, for example, enjoys the warm, sunny days that he spends there, but he also enjoys the legal right to rent or sell the property. With regard to this purely legal right to something, once we are in possession of the relevant legal titles (the deed to the land or a contract to rent the land), we can positively know the subject's legal enjoyment (as the right of use). But with respect to the actual gratification the subject takes in the enjoyment of that property, we remain in the dark. We can only suppose something about it. Maybe his time spent there is marvelous, or maybe he's actually miserable.

Just as the ninth commandment enjoins the subject to forswear lying despite its unavoidability, the tenth commandment, too, creates a constitutive contradiction. The moral subject is forbidden to covet the neighbor's enjoyment, but the prohibition itself is part of what sets the impulse to covet in motion. "In effect," says Lacan, "I would not have had the idea to covet it if the Law hadn't said: 'Thou shalt not covet it.' . . . The dialectical relationship between desire and the Law causes our desire to flare up only in relation to the Law."[42] Here we touch upon one of the constants of Lacan's teaching: desire and the law are inseparable from one another; indeed, desire is a kind of shadow of the law, called up by the prohibition the law lays down. He cites Paul's Letter to the Romans as the perfect expression of this paradox: "What shall we say, then? Is the law sinful? Certainly not! Nevertheless, I would not have known what sin was had it not been for the law. For I would not have known what coveting really was if the law had not said, 'You shall not covet.' But sin, seizing the opportunity afforded by the commandment, produced in me every kind of coveting."[43]

Lacan's borrowing from Paul here becomes more meaningful when we follow his suggestion to replace the reference to "sin" with "the Thing." The result is then: "I would not have known what the Thing was had it not been for the law." It is on that level that Lacan can say that "the law affirmed there, the part concerning the one's neighbor's wife at least, is still alive in the hearts of men who violate it every day." But the deeper issue concerns the relation to the unthinkable dimension of the neighbor's Thing. The Pauline teaching, Lacan maintains, "doubtless has a relationship to that which is the object of our discussion today, namely, *das Ding*."[44]

Living with the Law—the God Symptom

"In your Lacanian reading," suggests the critic, "by positioning the subject in relation to the One unnamable God, and in relation to the neighbor as a locus of unknowable enjoyment, Jewish monotheism introduces an unprecedented proximity to *das Ding*. That increased proximity to the Thing is the bottom line of what distinguishes Judaism from pagan polytheism. But precisely if you are right, shouldn't we expect that development to massively heighten anxiety? And mustn't we therefore expect to find powerful compensating measures to allay that anxiety?"

The critic exactly anticipates the conclusion. As Judaic monotheism brings its adherents incomparably closer to *das Ding*, the result is an inevitable increase in anxiety. To answer that challenge, what might instead erupt as unbearable anxiety is transformed into *guilt*. Otherwise said, Judaism invents what Freud called the superego.

As Freud insisted, the anxiety of legal fault functions as a defense against a more elemental and formless anxiety. In Lacanian terms, submission to the big Other of the law functions as a bulwark against a more direct and even more anxiety-producing confrontation with *das Ding*. The dynamics involved retrace the ground lines of obsessive neurosis. The obsessive's anxiety-ridden fussing with details functions to protect him from a much more primitive and destabilizing anxiety. The essential action is one of displacement. In the case of the relationship with Yahweh, the displacement effects a shift from direct engagement with the enigma posed by the desire of the Other toward an obsessive absorption with the letter of the law, a means of losing oneself in the minutiae of the relatively inconsequential requirements of behavior. The embodiment of these minutiae is readily recognizable: it is the Jewish halacha specified in the 613 laws (*mitzvoth*) that govern orthodox Jewish life.

From a psychoanalytic viewpoint, this giant catalog of regulations, detailing not only the oversight of rituals and management of the Sabbath but also everyday dress, diet, interaction with others, and so on embodies a massive symptom formation. And like any symptom, it performs two opposing functions at once. In this case, the symptom serves to manage the potentially anxiety-producing relation to the Law-Giver himself. Strict kosher observance protects the righteously behaving subject from a traumatizing exposure to the abyssal Other. The terrifying aspect of Yahweh draws off to a reassuring distance. At the same time, the fulfillment of the mitzvoth, an accomplishment that requires nearly moment-to-moment performance of all kinds of acts and observances, lends to the law-abiding subject a gratifying sense of closeness to God. The paradoxical effect of the symptom is to simultaneously create distance and intimacy. In this symptomatic compromise, we see quite precisely how the figure of Yahweh is divided between his role as an embodiment of the threatening Thing and the largely consoling and calming role as the big Other of the symbolic law.

But this description lays out only the bare mechanism of the symptom. What really makes it psychically effective is the way it establishes and maintains the social link. Here, we encounter the real-life fulfillment of Yahweh's promise to bring forth from Abraham a whole nation. In the community of observing Jews, we might say that everyone is implicitly deputized into the service of the deity. As deputized, the perceived behavior of every Other serves to police the conformity of the whole. One sees others in the group making all the proper motions and is reassured of the consistency of the group at large and of one's own place in it. Or better, the participating subject *supposes* such consistency. We thus return to the theme of the big Other's regulating influence over day-to-day life and see more exactly how that influence is exerted. The power and authority of the big Other is certified by the apparent obedience of everyone in the community—a consistency that is in large part pure supposition. One doesn't know for sure exactly what is being done behind closed doors; one isn't able to fully certify conformity to the law by direct inspection. On the contrary, one's sense of the obedience and conformity of the community is mostly merely assumed. As the subject supposed to know and the overseer of conformity to the law, the big Other is largely a tissue of social fiction.

In this picture of a generalized supposition concerning the Other we glimpse the way the big Other actually operates. We see, that is, how a triumph of the collective superego, overseen by the ultimate big Other, is actually stabilized by an act of pure supposition. Others are subjects supposed to obey. The subject does what it assumes everyone else is doing. In this way, the whole fabric of social relation and the larger laws that organize it are revealed to be based partly on what one *sees* the others do, but much more so on what one *believes* about what they do. Robert Pfaller has used the term "interpassivity" to name such positioning of oneself in relation to one or another supposition concerning the behavior of others. By means of interpassivity, the subject feels itself to be woven into the tapestry of community by means of a supposition, not merely about the big Other and its demands for obedience but even more importantly about conformity of the little Others, the aggregate of neighbors.

A side benefit of the suppositional regime of collective obedience is to enable a safe zone in which a whole array of decidedly *little* pleasures can be enjoyed. The whole process yields an effect of reassuring domestication. The wild and dangerous aspects of the Others that surround us can be put at bay by the supposition of conformity, opening the space that enables a comforting and deeply satisfying replacement by a thousand small gratifications. In the best-case scenario, what results is a stable, smoothly functioning collective neurosis.

6

Christianity

The Worship of Love

> In truth, there was only one Christian and he died on the cross.
> —Friedrich Nietzsche

Near the end of his life, in October 1974, Lacan gave an interview with a group of Italian journalists, parts of which have been published under the title *The Triumph of Religion*. In that interview Lacan astonishingly proposed that "the true religion is the Roman one. . . . [T]here is *one* true religion and that is the Christian religion. The question is whether this truth will stand up."[1]

Christianity is the one true religion? How to interpret this massively provocative claim? First, what can it possibly mean for a psychoanalyst and avowed atheist to refer to religion, any religion, as *true*? Lacan even goes out of his way to repeat the word three times. Were Freud to have heard it, one might readily imagine him making a joke about the disciple who three times denies his master. Then again, how are we to take the meaning of "truth" here? "True" in the sense of the best exemplar? Or "true" in a stronger sense, measured by some conjunction with reality? Lacan didn't specify.

Also puzzling is Lacan's wondering about "whether this truth will stand up." The question at issue was which of the two, religion or psychoanalysis, might best survive into the future. Lacan's prediction was that religion "will triumph not only over psychoanalysis but over lots of other things too. We can't even begin to imagine how powerful religion is."[2] For Lacan, the reason for that coming triumph is clear: it lies in the capacity of religion to "secrete meaning." "They can give meaning to absolutely anything whatsoever. A meaning to human life, for example. They are trained to do that. Since the beginning, religion has been all about giving meaning to things that previously were natural."[3] The great power of religion—and, for Lacan, especially Christianity—resides in its ability to answer to the challenges of the real with a profusion of meaning.

Let us frame the discussion in this chapter according to the two main questions that arise from the Rome interview. In what sense does Lacan propose that Christianity is the "one true religion"? And what, if anything, does that have to do with the capacity of Christianity to overwhelm other forms of thinking, including psychoanalysis, by an endless proliferation of "meaning"? What does religion's "secretion of meaning" even mean?

From the Jewish Religion to the "Jewish Science"

Viewed externally, the Jewish worship of the law can readily appear to be not only deeply obsessive but also conspicuously fetishistic. The scroll of the Torah, for example, is treated with elaborate fastidiousness. The scroll is stored in the holy ark, or *Aron Kodesh*, a special cabinet that forms a key fixture in the sanctuary of the synagogue. Not only is the ark fitted with doors that are closed until the Torah is called for in worship, but the doors of the ark are in turn typically concealed by an ornate curtain, the *parochet*. From this enclosure, the Torah is taken out only with dramatic and solemn ceremony. The scroll itself is usually further protected by an elaborately embossed metal outer casing, often capped with a special crown, or *keter*. Inside this casing, the contents are also dressed in an internal fabric sash or sheath, referred to as the Mantle of the Law. It is decorated with various symbols and flourishes, and is ceremoniously removed at the proper moment.

But even removal of this "robe" of the scroll often reveals yet another, lighter covering of linen or silk: the *wimpel*. The likeness of this more delicate inner wrapping to the penile foreskin is not lost on Jewish tradition. For Germanic Jews, the *wimpel* is traditionally made from the swaddling cloth in which a baby boy was wrapped for his *bris*, the ritual of circumcision.

Once it has been wholly freed from its wrappings, the scroll is then typically held high by the officiant and may even be slowly walked around the congregation before being placed on a special table or *bimah*, the real centerpiece of the sanctuary, to be unrolled and read. Once there, the scroll is manipulated by its upper and lower handles, with care taken not to touch the scroll itself with bare hands. Touching is further avoided by the provision of a pointer, the *yad*, with which particular words or passages can be indicated.

Despite what can easily appear here to be fetishistic ceremony at its most extravagant, it is crucial to acknowledge the sense in which the underlying intention of Jewish worship transcends mere fetishism. As we have seen, for the majority of Jewish traditions crucial questions remain about the true meaning of the holy scripture. Some measure of the unnamable character of the Jewish God trickles down into every increment of the law. Even if the bottom line of adherence to the covenant is never in question, all of the particulars admit of contestation. The rabbinic commentaries contained in the Talmud, Mishnah, and Gemara are the great testimonies to this free space of interpretive debate. To the extent that fetishism, as Freud defined it, functions to disavow uncertainty by appeal to the stabilizing influence of the fetish object, the Jewish relation to the word of scripture cuts against the fetishizing tendency by scrupulously maintaining an uncertainty about what the scriptural text actually means. If, as Freud taught, the fetish serves as a substitute to compensate and fill in for a lack, the Jewish posture toward the sacred text appears constantly to reopen and explore that very lack.

Particularly with this lack-driven necessity of ceaseless interpretation in view, it might reasonably be asked why, if Lacan were to champion any religion, he didn't choose Judaism.[4] In an important sense, the life pulse of Jewish faith is to be found precisely in the uncertain or wholly unknown dimension of the holy scripture, of God as unnamable, and of the Name as the ultimate mystery. These aspects of Jewish worship powerfully anticipate Lacan's own emphasis on the margin of indeterminacy that attends every iteration of the signifier. Viewed in this way, isn't Judaism the consummate exemplar of Lacan's theory of the unconscious, and particularly of *das Ding* and its enduring trace in the functioning of language? Seen from this angle, it is Lacan, the French Catholic *goy*, who most profoundly relinks psychoanalysis with the Jewish origins of Freud's new science. Lacan's linguistically inflected theory of the unconscious traces the roots of Freud's art of "interminable" interpretation into the deep soil of Judaic culture.

With all of this in mind, one might well wonder what room there is in Lacan's theoretical frame for Christianity. In Lacanian terms, what could Christianity possibly add? Which only redoubles the force of the question before us: What possible sense can we give to Lacan's remark about Christianity as the one true religion?

The Strangest God

The crucified Christ is unquestionably the most unlikely god ever conceived. To all appearances, Christianity offers the failed prophet, the beggar God, the loser God. It offers above all the dying God, who, after being spat upon, beaten bloody, and derisively paraded in the streets, is executed in one of the most excruciating and ignominious ways imaginable. His followers were understandably traumatized and scandalized by his crucifixion. Their initial reaction, coming in the wake of their teacher's promises of the imminent coming of the kingdom, was one of shattering disillusionment. In fact, it is clear that the divinity of Jesus was declared definitively only in retrospect, well after his death. And then the final, astonishing paradox: it was in no small measure the horrifically degrading manner of his death, the event that posed an extreme, virtually nonsensical inversion of the long-established logic of divine power as splendid and glorious, that most recommended him for a divine role.

The contrast of Christianity with both paganism and Judaism is striking in a number of ways. The first concerns appearances. The pagan gods evidenced themselves in the appearances of things, typically appearances that were in appropriate proportion to the enormity of the forces the gods personified. Yet those divine forces themselves ultimately emanated from an inaccessible beyond. In this limited respect, the Jewish God is akin to the pagan gods in that he remains in principle invisible, unimageable. In Jesus, by contrast, we have a God who unreservedly appears, and who appears *precisely in his very humble and degraded condition.* Christ is the only god who, as he does when he holds open his wounds to allay Thomas's doubts about his identity, willingly shows everything in plain sight. He has absolutely nothing to hide.[5] In this way, the Christian god might even be said to reverse the core principle of the Judaic prohibition of idolatry.[6] Precisely because the Christian God very purposefully assumes the form of a poor wanderer, Jesus is the God who *must* appear. Christ is thus the God of revelation par excellence, though only by way of an infinite paradox. What is revealed is the very opposite of everything anyone ever thought about the nature of the divine. In Christ, the strength and majesty of God is inseparable from his shockingly obvious weakness.

The apostle Paul immediately set about rescuing Jesus from such apparent contradictions. Paul's solution was to conceive of crucifixion as a redemptive sacrifice.[7] The apparent ignominy and failure of Christ's death was thereby turned into a triumph. Jesus's willing death becomes the means by which the sins of humanity are to be forgiven. The horror of his execution becomes the surest index of its redemptive power. But this retelling of the story, too, leaves us with a shocking contrast with both the pagan and Jewish traditions, which understood the meaning of sacrifice totally differently. The cultures of paganism and Judaism both assumed that it falls to mortal humans to offer fitting sacrifices to the god. In Christianity, the direction of sacrifice is reversed. It is God who sacrifices for man. If Abraham's willingness to sacrifice his son Isaac prefigures the sacrifice of Jesus, the parallel only works if we allow for a complete inversion of roles. In Christianity, it is God, not man, who offers his son in sacrifice. Moreover, in the Christian vision, unlike the drama between Abraham and Isaac, God not only proves himself *willing* to give up his only son in order to save humanity but *actually does so*.

Yet all of these strikingly distinctive features of Christian divinity pale in comparison with the definitive trait that sets Jesus apart from all other claimants. His message to his followers was radically, almost unimaginably, simple. It can be summarized in a single word: *love*. The teaching of Jesus of Nazareth reduces the meaning of the Jewish law to a single commandment: *Love thy neighbor as thyself.*[8]

To Love Thy Neighbor

Though the preaching of Jesus picked up on many themes central to the Jewish tradition, those who heard his teachings, both enraptured followers and wary traditionalists, were acutely aware of his departure from the established understanding of the Jewish covenant and the submission to the law that it demanded. In several key places in the Gospels, Jesus is asked to clarify his position. A crucial instance occurs in Matthew 22. Its essentials are echoed in both Mark and Luke.[9] Questioned by a Pharisee, Jesus is deliberately tested for his adherence to orthodoxy. "Teacher," he is asked, "which is the great commandment in the law?" Jesus gives a two-part answer. "You shall love the Lord your God with all your heart, and with all your soul, and with all your mind. This is the great and first commandment," he says. "And a second is like it," he continues. "You shall love your neighbor as yourself. On these two commandments depend all the law and the prophets."[10] The first part of Jesus's response appears to provide a kind of summary statement of the first five Mosaic commandments, relevant to the service of Yahweh as the one and only God to be honored and obeyed in all things. And if the first part of his answer covers the first tablet, the second part seems to sum up the laws of the second tablet, relevant to the neighbor.

But the question that hangs in the air after Jesus's answer to the

Pharisee is whether the two commandments—the first and the second, which "is like it"—are really two commandments or just one. That they are ultimately just one is suggested by another, almost immediately preceding passage from Matthew. A follower asks, "Teacher, what good deed must I do, to have eternal life?" Jesus's response leaves out specific reference to what we owe to God and concentrates instead on our duty toward our fellow human beings: "'Why do you ask me about what is good? One there is who is good. If you would enter life, keep the commandments.' He said to him, 'Which?' And Jesus said, 'You shall not kill, You shall not commit adultery, You shall not steal, You shall not bear false witness, Honor your father and mother, and, You shall love your neighbor as yourself.'"[11] Explicit mention of one's duties toward God is left out, as if those duties are already fulfilled by the love of the neighbor.

Another of Jesus's most famous quotations may also be taken to imply that his essential teaching brings divinity wholly down to earth, placing it not between the terrestrial valley here below and a heavenly beyond but rather wholly between loving persons. "For where two or three are gathered in my name," he says, "there am I in the midst of them."[12] The implicit reference here would seem to be to the Jewish *minyan*, the requirement for certain prayers and rites to be performed only among a quorum of ten observant Jews. Yet Jesus appears to skip the requirement of a minimum-size group, asserting instead that God may be fully present among any two or more right-hearted people. What is at stake is related to the essential reality that is Christ: the intersection of the divine and the human, the Word made flesh. The radical message of Jesus appears to forswear appeals to a transcendent God in favor of a wholly immanent one. As Jesus says, "The Kingdom of God is within you."[13] The same theme is audible in Jesus's words from Matthew about feeding the hungry, clothing the naked, and visiting the imprisoned: "Truly, I say unto you, as you did it to one of the least of these my brethren, you did it to me."[14]

The upshot of this discussion for my primary argument may by now be obvious. From a Lacanian point of view, the groundbreaking event enacted by the teaching of Jesus is to locate the divine directly and without qualification in the embrace of the neighbor-Thing—the person who is standing right in front of you. This radical move enjoins the followers of Jesus to drop the defensive posture toward what is unknown and anxiety producing in the Other in favor of a radical opening, an unhesitating and fully vulnerable acceptance of the Other. If Judaism succeeded in "making space for the Other," the revolutionary breakthrough of the young rabbi from Nazareth was to insist that the realization of divinity occurs when we positively engage the immediately present Other-Person and lovingly accommodate ourselves to them. The Christian subject must suspend all defensive barriers toward the Other, opening oneself even toward what appears to be threatening, alien, and anxiety producing. This posture of fearlessly reaching out to the strange is what grounds the Christian definition of love. Here we arrive at the explanation of the bon mot of Lacan in which he plays on the homophony of *étrange* and *être-ange*. For Lacan, the angelic arises in our welcoming reception of the strange Other-Person.

In the course of *Civilization and Its Discontents*, Freud famously rejects the Christian admonition to love the neighbor, which he judges to be a kind a thoughtless and even profligate squandering of one's affection. Freud thus writes:

> My love is something valuable to me which I ought not to throw away without reflection. It imposes duties on me for whose fulfillment I must be ready to make sacrifices. If I love someone, he must deserve it in some way. (I leave out of account the use he may be to me, and also his possible significance for me as a sexual object, for neither of these two kinds of relationship comes into question where the precept to love my neighbor is concerned.). He deserves it if he is so like me in important ways that I can love myself in him; and he deserves it if he is so much more perfect than myself that I can love my ideal of my own self in him.[15]

For Lacan, the problem with Freud's position is that it reduces love to an exchange in the imaginary, a relation that merely reflects my image of myself or of my ideal ego. Ironically, what is missed by Freud's approach is nothing less than Freud's own discovery of the unconscious. As Lacan says, "Freud makes comments about this that are quite right. . . . He reveals how one must love a friend's son because, if the friend were to lose his son, his suffering would be intolerable. . . . But what escapes him is perhaps the fact that precisely because we take that path we miss the opening on to *jouissance*."[16] For Lacan, the embrace of what is like myself merely flatters my narcissism. "It is a fact of experience," he says, "that what I want is the good of others in the image of my own. That doesn't cost too much."[17] By contrast, what is demanded by Jesus is a gesture that exposes me to something beyond my own reflection in the mirror, something that speaks to the threatening prospect, beyond mere pleasure, of *jouissance*.[18]

From a Lacanian point of view, the key to understanding the true meaning of Jesus's message about loving the neighbor thus resides in how we interpret the end of the phrase. When we are enjoined to love the neighbor as *thyself*, what is at stake is *the truth* of thyself. The appeal to "thyself" should be taken to indicate that a genuine opening toward the Other is inevitably tied to an opening to what is other, alien, and threatening *in oneself*. Psychoanalytically, that means an opening to the unconscious. What is strange in the neighbor calls up what I myself have repressed, what threatens the stability of my own ego. What is unknown in the neighbor therefore presents itself as tinged with evil, the most fearsome prospect of which is its correspondence with the "evil" that lies unacknowledged in myself. Thus Lacan concludes that "every time that Freud stops short in horror at the consequences of the commandment to love one's neighbor, we see evoked the presence of that fundamental evil which dwells within this neighbor. But if that is the case, then it also dwells within me. And what is more of a neighbor to me than this heart within which is that of my *jouissance* and which I don't dare go near?"[19]

. . . and Love Thine Enemy

My critic is unhappy. "It seems to me that you're peddling your own version of Jefferson's Bible, cutting out the miracles, and even the Pauline narrative of cosmic redemption, in favor of a radical focus on Jesus's gospel of love. But your claim about a distinctively Christian admonition to love one's neighbor doesn't hold up. It's fully Jewish. The very words are found in Torah: 'You shall love your neighbor as yourself.'"

Jesus's saying is indeed prefigured in the Torah. The critic quotes Leviticus 19:17. But as the context in Leviticus makes clear, this original appeal to neighbor love, like the commandments of the second tablet dealing with the neighbor, is based on a series of negative injunctions to respect the property and physical person of the neighbor. The immediately earlier lines of the text from Leviticus establish the baseline approach by directing the farmer harvesting his crop not to encroach on the neighbor's field. To provide an extra margin of safety, the passage even adds that "you shall not reap your field to its very border."[20] The Christian commandment, by contrast, is more substantively positive, laying down the challenge of an act of love that does not stop at refusing encroachment but calls for actively engaging the neighbor. What is called for is not merely refraining from harm (renouncing murder, theft, adultery, lies, and covetousness) but actively embracing the Other, extending oneself toward the Other in love.

If Jesus's commandment to love calls for more open and positive action toward the Other, it also calls for action that transcends all practical considerations. The love involved cannot be reducible to any mere service of utility. To fully acknowledge both these dimensions requires that we read Jesus's demand for love of the neighbor in conjunction with its almost impossibly challenging complement: love of the enemy. The true radicality of Jesus's teaching is thus to be located in Matthew 5:43–47: "You have heard that it was said, 'You shall love your neighbor and hate your enemy.' But I say to you, Love your enemies and pray for those who persecute you. . . . For if you love those who love you, what reward have you? Do not even the tax collectors do the same? And if you salute only your brethren, what more are you doing than others?"

Jesus's injunction to love the enemy has little antecedent in Jewish law. One passage of the Hebrew Bible that comes close is again from Leviticus: "The stranger who sojourns with you in your land, you shall not do him wrong. The stranger who sojourns with you shall be to you as the native among you, and you shall love him as yourself; for you were strangers in the land of Egypt."[21] But it is precisely here that a Lacanian perspective becomes most decisive. If we allow that the *jouissance* of the Other is what is truly at stake, then the love of the neighbor overlaps with the challenge of loving the enemy. By the measure of the unknown *jouissance* of the Other—by the measure of *das Ding*—*the neighbor is an enemy*. As Lacan puts it, "Perhaps the meaning of the love of one's neighbor that could give me the true direction is to be found here. . . . [M]y neighbor's *jouissance*, his harmful, malignant *jouissance*, is that which poses a problem for my love."[22] What is meant here is that even when I am dealing with people I know and trust, it is likely that I will at some point have to contend with something deeply strange in them, something beyond my comfort zone, even something threatening.

The challenge of loving the neighbor consists in accepting the Other's undomesticated *jouissance*, which inevitably means accepting some portion of one's own. This linkage between the *jouissance* of the Other and that of the subject—a linkage that forms the very spine of Lacan's cardinal dictum about human desire as the desire of the Other—enlarges upon the absolute heart of the Christian outlook: the emphasis on forgiveness. That is to say, we begin to see not only how forgiveness must be involved in extending love to the enemy—accepting what is weak, failed, or evil in the enemy—but also how such forgiveness must include an acknowledgment of one's own weakness, failure, and evil. Indeed, without such an acknowledgment of one's own kinship with the enemy, the gesture of love risks becoming at best an act of empty condescension, at worst a disguised and hypocritical form of self-congratulation.

It is the exhortation to love the enemy that most separates Christianity from Judaism. The embrace of the enemy is what breaks with the tribalism of Jewish community. Thus Paul's shattering declaration:

"There is neither Jew nor Greek, there is neither slave nor free, there is neither male or female, for ye are all one in Christ Jesus."[23] It is also what makes so poignant the story of the good Samaritan, the foreigner who stops to bind the wounds of the beaten man by the side of the road when others of the victim's own people had uncaringly passed by. Where the ostensible neighbors had looked away, the foreigner stopped and gave succor. Then again, it is what makes sense of the shockingly unconventional behavior of Jesus, who repeatedly seeks the company of outcasts, scapegoats, and pariahs. Jesus goes out of his way to extend himself not only toward the poor and forgotten but also toward the positively rejected and condemned: the whore, the leper, the criminal, the prisoner. It is with respect to this most challenging implication of Jesus's teaching that his own near-scandalous love for Mary Magdalene, the former prostitute, becomes such an important piece of the essential message of Christianity.[24]

From Circumcision to Crucifixion

Religious practices, said Nietzsche, require "three dangerous dietary demands: solitude, fasting, and sexual abstinence."[25] He could easily have added ritual mutilations of the body. It fact, corporeal mutilation might take its place on the list of familiar definitions of the human being— the animal that ceremonially maims its own body and that regards such mutilation as a gateway to the experience of the sacred. Lacan supplies a reason for what otherwise remains an enigma. The point of departure is the imaginary formation of the ego. Against the backdrop of imaginary identity, centered on the gestalt of the body's wholeness, bodily mutilation helps mark the shift from an imaginary to a symbolic register and, in so doing, enables an opening toward the real of *das Ding*. As Lacan says of it, "*Mutilation* serves here to orientate desire, enabling it to assume precisely this function of index, of something which is realized and which can only articulate itself, express itself, in a *symbolic beyond*, a beyond which is the one we today call being, a realization of being in the subject."[26]

In this light, we might pause and ask how the two most conspicuous bodily mutilations in Judaism and Christianity—circumcision and crucifixion—symbolize something different. We have already considered the meaning of Jewish circumcision. The choice of the organ is not accidental. Accepting a symbolic mutilation of the male organ of procreation signals an acknowledgment that true paternity belongs not to a human but to a divine father. Cutting the *penis* establishes the signifier of the *phallus*, which for Lacan means pointing toward a signified that cannot be fully specified.[27] In this way, the ritual of circumcision helps to symbolically establish the regime of signification itself, holding it open to meaning-as-yet-to-be-determined. Accepting circumcision becomes in itself a testimony to the ineffable character of God.

What, then, is the significance of the specifically Christian mutilation of crucifixion? The first key to grasping its function is to recognize its phantasmatic status. Whereas circumcision must actually be performed, crucifixion is purely symbolic, that is, merely to be *contemplated*. The follower of Jesus is enjoined to identify with the manner of his grisly death. What he suffered, his disciples, too, must suffer, at least figuratively. As Matthew recalls, "Jesus told his disciples, 'If any man would come after me, let him deny himself and take up his cross and follow me.'"[28] All must find and accept their own crucifixion.

But what does such willing acceptance of suffering mean? For the mainstream Christian tradition, its significance aligns with the Pauline interpretation of Jesus's death as a redemptive sacrifice. Faithful followers are invited to follow the Messiah in offering their own lives in the cause of universal atonement. True disciples must throw themselves on the great funeral pyre whose purifying flames will finally redeem humanity and win immortal life.

This interpretation is attested by many monastic traditions, for which the voluntary acceptance of pain and deprivation becomes in itself an index of saintliness. The history of Christianity has thus spawned myriad cults of pure-minded suffering in the service of salvation. Viewed psychoanalytically, however, the phantasmatic structure of this ascetic trend risks merely blending narcissism with masochism. At one point, Lacan analyzes the dynamic involved by suggesting that Christian piety is a mode of identifying oneself with the scrap of severed foreskin. That scrap represents the inexorable remainder, the leftover of the signifying process: the *objet a*. The Christian masochistically identifies in toto with this "waste object," sacrificing itself to the greater glory of God.

> What is the remainder? It is what survives the ordeal of the division of the field of the Other through the presence of the subject. . . . [T]he Christian solution was . . . none other than the mirage that is attached to the masochistic outcome, inasmuch as the Christian has learnt, through the dialectic of Redemption, to identify ideally with he who made himself identical with this same object, the waste object left behind out of divine retribution. . . . [T]he crux of masochism, which is an attempt to provoke the Other's anxiety, here become God's anxiety, has become second nature in the Christian.[29]

"But wait," protests the critic, "isn't the *objet a* Lacan's definition of the object-cause of desire? In identifying with that object, don't Christians effectively offer themselves as a special object of desire?"

That is exactly the point. Insofar as saintly Christian martyrs become caught up in this structure, they embody the very blend of narcissism and masochism we just referred to. In this self-flagellating identification with the *objet a*, Christian ascetics offer themselves as the privileged object of desire. Yet for that very reason the underlying structure becomes essentially perverse. As Slavoj Žižek compellingly argues, the basic strategy is comparable to that of the fireman who deliberately sets a house on fire so that he may play the hero who arrives just in time to put it out.[30]

The irony is that the amalgam of narcissism and masochism that often passes for saintliness may function to sidestep Jesus's exhortation toward love of the Other. Can we not glimpse such a refusal of real engagement with the Other in the famous story told about Saint Catherine of Siena? Disgusted by the pus that flowed from the festering wound of a soldier she was nursing, Catherine gathered a cup of the pus and drank it. It is almost impossible not to suspect that this gesture of extravagant self-punishment derived more from Catherine's fervent desire to stage a spectacular demonstration of her own piety than from any real concern for the patient she tended.

Embracing the Cross

So is there another, somehow more authentic function performed by the fantasy of crucifixion that better symbolizes the essential spiritual meaning of the Jesus gospel? Lacan does not expressly provide an answer to this question, but we can venture a hypothesis on the premises that we have been unfolding. The crucial thing is to recognize in the image of crucifixion an emblem of the subject's embracing precisely what is foreign and threatening in the Other, *not just as occasion for forbearance or forgiveness of that Other but as an opening to what is foreign and threatening in the subject her- or himself.* In this embrace, the subject "dies" away from its accustomed understanding of itself as it is opened toward what is other in itself. Such "dying away" can be understood as relinquishing the claims of the ego in favor of an opening toward the unconscious. In this way we can reread the famous passage from Matthew in which Jesus calls his followers to achieve new life by dying. "If any man would come after me, let him deny himself and take up his cross and follow me. For whoever would save his life will lose it, and whoever loses his life for my sake will find it."[31]

The paradox expressed in the saying runs parallel with Lacan's rereading of Freud's epigram *Wo Es war, soll Ich werden.* Where the defensive *ego* was, there the *subject* (reliant on what is alien in the Other as the clue to what is unknown and alien in oneself) shall come to be. If the defended ego succeeds in fully preserving itself, the desiring subject never comes to life.

Hegel, whose thought is everywhere profoundly informed by a Christian sensibility, fully endorses the view that the distinctive core of Christianity is the commandment to love one's neighbor, while also insisting that true love must engage precisely what is most other in the Other. The all-important consequence of such loving is the way the opening to the Other is inevitably challenging for the established identity of the self. To truly love is to be transformed, as the engagement with the Other allows for the subject's encounter with what is other and unknown in itself. In a superb book on Hegel, Todd McGowan provides a succinct account of this crucial dimension of Hegel's thought. In Hegel's conception, McGowan observes,

> Christianity becomes the most revolutionary religion ever conceived. It embraces love as the actualization of the law, an actualization that makes possible a new way of communal living. Rather than relying purely on the restrictiveness of the law to bind us together, we recognize the bond that occurs through love. Love reveals that our relation to the other is never an external relation but always an internal one that shapes our own identity. Love announces the subject as divided in itself and thereby invaded by the other. The Christian commandment of universal love becomes in Hegel's eyes the enactment of contradiction. I am both myself and other. It enables subjects to engage with the disturbance of the other as constitutive of their own identity.[32]

McGowan is right to see that the true core of Hegel's philosophy resides in the embrace of contradiction, the willingness to submit oneself, in Hegel's words, to "the tremendous power of the negative."[33] McGowan compellingly shows that Hegel's appeal to rationality, ridiculed by generations of critics as a ham-fisted attempt to cram the complexity of life into the straitjacket of the universal concept, is in fact intended to retain the tension of contradiction and Otherness that animates every moment of the life of the spirit. Hegel's ultimate category—variously called the Absolute, the Idea, the Concept—not only includes Otherness but is radically founded upon it. McGowan draws the correct implication for Hegel's concept of love, which in Hegel's view is the best single name for the subject's relation to the Absolute.

> Love for Hegel has nothing to do with narcissistic self-affirmation
> through the other. It is rather a profound disturbance for the subject's
> identity. Hegel's definition of love has a radicality that he would sustain
> in his love-inspired definition of the concept. He writes, "Love can
> only occur against the same, against the mirror, against the echo of
> our essence." When the subject loves, it doesn't just seize the other but
> encounters the other as a disturbance of the self. In this way, love defies
> the mirror relation to which critics would want to confine it.[34]

Interpreted in the spirit of Hegel's conception of love, crucifixion
becomes the most extreme image of the suffering the subject must accept
in truly loving the Other. What is revealed by the dance of identity and
difference that love enacts is the otherness of the subject to itself. In this
way, the meaning of crucifixion ceases to be a mere fantasy. It becomes
something one actually goes through. With this necessity of subjective
destitution and rebirth in mind we can now read the famous lines from
the preface to Hegel's *Phenomenology*, granting them a fuller portion of
their true meaning: "The life of the Spirit is not the life that shrinks from
death and keeps itself untouched by devastation, but rather the life that
endures it and maintains itself in it. It wins its truth only when, in utter
dismemberment, it finds itself."[35]

This Hegelian perspective, as Hegel himself recognized, refuses the
Pauline appeal to the afterlife as the justification of Christ's death. The
stakes of love for Hegel reside entirely in this life, not some other one.[36]
In Paul's telling of the Christ story, rebirth is understood as occurring
after the crucifixion. Christ's crucifixion is the event by means of which
all humanity is thenceforth spared from death. Yet this understanding of
crucifixion risks being drawn back into the orbit of pagan sacrifice. Christ
becomes the sacrificial victim, the Lamb of God, offered for slaughter
to achieve the salvation of human beings. The words of Jesus himself
completely belie this view. Jesus presents himself as the example to be
followed. His acceptance of grisly death points toward the necessity of
our own voluntary self-abnegation, the acceptance of our own crucifixion, which opens our own salvation. The true Christian is called to the
self-sacrifice demanded by love. As the symbolic stand-in for being truly
opened to the Other and transformed by it, crucifixion marks the event
of rebirth in the here and now.

The extremity of crucifixion is appropriate for the Christian challenge of loving the enemy. A genuinely Christian stance means resisting
the temptation merely to react defensively to what seems foreign and
menacing in the enemy. Instead, we are called to give Others the benefit

of the doubt concerning their motives in an attempt to understand our enemies as they understand themselves. Such a stance is the true meaning of Jesus's admonition to "judge not, lest ye be judged."[37] The indispensable thing is to distinguish the two ways in which we use the word "judgment." The most common meaning is that of making an either/or evaluation: useful or useless, attractive or unattractive, guilty or innocent, good or evil. It was judgment in this sense that Jesus called upon his followers to resist. His true teaching asks us to enact a different kind of discrimination, judging persons and things in accordance with internal considerations.

Hegel focuses on this second meaning when he points to the inner wisdom reflected in the German word for judgment, *Urteilung*, built around the root word *Teil*, or "part." The trap to be avoided is thinking that judgment is merely a matter of dividing things up into neat categories—these things go in this box and those in the other box. True judgment refers instead to discerning the way each thing is always already internally divided. Judgment is the act of assessing the tensions internal to the thing itself. In order to follow the Christly admonition and resist the first, categorizing usage of judgment, we need to employ the second, more dialectical meaning.

On this reading, the genuinely Christian injunction might be rephrased as "never allow things to become black and white." Christianity calls upon us to see how every subject is internally partitioned and complicated. Nothing is simple. In this sense, the categorical judgment that simply lumps something or someone into the bin of a univocal category is always false. The truth, as Hegel said, always lies in the whole (*Das Wahre ist das Ganze*: the truth is the whole) but only because the whole is always divided in some way, inflected by the negative. The inner secret of the Hegelian notion of love always involves a judgment of internal complexity. The point is not a matter of merely finding the underlying goodwill in my fellow human beings. On the contrary, the point is that the Other, like myself, embodies contradiction. When the experience of love connects the subject to the dimension of the Thing, the result is a violent shudder of the subject's being. "In the phenomenon of love," says Lacan, "at every step of the way one encounters the wrenching and discordance associated with it. No one needs, for all that, to dialogue or dialectize about love to be involved in this gap or discord—it suffices to be in the thick of it, to be in love."[38]

To put the point in Freudian terms, the act of love must in some way engage a *complex*, in oneself and in the Other. We here encounter a profound point of intersection between psychoanalysis and Christianity. The first rule of being an analyst precisely follows Jesus's teaching: do not judge the analysand, at least in the first meaning of the term, which seeks to put things into discrete categories. Allow no simple division into black and white, good and evil, healthy and unhealthy. The whole aim and effectiveness of analysis is conscientiously to apply the second meaning of judgment. Open the space for the internal complexity of the analysand, allow for the self-contradiction of the symptom. Facilitate analysands' own entry into that space, enabling their ownership of contradiction, and you will probably have done everything that is in your power to do for them.

The True Religion Is Atheism

"There is *one* true religion and that is the Christian religion." It is now possible to make sense of Lacan's provocative remark. In different ways, both Greek paganism and Judaism were centrally engaged with the unknown Thing, but both avoided too direct a confrontation with it. Paganism projected the vortex of the unknown outward into the field of great and unpredictable forces that animate the external world, then invested itself in adopting a heroic posture of redoubtable self-possession in the face of that unknown. By contrast, Judaism located the Thing in the fearful intervention of a single deity who proposed a law-governed covenant with the Jewish people but remained himself shrouded in mystery. The elaborate regime of the halachic law demanded by the covenant then served to stabilize the social link, pacifying relations between subjects by reassuringly referring them to a third position, the divine big Other.

The teaching of Jesus focuses religious life directly and unflinchingly upon the Other-Thing itself. Where other religions spared a direct encounter with the neighbor-Thing by triangulating the relation to it by reference to one or another deity, the gospel of Jesus directly identifies divinity with accepting the threatening unknown in the fellow human being and, by extension, in oneself. The core intention of Jesus's teaching can thus be summed up in two unprecedented formulas: (1) embrace with love precisely what makes you anxious in the Other, and (2) revere that very embrace as the entry of the divine into the world.

We have seen how Hegel defines Christian love in exactly this way. For Hegel, the salutary effect of love consists in the way the discovery of contradiction in the Other should lead to the revelation of the contradiction in oneself, the genuine encounter with which ushers in a personal transformation. It is with reference to this conception of love as an embrace of the enemy that we should read Hegel's uncompromising remark that "a human being who has not the truth of the Christian religion has no truth at all; for this is the one and only truth."[39]

The same series of considerations leads us to the most radical and sweeping Hegelian conclusion about Christianity. For Hegel, Christianity is the most profound and revolutionary religion—the truest religion—precisely because Christianity announces the death of the god who is supposed to dwell in an inaccessible, transcendent beyond. What the crucifixion communicates is nothing less than the event of God's fully entering the human, of the infinite becoming coincident with the finite. The Christian god is the deity who, motivated by the power of love, willingly abdicates his transcendent status. God now becomes coterminous with the quintessential movement of Hegelian dialectic. Only by closing the distance between the transcendent and the immanent, the divine and the human, does God become what he truly is. As J. N. Findlay summarizes this central point, "To be conscious of himself in a finite, sensuous, human individual does not represent a descent for God but the consummation of his essence. For God is not merely an abstract being, remote from concrete sensuous instantiation: he is only fully and completely himself in an instance."[40] What distinguishes Christianity for Hegel is its radical embrace of God's self-abdication. In the language of Christian theology, the Christ event marks the self-emptying or kenosis of God. To take this kenotic movement fully seriously is to be faced with the paradoxical result that Christianity is the religion that gives birth to atheism from out of its own conception of God. While Lacan seldom refers his own conception of Christianity to that of Hegel, usually preferring to keep a guarded distance from Hegel's dialectic, he clearly offers a parallel view.[41] One of the unique things about Christianity, Lacan writes, is that "there is a certain atheistic message in Christianity itself, and I am not first to have mentioned it. Hegel said that the destruction of the gods would be brought about by Christianity."[42] And elsewhere: "Christ is a god," Lacan says, "but in the end, he's not just any god. . . . This is the true dimension of atheism. The atheist would be he who has succeeded in doing away with the fantasy of the Almighty."[43]

The atheistic turn of Christianity is rooted in its teaching of love. In defining devotion to God in terms of love for the neighbor, insisting that the truly divine act is consummated in the love one human subject risks for another, Christianity collapses the defensive triangulation that was effected by both pagan and Jewish religiosity. The middleman—God himself—gets cut out. In Christianity, one loves God by loving one's fellow human being.

"But surely what you jokingly call 'cutting out the middleman' overstates the case," complains the critic. "Shouldn't Christianity retain the reference to God as the source and inspiration for loving the Other? Doesn't the reference to God continue to be necessary in order give love its truly transcendent dimension?"

Of course, there's nothing about Christianity that unavoidably *requires* atheism. Atheism can become as rigidly dogmatic as the theism it opposes. But to demand that we retain some vestige of the traditional transcendent God as a divine hand-holder as we assume responsibility for loving the neighbor as ourselves is to miss the radical import of the Christian event. The crucial thing is to see how the Christian love of the neighbor breaks the mold of the Judaic law. The distinctiveness of the Christian message resides first of all in the way it transcends the merely negative injunctions of the Decalogue, passing beyond the commandments' repeated formula of "thou shalt *not*." The Christian teaching calls upon us to do something positive. In fact, Jesus's exhortation to love one another is not really a *commandment* at all. Jesus doesn't bring a new law but rather the "good news" of the gospel. The reason is that love is not something demanded by God. Love *is* God.[44] Love is the very heartbeat of the divine, its living essence. In loving the Other as oneself, human beings bring God into the world.

For both the pagan and the Jew, divine power is bestowed on human beings from above and beyond the human realm. The most humans can do is to prepare appropriate sacrifices, conduct themselves in a manner pleasing to the god, and hope for the best. Christianity ushers in an entirely new relation between the mortal and the divine. For the first time, the entry of God into the world occurs not just in response to the actions of human beings but substantively in and through those actions. Quite literally, human action is the power that opens the door for God's entry into the world. The closest pre-Christian religion came to something like this view might be found in the Jewish mystical tradition of Kabbalah, which risked the assertion that God deliberately leaves his creation unfinished in order that humanity may actively participate in its completion.[45]

The Abyss of Freedom

Yet the Christian outlook takes a further, even more radical step. The love message of Jesus, whispered into the ear of humankind before he was killed, is inseparable from the idea of human freedom. For love to remain true to its own essential nature, it must be freely given. Not only is it the case that Jesus's teaching doesn't make neighbor love into a commandment; his teaching ineluctably includes the idea that love in principle *cannot be commanded.* Love is its own recommendation, its own quiet strength, its own raison d'être, or it is nothing at all. The voluntary character of love is not incidental to its nature but belongs to it absolutely. To command love, to order it done, generates a contradiction in terms. It is in this radical sense that we should interpret Jesus's claim not to add to the law but to "fulfill" it.[46]

"But doesn't this explanation still leave room for my point?" asks the critic, impatient to know if there isn't still some way to retain a role for the worship of a transcendent God, if only as the heavenly wellspring of love. "Doesn't Jesus himself talk this way? Even Kant, who declares that morality does not need religion, allows for reference to the representation of God as a source of moral encouragement."

It's true that Kant leaves room in his *Religion within the Limits of Reason Alone* for appeals to God as a source of moral inspiration. But he also signals the danger of such appeals. In conceiving of ourselves as "serving" God, we risk losing the very self-determination that gives ethical conduct its sublime moral stature. Yet we also have to acknowledge that Lacan's ethics of psychoanalysis and the ethics of Kant are not the same thing. While Lacan is certainly appreciative of the Kant's breakthrough, at least insofar as he recognizes that submission to the law is an indispensable stage for the becoming of the subject, he also moves decisively beyond Kant's conception. For Lacan, the key to that beyond, a beyond ultimately linked to Freud's beyond of the pleasure principle, can be situated in relation to the Christian ethic of love for the Thing. Love, he says, is ultimately "a way of rediscovering the relationship to *das Ding* somewhere beyond the law."[47]

It now remains to make explicit that love and freedom are inextricably bound up with unknowing. In his twentieth seminar, Lacan compares his own *Écrits* to "mystical jaculations." There he recalls Bernini's sculpture *The Ecstasy of Saint Teresa,* about which Lacan says that it's obvious that "she's coming. There's no doubt about it. What is she getting off on? It is clear that the essential testimony of the mystics consists in saying that they experience it, but know nothing about it."[48] In the same sentence, Lacan also refers us to a more obscure figure, the fourteenth-century Beguine, Hadewijch of Brabant. Lacan may well have been familiar with the following astonishing passage from one of Hadewijch's letters in which love, freedom, and unknowing are provocatively entwined: "If it maintains its worthy state," Hadewijch writes, "the soul is a bottomless abyss in which God suffices to himself. . . . Soul is a way for the passage of God from his depths into his liberty; and God is a way for the passage of the soul into its liberty, that is, into his inmost depths, which cannot be touched except by the soul's abyss."[49] The most striking thing about this extraordinary fragment is the way it attributes to God himself an unknown depth in which lovers of God find their own unknown dimension.

As Slavoj Žižek rightly claims, it is this unknowability of God to himself that distinguishes Christianity from Judaism. "Judaism remains at the level of the enigma of God," he says, "while Christianity moves to the enigma in God himself."[50] The wrenching, most profoundly revealing moment is when the crucified Christ calls out, "My God, my God, why hast thou forsaken me?" As Žižek comments, "In that terrific tale of the Passion there is a distinct emotional suggestion that the author of all things (in some unthinkable way) went not only through agony, but through doubt."[51] G. K. Chesterton was right to say that in that moment of supreme affliction, God himself appears for a moment to be an atheist.

In summing up his Lacanian position, Žižek again refers to Chesterton's characterization of Christianity as the religion that terrifies people with the consequences of four words: "He was made Man." In the face of these four words, says Žižek,

> what really frightens them is that they will lose the transcendent God guaranteeing the meaning of the universe, God as the hidden Master pulling the strings—instead of this, we get a God who abandons this transcendent position and throws himself into his own creation, fully engaging himself in it up to dying, so that we, humans, are left with no higher Power watching over us, just with the terrible burden of freedom and responsibility for the fate of divine creation, and thus of God himself. Are we not still too frightened today to assume all these consequences of the four words? Do those who call themselves "Christians" not prefer to stay with the comfortable image of God sitting up there, benevolently watching over our lives, sending us his son as a token of his love, or even more comfortably, just with some depersonalized Higher-Force?[52]

Precisely the same dynamic between knowing and unknowing informs Lacan's conception of the psychoanalytic transference, which, as Freud insisted, is also an experience of love. For Lacan, the default position of the transference construes the analyst as a "subject supposed to know." But this supposition is erected in response to a void of unknowing. Seated invisibly behind the couch and saying little or nothing while the analysand prattles on about his or her dreams, memories, feelings, and so on, the figure of the analyst remains an inaccessible enigma. This anxious unknowing is transformed by the analysand into its opposite. The analyst is turned into a special locus of purely supposed knowing. The analysand becomes convinced that the analyst possesses the inner secret that the analysand her- or himself cannot articulate. Such supposed knowledge arises from a defensive reaction. It represents an attempt to fill in what is unknown in the Other. A primary index of the progress of analysis therefore lies in the extent to which this project of compensatory supposition is eventually given up and the void of unknowing about the analyst is allowed to yawn open. Such a retrieval of the unknown dimension in the analyst opens the space in which analysands can begin to discover a greater portion of their own unconscious desire.

Dogma: The Real Immaculate Conception

The critic is now just plain grumpy. "I've lost the thread here. Why make such a big deal of the way in which love, which you say is born in the abyssal unknowing of freedom, tends toward a phantasmatic supposition of knowledge?"

The answer is not going to make the critic happy. We've put forward a radical version of the Christ message, not only focused on love of the neighbor but also crucially centered upon unknowing, an experience best emblematized not in love for the neighbor but in love for the enemy. We now need to absorb the way the history of Christianity has turned away from that abyssal confrontation in the direction of a diversionary over-investment in reassuring "knowledge." The truly revolutionary message of Jesus was about love as an unhesitating embrace of the Other-Thing. We now turn to the defensive obverse of that radical breakthrough: the Christian embrace of orthodox doctrine and belief.

From the perspective I am putting forward here, the Christian investment in dogma becomes explicable as a defensive response to the prime directive of Jesus's teaching.[53] That directive presents the follower of the Nazarene with an ideal that is not only practically impossible to fulfill but also profoundly anxiety producing. Resort to dogma becomes the near unavoidable recourse in the face of such a deeply unsettling challenge. We here encounter the underlying reason for Nietzsche's trenchant observation that the "there was only *one* Christian and he died on the cross."[54] It is also on this basis that we can now make sense of Lacan's remark that Christianity, even more than other religions, finds it almost impossible to resist an unending "secretion of meaning."

The Christian "secretion of meaning" refers primarily to the proliferation of canonical beliefs and derivatives thereof. The irony is that such expanding webs of belief, while offering means for Christianity to defend itself against the competing views of rival religions or for one Christian sect to define itself against another, represent at a deeper level a reactive defense against the inner core of Christianity itself. It is with this dynamic in view that we grasp the cold, fish-eyed perception at the heart of Lacan's assessment of Christianity. To the extent that it connects the subject most directly with the agitating mix of anxiety and desire that emanates from the Other-Thing, Christianity might indeed be said to be the one true religion. Yet for that very reason, it becomes almost impossible for Christianity to avoid betraying itself. Organized, theologically articulated Christianity almost inevitably functions as its own Judas.

The core idea at stake here is by no means original, either to Lacan or to this book. The notion that the essential Christian vision, embodied in the life and teachings of the strange man from Nazareth, has been undermined by the institutionalization of the church is hardly new. It was precisely such a critical sensibility that informed Hegel's youthful attack on what he called the "positivity" of Christian religion.[55] For Hegel, too, the Jesus teaching, entirely focused on the soul adventure of love, was ultimately undone less by the bitter kiss of Judas than by the "constructive" work of Peter and Paul. Kierkegaard's *Attack on Christendom*, in which the existential challenge of faith is contrasted with the dogmatically calcified ecclesial hierarchy and its fetishism of orthodoxy, is an especially articulate and provocative argument along similar lines.[56]

The traumatizing impact of Jesus's call for love prompted an intense need for restabilization. And what better way to reassure the subject threatened with the unknown than to expand the realm of the known? Put in Lacanian terms, the Christian demand to embrace the enigma in the little Other led to a new and far-reaching compensatory reinvestment in the symbolic big Other. It remains to elucidate some primary dimensions of that defensive reaction.

1. The first and most obvious point to be made is the way Jesus's disarmingly simple and direct identification of divinity with love of the Other appears betrayed by the intensive effort of Christian theology to relaunch the fully transcendent status of God. Relying on the framework of Greek metaphysics, centered on the chasm between finite, material reality and the ontological purity of the supersensuous, Christian theologians sought to restore the transcendence of the deity, enumerating a long list of God's supernatural and emphatically extrahuman characteristics. In addition to the more familiar traits of omnipotence, omnibenevolence, omniscience, and omnipresence, for example, God is thought to possess aseity (he doesn't need us), immutability (he cannot change), impassability (he cannot experience emotion), incorporeality (he is pure spirit, utterly lacking any material composition), and unity

(despite his triune character, he is absolutely one). The striking thing about these last five attributes, whatever their pleasing conformity to the demands of pure logic concerning an infinite being, is the way they appear almost systematically to deny divinity a whole cluster of characteristics that might most readily be associated with the existential reality of love. In relation to this theological infatuation with the infinite, concrete relations with other human beings not only become something of an afterthought but are also hard to imagine in relation to the characteristics attributed to divine being.

2. Alain Badiou's stirring defense of Saint Paul as a hero of the universal has spawned a veritable cottage industry devoted to positively reevaluating Paul's contribution. Though my purpose here is not to repudiate that approach, my argument in these pages inclines me to reaffirm Nietzsche's scathing critique. For Nietzsche, Paul's interpretation of the Crucifixion as the cosmic price required to redeem humanity from sin represents a near-complete reversal of Jesus's core teaching.[57] In the Pauline version of the gospel, the loving embrace of the Other takes a backseat to the really important desideratum: getting into the cosmic lifeboat of the hereafter. In Paul's hands, the sublime Christian teaching of the free gift of love is reduced to a kind of mortgage payment on an other-worldly reward. Selfless love is converted into piously justified self-service. While there are many genuinely uplifting views expounded in Paul's epistles—and there are indeed many of them—his central message of salvation opens the door to replacing Jesus's appeal to love with an ultimately selfish concern wrapped deceptively in a pious pose.

3. Christian doctrine lavishes enormous attention on questions of what is proper and improper in the love relation. Not surprising, one might say, given that love is the very core of the Jesus's teaching. Yet it is also palpably clear that this intensity of fretful concern with matters of love reflects the adoption of a fundamentally defensive posture against the most direct and disconcerting forms of loving engagement with the Other. We see it first in the way Christianity, given the three basic forms of love identified in the Greek words *eros, philia,* and *agapē,* celebrates the last of the three as the cardinal Christian virtue. Of course, it is possible to see in this choice to privilege charitable love some vestige of the special status of love for the truly Other, since the fellow human being toward whom the hand of charity is extended is generally someone in far different circumstances than oneself. Yet the posture adopted by the charitable caregiver is all too compatible with maintaining a comfortable distance from the Other, recognizable in the condescension that anyone who has ever worked in a soup kitchen knows to be an occupational hazard of service to the less fortunate. The danger is that of outwardly lavishing loving at-

tention on the Other, all the while, however surreptitiously, adopting a morally superior, self-congratulatory, and distinctly distant posture.

4. Finally, it is telling that the entire framework of dogmatic theology, the "knowledge" of Christianity, remains everywhere expressly attached to "mystery." "Mystery" is the last word, the final refuge of the beleaguered debater in every contestation of Christian doctrine. This appeal to mystery functions in theology in almost perfect parallel to Freud's description in *Negation* of the way a negative proposition, in and through the signifier of negation, maintains a link to the very thing being denied. It stands there, Freud says, like a label of origin, like the little sticker that says "Made in Germany." The Christian theological appeal to mystery arguably functions in a similar way, pointing as a sympathetic afterthought toward the abyss of the Thing, which theological elaboration is more often concerned with covering over.

Credo: How Christianity Invented Ideology

The reader may be surprised to hear that I don't expect the preceding list of points to be completely convincing. At a minimum, it will be objected that my bare-bones arguments cry out for more extended examination, illuminated by the history of theology. The reason I'm not overly worried about that deficit is that even a much more elaborate, theologically informed accounting would remain beside the main point. In the larger scheme of things, the specific *content* of Christian belief is less decisive than its pure *form*. Less important than any particular doctrine is the more general Christian appeal to personal faith. What remains untouched by the minutiae of theological argument is the more elemental fact that Christianity introduces a novelty into the history of religion: the centrality for spiritual life of *belief itself.*

The Nicene Creed, the first version of which was hammered out at the Council of Nicaea in 325, probably comes closest to offering a prototypical expression of Christian belief. The standard Roman Catholic version of the creed runs as follows:

> I believe in one Lord Jesus Christ, the Only Begotten Son of God,
> born of the Father before all ages. God from God, Light from Light,
> true God from true God, begotten, not made, consubstantial with the
> Father; through him all things were made. For us men and for our sal-
> vation he came down from heaven, and by the Holy Spirit was incarnate
> of the Virgin Mary, and became man. For our sake he was crucified

under Pontius Pilate, he suffered death and was buried, and rose again on the third day in accordance with the Scriptures. He ascended into heaven and is seated at the right hand of the Father. He will come again in glory to judge the living and the dead and his kingdom will have no end. I believe in the Holy Spirit, the Lord, the giver of life, who proceeds from the Father and the Son, who with the Father and the Son is adored and glorified, who has spoken through the prophets. I believe in one, holy, catholic and apostolic Church. I confess one Baptism for the forgiveness of sins and I look forward to the resurrection of the dead and the life of the world to come. Amen.

The history of Christianity presents a series of convulsive divisions over competing articles of belief. The Nicene Creed itself has undergone a rather torturous series of alterations, adopted in various periods by a range of denominations and sects. But the spectacle of this schismatic history, too, threatens to obscure the key underlying fact: for the Christian soul, the particular content of belief is less important than dedication to the act of believing itself. The common thread for all Christian churches is that faithful subjects commit themselves to a credo. The most important words of the Nicene Creed are thus the first two: "I believe." For the religious tradition instituted in the name of Jesus, the messianic event has become virtually identical with the moment of the subject's assent to belief, the moment when, in the shattering ecstasy of spiritual conversion, the tormented soul cries out, "Yes, I believe!"

"But surely this claim of a distinctive Christian investment in belief is bogus," the critic charges. "The Greeks and the Jews had beliefs of their own."

Of course, in a certain sense, possession of some sort of belief, far from being exclusive to Christianity, could and should be taken as a key part of the definition not only of paganism or Judaism but of the human being in general. Yuval Noah Harari has good grounds for suggesting that what most distinguishes *Homo sapiens* from other primates and early hominids is our investment in shared fictions.[58] Community is built on the foundation of common purpose, informed by shared beliefs. In this sense, pagan and Jewish society, too, had their respective beliefs. We can also safely say that the most strident and orthodox minorities of a given social and cultural formation quite typically are the most committed to cognitive investments of various sorts that distinguish them from other groups. But we should nevertheless recognize the Christian dedication to belief as a new development. To characterize it, we can again lean upon the Hegelian distinction between *an sich* and *für sich*. The pagan Greeks generally believed that something like gods existed. The Jews believe in the existence of an inherited covenant with Yahweh. But such beliefs merely provide the rough frame for the central reality of pagan and Jewish religious life, which focuses less on belief than upon action.

For the Greeks the action required by piety was the performance of sacrifices. What exactly one believed about such sacrificial rituals, or even whether one *believed* anything at all about those rituals beyond a vague hope for their efficacy, was generally a matter of indifference. To have suggested to an ancient Greek that salvation might accrue from the adoption of a mere state of mind would have triggered a response of utter incomprehension, or maybe more likely, utter derision.

Jews, too, actively participate in belief. To be a Jew requires some baseline acceptance of the reality of a binding covenant with "the God of our fathers." Beyond that initial premise of shared belief, however, most of the Jewish community sponsors and even prides itself on ceaseless debate concerning the precise terms and meaning of the covenant. Moreover, in accepting "the God of our fathers," the emphasis often falls less on the first part of the phrase than on the last. Judaism has always been a quasi-tribal formation in which belonging is almost exclusively a matter of being born into it. And like the pagan Greeks, the religiosity of the Jews is arguably focused more on action than on any particular content of thought. Faithfulness consists less in any mere mental disposition than in conscientious obedience to the halachic laws that govern everyday life.

With the emphasis on action over thought, both ancient paganism and Judaism can be said to grant to their adherents a certain free space of mental life. The fulfillment of one's religious duty depends more upon the performance of prescribed behaviors than upon any rigid standardization of thought. From this point of view, the Christian elevation of belief to the status of the sine qua non of religious life might even be recognized as part of what the ancients found shocking about the new religion, a key part of what made it appear as "madness to the Greeks and scandal for the Jews." With the rise of Christianity, *belonging* becomes for the first time primarily a matter of merely *believing*. The question then becomes: What does "believing" really mean and how are we to evaluate the appeal to believing in relation to the original message of the original Christian?

To advance farther, we need to put ourselves freshly, even a bit naively, before the question: What exactly is belief? How does it function psychically?

Only a moment's reflection is needed to see that belief is an exceedingly strange psychic state, fraught with odd internal complications, even outright contradictions. As Lacan says of it, "Nothing is more ambiguous than belief."[59] An initial feature of that strangeness appears as soon as we recognize that holding a belief need not at all mean that the believer understands what is believed. In a large Catholic congregation reciting the Nicene Creed, for example, how many of the assembled actually understand what they are mouthing? How many appreciate what is at stake in the opening distinction between "begotten" and "made"? How many understand what is at issue in saying that the Son is born from God "before all ages"? How many have any clear conception of what it means that the Holy Spirit, said to "proceed from the Father and the Son," is also credited with making possible the virgin conception of Mary? Almost certainly very, very few. But, then again, it doesn't matter. Belief is less a mode of knowledge than a psychical means of compensating for the lack of it. Indeed, far from replacing ignorance with knowledge, belief appears on the contrary to cover over and defend against a baseline unknowing. It is as if the unacknowledged yet archetypal claim of all belief is something like "Precisely where I don't understand, I decide to believe."

On reflection, belief turns out to be a shadowy affair in which rigidity of conclusions is by no means bound to the clarity of underlying premises. In fact, not only does belief quite typically cohabit with a lack of real understanding of its own position; rather, belief is essentially tied to uncertainty. We only claim to "believe" things about which there is some palpable margin of doubt. It would be absurd to say that I *believe* 2 + 2 = 4, or that I *believe* the ocean is salty. Belief only concerns things that are contestable. There is, therefore, a doubting Thomas at the heart of every believer. Indeed, uncertainty is the hidden force that actually *motivates* belief. Among other things, this means that belief is a psychic attitude that pushes back against something. Is this something against which belief asserts itself merely an uncertainty? Does the force of belief merely set up a counterposition to an intellectual deficit, or is there something else at stake?

The answer to this crucial question about the essential push back that gives belief its center of gravity is that belief is ultimately less an intellectual stance than a social one. At the most basic level, belief is a mode of positioning oneself in relation to one's fellow human beings. What is pushed back against is *other people*. In a world composed of a single person, belief would not exist. The posture of belief is ineluctably dependent upon an assumption concerning *others who do not believe as I do*. To put the point in parallel to Lacan's characterization of the analyst as the subject supposed to know, believers position themselves in relation to *the subject(s) supposed not to believe or to believe otherwise*. Belief introduces an implicit line of division into the social body. It segregates the believing subject from some group of Others who are supposed to lack it.

When belief rises to the level of an express credo, belief takes the crucial step in the direction of an explicit opposition to those who fail to believe. That throng of unbelievers can be referred to as infidels, as those who have no faith, no *fides*. As such, the infidel becomes the exception that proves the rule, the truly *other* Other, whose existence in the world helps define and stabilize the very being of the believer. That we are here dealing with something purely supposed is indicated by the following consideration. Just as belief need not be fully clear about exactly what is believed, so, too, belief typically postures itself in opposition to Others who are very typically only vaguely specified. Indeed, the fact that the counterbeliefs of such Others may remain largely undefined and indistinct, far from disqualifying them from serving as a foil that fortifies the believers' own conviction, outfits those shadowy Others all the more effectively for the role they perform.

Belief is a fortification at the limits of knowledge, a defense against the threat of unknowing. At some level belief is nothing more than an arbitrary assertion in the face of not really knowing at all. The unavowed form of belief is "I don't really know, but for that very reason I assert emphatically and unequivocally that I believe." It is a formula that not accidentally recalls that of Tertullian, derided by Freud in *The Future of an Illusion*: *Credo quia absurdum*. The Latin phrase does not mean "I believe something absurd" but rather "I believe *because* it is absurd."[60]

In the context of our approach to Christianity, centered on Jesus's exhortation to lovingly embrace what is unknown in the Other, it becomes possible to read these strange and contradictory features of belief in a consistent way. Belief all too easily becomes a means by which the unknown in the Other is psychically defended against. By the measure of belief, potentially threatening Others are domesticated insofar as they may be divided into one of two camps: those who share my beliefs versus those who do not. The first group ceases to be threatening to me because their beliefs are the same as mine. This Other is assumed to be a replica of myself. But in the case of the unbeliever, the threatening otherness of the Other is reinforced. The "Other" is thus whatever fails to align with my own position of belief. All such Others thereby cease to have any claim to my love. Either way, in relation to either group, Jesus's challenge to embrace what is unknown in the Other is defused.

Unfolding the Christian reliance on belief, we recognize how a second possible interpretation might be offered for Lacan's shocking claim that "the one true religion is the Roman one." Precisely to the extent that Christianity inaugurates a new demand for belief, the stance of the Christian worshipper becomes entangled in competing truth claims. Acts of love and charity make no such demand. Risking the gift of love requires no truth. But as soon as faith is put to the test of an ultimate and eternal verity, the stage is set for an endless series of battles about which sect can properly lay claim to it. By this path, the gospel of love is transformed into the religion of competing orthodoxies.

With these considerations in view, we glimpse another of the great ironies of Christian religious life. The Christian investment in belief becomes in itself the primary means by which the church betrays the original teaching of Jesus. It remains, however, to unfold the most decisive feature of that irony. It centers on the problem of evil.

The Manichaean Temptation

Over the two millennia of Christian history, theologians have wrestled mightily with the problem of evil. Augustine formulated the key question: if everything that exists was created by a Supreme Being that is both infinitely powerful and infinitely beneficent, how we can explain the existence of evil, suffering, and death in the world? The problem simply didn't exist for the pagan Greeks. In the first place, they never attributed existent reality to the creative act of a single creator. Moreover, they assumed that all existence, even that of the gods, was ruled by Fate, the dice throw of chance, where bad outcomes are as likely as good ones. Nor was the problem of evil—what came to be referred to as the problem of God's justice, or theodicy—an issue for the followers of the third-century Persian prophet Mani. Manichaeism, a variant of Gnosticism, envisaged a fundamentally dualistic universe in which the power of God, associated with Goodness, Light, and Spirit, was locked in eternal battle with the forces of Evil, Darkness, and Matter. For Manichaeism, it's no mystery that terrible things happen in the world. Evil has been half of the game from the start.

Augustine's solution insists that it is human beings, not God, who are responsible for the presence of evil in the world. Evil steals into the world through human sin, which is in turn made possible by the divine gift of free will. Of course, this answer gives rise to a second question: if God grants human beings the power of free will, and they in turn abuse that power to sin, isn't God at least indirectly culpable? Surely a parent who leaves the kids at home alone with a box of matches and a pile of fireworks on the coffee table shares a heavy portion of responsibility when the house burns down. At bottom, the Augustinian answer is that the dispensation of free will is justified, even in the face of potentially generating evil, insofar as true love is possible only through uncoerced choice. The priceless treasure of love is to be had only at the price, however grim, of evil entering the world.

For Augustine, the greatest value of this solution, and surely its most far-reaching consequence, consisted in denying the substantive reality of evil. Here Augustine hoped to make a complete break with his own youthful embrace of Manichaeism. If the unqualified infinity of God is to be vouchsafed, evil can have no substantive existence of its own. The infinitude of divine illumination cannot be compromised by a substantive countervailing power of darkness. The conclusion must be that evil is nothing in itself. It is merely a privation of good, in the same way that darkness is merely the absence of light. Evil arises only when human beings turn away from God.

Toward what, then, does the sinful soul turn when it turns away from God? It turns, Augustine says, in the only direction available to it: toward some feature of the finite creation itself. Evil consists in illicitly substituting something created for the dignity of the Creator himself. Such turning toward creation instead of toward the Creator is in the literal sense a "perversion." Sinners' implicit aim is to place themselves in the position of God. Thus Augustine's formula for evil: sin is a perverse imitation of God.[61] Even the impulse toward evil is therefore rooted in the love of God, albeit in a manner that is twisted and self-serving. Ultimately, we cannot stray from our love of God. The only question is whether that love is rightly and straightforwardly directed toward the true source and power of creation—the Creator himself—or whether it takes a perverse detour, satisfying its hunger for God by waywardly gorging itself on one or another merely finite piece of his creation.

Following out the full measure of the consequences of his own argument, Augustine arrives at the deeply counterintuitive notion that evil has no material or substantial existence at all. Evil arises as a kind of a distorted shadow when human willfulness ignores the reality of God. This conclusion requires us to deny the real existence of any substantive agency behind temptation, be it named the Devil, Satan, Lucifer, Beelzebub, the Prince of Darkness, or something else. In the wake of Augustine's breakthrough, all such conceptions of substantialized evil are to be rejected not only as misunderstandings but as failures to honor the true infinitude of God. If we must continue to speak of an agent of evil, the only agency involved is the failure of our own steadfastness in praise and service of the good.

Such fine points of orthodox Christian doctrine contrast markedly with what might be gleaned from some of the sayings attributed to Jesus. Despite the famous story about holding his own in discussions with the wise men in the temple, Jesus was no theologian.[62] He didn't offer a conceptual solution to the problem of the nature and reality of evil. He arguably did suggest, however, that whatever evil may be in itself, we all participate in it. Perhaps the best expression of this view occurs in his response to the threatening crowd surrounding the woman taken in adultery.[63] "Let he among you who is without sin cast the first stone," he says. One by one, the would-be punishers slink away. "Woman, where are they?" Jesus then asks. "Has no one condemned you?" "No one, sir," she answers. To which Jesus replies, "Neither do I condemn you. Go your way, and sin no more."

Clearly implying that there is no one free from sin, the story of the woman accused of adultery is a close cousin to the text in Matthew in which Jesus admonishes his followers to "judge not, that you be not judged."[64] The larger point is a rejection of any clear division between the "righteous" and the "sinners," of any simply dichotomy between good and evil people. Whatever its distance from the rationalizing constructions of the theologians, Jesus's teaching is emphatic in its rejection of any simple dualism.

Of course, Christians routinely profess to accept such a view, mouthing pious admissions about how we are all sinners. But when the going gets rough, such glib pieties routinely give way to self-righteous, finger-pointing condemnations. The American response to the attacks of 9/11 offers a spectacular example. In the wake of the attacks, President George W. Bush, careful to invoke a Christian warrant for his judgment, identified the perpetrators of the attack as embodiments of pure evil. He went on to identify three countries—Iraq, Iran, and North Korea—as the "axis of evil" on earth. That declaration smoothed the road for the disastrous invasion of Iraq. A response more in the mold of Jesus himself—a response that is admittedly hard for us to imagine in the contemporary context, though it would have been more rational as well as more truly Christian— might have paused to take some note of how the actions of the largely Saudi attackers on 9/11, however wrongheaded, however terrible, were undertaken in response to a long-standing pattern of American actions in the Middle East aimed at protecting US oil interests, actions tied to the deeply repressive Saudi regime. Such a response would truly, as Jesus himself put it, have pointed to the log in our own eye instead of complaining about the splinter in the eye of the Other.

As regards the question of evil, the belief of mainstream Christians tends to disregard both the architects of orthodoxy *and* the teachings of Jesus in the direction of a gnostic dualism that imagines a kind of "dark lord" who draws otherwise well-meaning people into the nets of malevolence. Even Augustine himself shows signs of cheating on his own conclusion concerning the nonsubstantiality of evil, allowing that something like Satan does exist, albeit calling for a rather tortured explanation.

Precisely such a gnostic vision of the powers of good locked in mortal combat with the forces of evil informs the theological framing of the *Star Wars* franchise. At first glance, it is tempting to think of the mythic architecture of George Lucas's creation as a mix of Christianity and Taoism, with Luke Skywalker representing a messianic Christlike redeemer and Yoda in the role of a Taoist sage who counsels Luke that the secret of true power resides in renouncing all ego-driven effort in favor of merely channeling the Force and allowing it to do the work.[65] "Do or do not," Yoda says in a comically Asiatic pidgin, "there is no try." But the fact of the matter, and no doubt a huge part of the popular appeal of the *Star Wars* mythology, is that these Christian and Taoist threads are combined with a more decisive gnostic strand that materializes evil. The positive and redemptive powers in the universe are locked in combat with "the dark side of the Force," embodied in the evil emperor and his henchman, Darth Vader. Lucas's galaxy "long ago and far away" is a Manichaean universe.

Of course, the fact that the popular reality of Christianity through the centuries has tended to retain such a deeply gnostic investment in the dualism of good and evil is in no small part a function of the high abstraction and intuitive implausibility of the Augustinian position, which denies evil any substantial reality of its own. It is far less intellectually challenging, and above all far more emotionally satisfying, to suppose that there really is a Devil-Power that leads us astray with the seductive force of wickedness. But we might still wonder why the gnostic account retains such appeal. How and why do such large numbers of Christians ignore church orthodoxy and cherish deeply gnostic assumptions?

The Lacanian perspective we have opened up suggests a disturbing part of the answer: the Christian tendency toward the substantialization of evil is powerfully energized by *the requirement of belief itself*. And it is not difficult to imagine how and why this trend gains traction. The key resides in our earlier observation about the way belief relies implicitly or explicitly on a supposition about others who fail to believe, or believe differently. That divide is nothing other than the psychic architecture of belief itself. We are then given to wonder whether the tendency of Christianity toward gnostic dualism is founded upon that very structure. The tension between believers and unbelievers assumes the shape of the struggle between good and evil.

The gnostic tendency among Christians marks a stark contrast with Homer's depiction of vengeful violence. The drama of the *Iliad* establishes the basic pattern of the contemporary revenge movie. Who would have guessed that the conventions of Hollywood derive from an archaic Greek poet? In one way or another, the hero hangs back until a relatively innocent and likable figure—modeled on Akhilleus's bosom friend, Patróklos—is harmed or killed. The hero then assumes his true stature and delivers a hugely satisfying explosion of vengeance. Howard Hawks's classic 1944 film *To Have and Have Not*, based on a novel by Hemingway, offers a typical retelling of the Homeric story. Harry Morgan (Humphrey Bogart) remains aloof as the political tensions of World War II begin to roil even the sleepy corners of the Caribbean, until his rum-sodden buddy (Walter Brennan) is abducted and tortured by Vichy agents of the Nazis. At that point, Harry rises gratifyingly to the occasion, dispatching the despicable Nazi henchmen and then using his fishing boat to run guns for the partisan opposition.

With overwhelming predictability, the distinguishing feature of such modern remakes of Homer's plot is the obscene villainy of the enemy. In Homer's tale, the Trojans are anything but evil. If there is a truly noble and fully respectable figure in the *Iliad* it is Prince Hektor, the very one upon whom the vengeful rage of Akhilleus falls. But in modern, post-Christian restagings of the revenge plot, the enemy is almost always a grotesque caricature of malevolence. Sam Peckinpah's spectacularly violent western *The Wild Bunch* offers an example. The youngest and most tender member of Pike Bishop's gang of gunrunners is the Patróklos figure, appropriately named Angel. When Angel is seized and tortured beyond recognition by the slobbering and sadistic Mexican general Mapache, Pike's anger finally boils over. In the climactic scene, he and his crew mow down half of the local Mexican army garrison in a suicidal paroxysm of bloodletting. Unlike Homer's noble depiction of Hektor, the Mexicans are sketched in Peckinpah's film as filthy, debauched, and utterly despicable vermin. The final scene of Pike ripping into them with a blazing Gatling gun offers the giddy satisfaction of watching the extermination of a teeming nest of rats.

If the belief of many ordinary Christians departs from theological orthodoxy in substantializing evil, it also fails to align with the Jesus's admonition to give oneself wholly to the loving embrace of the stranger, not allowing the fear of evil to sire even a moment's hesitation. So radical is this gospel of love that it prompts us to reread the lesson of the *pericope adulterae*. On a first glance, we took the story to assert the universal distribution of evil, the way we are all implicated in it. Participation in evil is the one thing we all share. Yet the deeper message of Jesus, modeled by his defense of the adulterous woman, is rather that of our own failure to love. Evil is nothing but the hesitation, born of fear, to open ourselves in love for the Other.

7

Other Paths, Other Gods

Freud is consistent with himself in also pointing, at the limit of
our experience, to a field in which the subject, if he exists, is
incontestably a subject who doesn't know in a point of extreme,
if not absolute, ignorance. One finds there the core of Freudian
exploration.

—Jacques Lacan, *The Ethics of Psychoanalysis*

Beneath the obvious differences separating Greek paganism, Hebrew
monotheism, and Christianity lies the shared function of stabilizing the
subject's relation with *das Ding*. Yet religions variously stylize the relation
to unknowing. Moreover, among the trio of religions we have considered,
the broad outline of an underlying trajectory can be discerned in which
the unknown Other-Thing is approached with increasing directness.[1]

For Greek paganism, the will of the gods and the dictates of fate
remained shrouded in darkness. Yet noble conduct for human beings
required courageous and honorable self-possession precisely in the face
of that darkness. The redoubtable hero retained poise and dignity even
in the teeth of death.

Jewish religiosity, by contrast, took a crucial step toward a direct
confrontation with *das Ding* by locating the unknown in the inscrutable
will of a single, implacable deity, whose covenant demanded scrupulous
observance even if its ultimate meaning remained undecidable. The
very namelessness of the Judaic God is an index of his proximity to the
Lacanian Thing.

Only with the arrival of Christianity was the dimension of the unknown fully restored to its original, most truly abyssal site. When Jesus
of Nazareth identified divinity with love of the enemy as much as of the
neighbor, challenging his followers to fully embrace what is unknown
and potentially threatening in every human being, he sparked a revolution by focusing directly upon the primordial locus of the anxiety-
producing Thing. Jesus brought the enigmatic call of divinity fully down

to earth, alarmingly pinpointing it in our relations with the actually existing human Other. If Kant's motto for enlightenment was *Sapere Aude*, dare to know, the challenge of Jesus was *Amare Aude*, dare to love, above all where you do not know.[2]

The Religious Symptom

Precisely to the extent that religions elicit the specter of the unknown Thing, they also deploy defenses against their own potential for anxiety. We can now summarize how the three traditions each responded with a unique symptomatic formation.

The ethos of Greek polytheism deserves to be called *imaginary* in the properly Lacanian sense. The Greek hero's comportment of honor and nobility was essentially a struggle for recognition, a game premised on the goal of impressing other people. In effect, the hero painted himself into the magnificent tableau of myth, the dazzling veil that helped conceal the abyss. The resulting regime was a culture of sublime egoism, embodied in legendary figures but available even to the common man through identification.

Judaism is unquestionably the great religion of the *symbolic*, the worshipful sublimity of the Word. That apotheosis of the symbolic function was set in motion by an unnerving proximity of *das Ding*, made audible by the covenant with a solitary, imperious, and inscrutable deity. Massively expanded regulation of behavior protected believers from the unnerving approach of the God-Thing. In Judaism, the confrontation with unknowing tends, like a fluid drawn into a sponge, to be absorbed within the warp and woof of the law. The cultural product of this symptomatic compromise was a new and more stable configuration of the social link. Judaism offers a reassuring, even mildly ecstatic, fraternity of obedience.

The revolutionary event of Christianity consisted in Jesus's direct solicitation of the real in the neighbor-Thing. This event presupposed the background of the Jewish regime of halachic law to the extent that it effected a measured rejection of the prescribed rules governing social life in favor of demanding direct vulnerability to the fellow human being, emphatically including an exposure to the Other's foreign and threatening potential. This fulfillment of the law in love was unavoidably traumatizing. The teaching of Jesus turns every person we meet into a burning bush. It was this radical exhortation to directly embrace *das Ding* that prompted Lacan to call Christianity the one true religion, the religion of the *real*. In the face of this uniquely pointed threat, the Christian tradition has responded with a range of defenses, the first of which was an effort to retranscendentalize divinity. In effect, Peter denied Jesus a fourth time, building a church heavily invested in restoring divinity to an ever more resplendent and heavenly status. Just as Christian cathedrals over the centuries couldn't be built high enough, so too theologians couldn't resist reinflating the sublimity of God. The Kingdom among us proclaimed by Jesus was reelevated into an Otherworldly Beyond.

In tandem with this transcendentalizing trend, Christianity adopted new defensive investments in both imaginary and symbolic forms. On the side of the imaginary, Christian piety blossomed forth a veritable forest of fascinating images and icons, from the predominantly Catholic figure of the tortured and crucified body of Jesus, to the Christ *pantokrator* icons of the Eastern church, to the more general explosion of images of the Madonna, with or without child. This theater of visions functions to displace Jesus's challenge of embracing the unknown Other in front of me in favor of one or another mesmerizing representation of the divine family.

On the other, symbolic side arose an unprecedented investment in the posture of belief, accompanied by a correlative elaboration of doctrinal orthodoxy. This massive inflation of the subjective value of dogmatically informed belief represented a new and extensive elaboration of the symbolic, leading not, as in Judaism, toward renewed devotion to the contested meaning of the law, but rather toward a spiritual heroism of faith. In this way, the Christian religion transformed the authority of the symbolic big Other, extending its surveillance beyond outward obedience toward an unparalleled, inwardly directed self-consciousness.

It is with a view to this proliferation of defenses against its own breakthrough that Christianity deserves to be considered the most extravagantly symptomatic religion, the religious formation that most spectacularly displays the tension of opposing trends.[3] A prime index of this symptomatic conflict is the veritable river of blood that has flowed over the centuries in the name of Christ. Even a modicum of honesty forces a sobering judgment upon the unrivaled history of violence attributable to overheated Christian faith.[4] That historical record includes the murderous persecutions of apostates and heretics; the deadly pogroms undertaken against Jews, which reached their horrendous climax in the Nazi Holocaust; the brutal, genocidal conquest of tribal peoples in the Western Hemisphere; the centuries of African slave trade carried on by Christian nations; and the massive and lethal waves of officially sanctioned crusades against the rise of Islam, crusades that, even now, may not be fully over. We need to unflinchingly acknowledge this dark side of the Christian legacy and to take account of the paradox it presents. A long and bloody history of systematic torture and murder was conducted in the name of the quintessential religion of love. The horrors perpetrated under the banner of the cross arose precisely in response to Jesus's demand for love. I take it to be a prime recommendation of the perspective put forward in this book that it theoretically illuminates the almost unbearable irony of this world-historical contradiction.

Many definitions of the human being have been proposed: the naked ape, the two-legged animal, the animal that speaks or laughs, the animal aware of its own death. The perspective I have adopted in this book illuminates another definition: the animal that worships. But the main thesis put forward here is that worship is fundamentally a posture toward *das Ding*. At its core, the sense of the sacred arises in relation to the darkness of the unknown. In this respect, the outlook I have limned here is deeply akin to that of Heidegger: the human being is the animal capable of knowing that it doesn't know, the animal that is a question to itself. In worship, that question is transfigured into the stuff of divinity.

Insofar as the unknown Thing forms the central, if hidden, focus of the passion of worship, against which some sort of defensive reaction becomes almost unavoidable, it becomes possible to venture the conclusion that religion is the most elemental and ubiquitous symptom of the human condition. Human beings can wean themselves from the religious symptom only through other forms of sublimation—one or another means of "raising the object to the dignity of *das Ding*"—the most dependable of which are to be found in making love, art, science, or war.[5]

A Broader View?

"You want to defend a sweeping conclusion about religion as the master symptom of the human being," says the critic, "yet you've presented just three examples. Can your perspective offer anything to illuminate other world religions?"

My response is bound to disappoint. I've focused on the three primary religious traditions of the West for two reasons. First, quite simply, it was about them that Lacan had the most to say. Second, when those three traditions are compared with one another what unmistakably emerges is a quasi-historical progression toward a more intimate (and anxious) approach to the unknown neighbor-Thing. To go beyond that itinerary to provide even a minimally adequate treatment of other religions would require another book altogether. Mindful of that caveat, however, we might venture a few very brief notes, if only to crudely sketch some key points at which a handful of other traditions can be seen to reflect themes and dynamics akin to what we have discerned in the three primary formations of the West.

The challenge of responding to the critic's question is on vivid display in the case of Hinduism. Often cited as the world's oldest religion, it is also among the most diverse and complicated.[6] The difficulty of defining Hinduism by any single measure was noted by the Supreme Court of India. "Unlike other religions in the World," the court said, "the Hindu religion does not claim any one Prophet, it does not worship any one God, it does not believe in any one philosophic concept, it does not follow any one act of religious rites or performances; in fact, it does not satisfy the traditional features of a religion or creed. It is a way of life and nothing more."[7] Against the backdrop of Lacan's thought, however, it is tempting to risk a remark concerning one of the more conspicuous red threads linking many Hindu traditions, that of the goal of achieving liberation, or *moksha*. The objective is to sever attachment to the ego, the pawn of petty, transitory impressions, inclinations, and attachments, in favor of encountering a more transcendent level of reality. The beleaguered self of everyday life must be set aside in favor of an experience of the one's innermost self, the soul-seat of consciousness, or Atman. When the essential spirit of Atman has been sifted from the detritus of the mundane ego, the wayfarer on the path of wisdom is opened to a union with the eternal and unlimited cosmic reality of Brahman.

While he never develops it in any detail, Lacan clearly plays with this idea. In the last paragraph of his famous essay on the mirror stage, an essay the culmination of which is concerned precisely with the transcendence of the ego, Lacan quotes the ultimate expression of Hindu experience: "*Tat Tvam Asi!* Thou Art That!"[8] Hindu *moksha* consists in the realization that there is in me something more than me, indeed something infinitely more than me. For the·Hindu tradition, this something more is the Godhead itself. The basic point is well spoken by the verses of the eighth-century *Vivekachudamani*:

> That which is without name and form, beyond merit and demerit,
> That which is beyond space, time and sense-objects,
> You are that, God himself; Meditate this within yourself.[9]

The precise nature of the relation between Atman and Brahman is posed somewhat differently among different Hindu sects. In the Advaita Vedanta tradition, however, that relation is conceived in a manner that is especially interesting from a Lacanian point of view. For the Advaitin, the ultimate spiritual realization is achieved when one's innermost sense of selfhood is experienced as identical with the eternal and transcendent reality of Brahman, where Brahman is itself understood as an infinite, cosmic self. *Moksha* thus becomes less a complete erasure of one's sense of self than an ecstatic transformation of it. Advaitan religiosity thus appears to offer the means by which the subject not only identifies itself with an unlimited horizon but realizes its fusion with an infinite self. Liberation consists in the passage by which one's own sense of self becomes indistinguishable from the all-embracing and boundless Self.

In the Vedas we also find the idea not merely that the Godhead remains utterly beyond our capacity to know, but more so that the divine Self, too, may be suspended in unknowing. As the "Hymn of Creation" sings:

> Who knows for certain? Who shall here declare it?
> Whence was it born, and whence came this creation?
> The gods were born after this world's creation:
> Then who can know from whence it has arisen?
> None knoweth whence creation has arisen
> And whether he has or has not produced it:
> He who surveys it in the highest heaven,
> He only knows, or haply he may not know.[10]

In *moksha*, the subject achieves the ultimate sublimation, the sublime transformation of the ego itself. In the experience of oneself in kinship with Brahman, or even identical with it, some trace of the subject's own ego is raised to the dignity of *das Ding*. The unknowable ground of one's own being, the way we remain a mystery to ourselves, is taken up into the relation with a supreme Self, the locus of the infinite mystery.

Buddhism, one of the primary offshoots of the Hindu tradition, is commonly interpreted as rejecting selfhood altogether, regarding all attachment to self as a source of *dukkha*—suffering, pain, and dissatisfaction. The Buddhist doctrines of *anatta* or *anatman* thus reject all retention of self in the achievement of nirvana, the rough Buddhist analogue of *moksha*. From a Lacanian standpoint, this Buddhist twist of the Hindu sensibility might be interpreted as a matter of stripping away from the subject's orientation toward the Other-Thing all vestiges of its imaginary husk. Personification of any sort is expressly resisted. In nirvana, all traces of separation and discreteness dissolve into an experience of perfect cosmic unity in which all things have their integral part and place.

If Buddhism tends to deny all personhood in favor of engaging an infinite void, it is no accident that it emphasizes in equal measure the abyssal unknowability of that void. The result is deeply paradoxical as the apex of enlightenment reveals an ineluctable dimension of unknowing. Such enlightenment aims to attain a "beginner's mind" that restores the wonder and sanctity of all experience.[11] In this respect, Buddhism appears dedicated to splitting Freud's "perceptual complex" of the *Nebenmensch,* focusing completely on the void of unknowing while refusing altogether any imaginary reference to another subject, another self. Religious experience becomes oriented toward cultivating an exposure to utter emptiness. The objective is a clearing of consciousness in the service of achieving an ever more open and receptive cast of mind. Thus the practitioner of Zen meditation adopts a pose of absolute stillness in which a single-minded focus on breathing effects a transformative suspension of attention, a kind of radical distillation in which the intentionality of consciousness dissolves into a sublime emptiness, an ecstatic vacancy.

The teachings of the Kyoto School of Japanese Zen Buddhism shed an especially interesting light on this discussion, perhaps nowhere as impressively as in Keiji Nishitani's monumental work *Religion and Nothingness.*[12] Nishitani's nuanced attempt to integrate Eastern and Western philosophical traditions takes its point of departure from the modern crisis of nihilism that unfolds in European thought from Descartes to Nietzsche. For Nishitani, "pessimistic nihilism represents the greatest issue facing philosophy and religion in our times."[13]

The elegance of Nishitani's solution is to assert that the path to spiritual revitalization—in Western terms, nothing less than the rediscovery of God—consists not in dogmatically resisting nihilism but rather in entering unflinchingly into its darkest depths, enabling the hopelessness of "nihility" to be opened toward a transformative experience of absolute emptiness or *sunyata.*[14] Nishitani approvingly quotes Meister Eckhart, who also insists that the Godhead resides precisely in such absolute nothingness.

Nishitani finds a deeply confirming perspective in Heidegger's radicalized phenomenology of human *Dasein* "held out into the nothing."[15] On the first level, what is at stake is the primal ground of consciousness, itself inaccessible to becoming fully conscious, in which the field of *sunyata* yawns open as a pure void. Thus Nishitani asserts that "all consciousness as such is empty at its very roots: it can only become manifest on the field of emptiness. Consciousness is *originally* emptiness. . . . Put in more general terms, there is a *non-consciousness* at the base of all consciousness."[16] For Nishitani, all being wells up from the depths of nothingness. "The field of emptiness," he says, "stands opened at the very point that things emerge into being."[17]

Appeal to this aboriginal shining forth of being from out of absolute emptiness allows Nishitani to assert the absolute unity of being—that all things are ultimately one. "All things that are in the world are linked together, one way or the other," he writes. "Not a single thing comes into being without some relationship to every other thing."[18] Yet the very same ground in absolute nothingness also allows us to draw a crucial, deeply paradoxical correlate. All things are one, everything is thoroughly interconnected in a web of all-embracing "circumintercessionality," yet each instance of being is ultimately singular and unique. Nishitani can thus conclude that "it is only on a field where the being of all things is a being at one with emptiness that it is possible for all things to gather into one, even while each retains its reality as an absolutely unique being."[19]

If one pole of the doctrine of *sunyata* as absolute emptiness is to be located in a kind of radicalized phenomenology in which nothingness becomes the *Urgrund* of consciousness, itself unconscious, the complementary pole refers the emergence of all beings to the kenotic, self-emptying act of divinity.[20] All things are enabled to come forth in their uniqueness as the divine power steps back in self-effacing withdrawal. Divine creation is therefore a profound "letting-be," enabled by an act of self-evacuation. Nishitani thus insists that "the meaning of self-emptying may be said to be contained within God himself. In Christ, *ekkenosis* is realized in the fact that one who was in the shape of God took on the shape of a servant."[21]

The two sides—the abyssal ground of consciousness and the kenotic self-erasure of divinity—are ultimately two sides of the same reality. Again, Eckhart clearly recognized the infinite paradox involved. As Nishitani quotes him, "The ground of God is the ground of my soul; the ground of my soul is the ground of God."[22] Taken together, these premises point to the ultimate unknowability of both object and subject.

> That nihility opens up at the ground of a being means that the field of that being's 'existence,' of its essential mode of being, opens up. In nihility both things and the subject return to their respective essential modes of being, to their very own home-ground where they are what they originally are. But at the same time, their 'existence' itself then turns into a single great question mark. It becomes something of which we know neither whence it comes nor whither it goes, something essentially incomprehensible and unnameable. Each and every thing, no matter how well acquainted the self may be with it, remains at bottom, in its essential mode of being, an unknown. Even should the subject itself, as subject, seek to return to its home-ground, to is very existence as such, it becomes something nameless and hard to pin down.[23]

In light of these considerations, Nishitani's analysis very suggestively aligns with the perspective we have unfolded, according to which an engagement with unknowing animates the heart of religious experience. Yet the upshot becomes even more suggestive when we find him reconceiving the role of self in the whole drama, as if calling up a particularly sublime echo of the Advaita Vedanta doctrine of self-transcendence. Though his account deserves a far more careful explication that I can enter into here, Nishitani is emphatic in not wanting to lose all reference to self. "The idea of man as person," he insists, "is without doubt the highest conception of man yet to appear. . . . Person is an appearance with nothing at all behind it to make an appearance. That is to say, 'nothing at all' is what is behind person; complete nothingness, not one single thing, occupies the position behind person."[24] There is, we might say, nothing but person. Correctly understood, however, "person" is at bottom nothing at all. Nishitani thus plays on the original meaning of *persona* as the mask from behind which the actor projects a voice. "We can understand person as *persona*—the 'face' that an actor puts on to indicate the role he is to play on stage—but only as the *persona* of absolute nothingness."[25]

Of course, such insistence on the primal reality of self does not at all obviate the necessity of transcending the selfish gravity of mundane ego. But when such transcendence is achieved, what steps forth is a new, absolute and universal selfhood. What is involved, says Nishitani, "is a complete conversion from the standpoint where the self is an autotelic person to the standpoint where the self is a means for all other things. The self that has returned to the original self, that (while taking a firm stand on the universality of moral law) finds its *telos* in the self itself, must break its way through that standpoint as well and revert to a self that finds its *telos* in all other beings."[26] The conclusion to be drawn articulates the most profound paradox: "Non-ego does not mean simply that self is not ego. It has also to mean at the same time that non-ego is the self. . . . '[S]elf is not self (self is non-ego), therefore it is self.'"[27] "True emptiness is nothing less than what reaches awareness in all of us as our own absolute *self-nature*."[28]

At least with the teaching of the Kyoto School in mind, it is possible to see in both Hinduism and Buddhism a doctrine of cosmic selfhood that is deeply inflected with paradox, not only between self and nonself but also and crucially between knowing and nonknowing. For Nishitani, the ultimate meaning of Zen enlightenment, or satori, is to recognize and embrace "a knowing of non-knowing, a sort of *docta ignorantia*."[29] The assertion of this paradox of nonknowing as central to the deepest encounter with things and with others, as well as with oneself, points us back a final time in the direction of the Lacanian notion of *das Ding* as the unknown dimension of the *Nebenmensch*.[30] Nishitani is at pains to show that we remain in a state of profound unknowing, not merely in relation to strangers but also in the case of our most intimate loved ones.

> We like to feel that we are close to our family and friends and know
> them well. But do we really, after all, essentially know those whom we
> are most familiar with? . . . . We no more know whence our closest
> friend comes and whither he is going than we know where we ourselves
> come from and where we are headed. At his home-ground, a friend
> remains originally and essentially a stranger, an 'unknown.' . . . Es-
> sentially speaking, then, all men, be they the most intimate of friends
> or the most distant of acquaintances, are exactly to the same degree
> 'unknown.'[31]

The deepest crux of this Buddhist teaching concerns the relation to God,
who, as Augustine claimed, is closest to us—most absolutely intimate,
closer to us than we are to ourselves—and yet who remains massively unknown, the locus of the ultimate mystery.

Along the Path of the Fourth Prophet

What, then, might be said of Islam? Despite contemporary tensions between the Muslim Middle East and Israel, Islam's likeness to Judaism is
striking in more ways than one, beginning with its emphasis on the un-
graspable depth and mystery of God. Appropriately enough, there has
been debate among scholars about whether the name Allah derives from
the Hebrew and Aramaic words *El* and *Elah* for "God," or rather from
L-ah (or *lyh*), meaning "lofty" or "hidden." Like Judaism, Islam passionately maintains an acute sense of God's ineffability. While the often repeated Islamic announcement of faith, *La ilaha illa 'llah!*—"There is no
god but God!"—might readily seem almost the opposite of the Jewish
prohibition of naming the Lord, the near-tautological character of the
Arabic phrase can readily be taken to announce the unspeakable. To
make a companion point from another angle, where Judaism prohibits
speaking the name of God, Islam seems to underscore the utter sublimity of Allah by calling him by a hundred names, as if the very profusion of names emphasizes that no title is sufficient to encompass his
divine majesty.

Though arising in the wake of Christianity, Islam displays a return
to the fear of God more characteristic of Jewish than of Christian faith.
Like Judaism, the religiosity of Islam centers upon a shatteringly direct
encounter with the Supreme Being himself. The mercy and compassion
so passionately attributed to Allah is counterbalanced by an emphasis
on the terrifying prospect of his wrath. In the face of the overwhelm-

ing experience of his presence, power, and commanding authority, the worshipper can only submit. It is deeply fitting that the very name Islam derives from the root *s-l-m*, which signifies "peace" but also "surrender."

The unknowable character of the Islamic God is well signaled by the Kaaba. Every day, observant Muslims prostrate themselves five times in the direction of Mecca or, more precisely, in the direction, or *qibla*, of the black cube of the Kaaba that occupies the center of the Great Mosque. At the climax of the annual pilgrimage of the hajj, the devout circle seven times round the Kaaba. Entered only once a year by a select few, the Kaaba is almost literally a pure black box. It is very nearly empty of contents. As such, it would seem to be the perfect locus for something purely supposed, something unknown—a true house of God. As if to heighten the effect, the square granite structure is completely enveloped by a black shroud, ornamented only with verses from the Qur'an. The Kaaba is thus not only a closed box but a box concealed beneath a black curtain festooned with signifiers. It's hard to imagine a more perfect material embodiment of *das Ding*.

In the text of the Qur'an we find some forty references to an absolutely key concept of Islam, that of *al-Ghaib*, which variously means the unseen, the hidden, or the unknown. The centrality of *al-Ghaib* for Muslim spirituality is hard to overstate, as it names the core commitment to the infinite transcendence of Allah.[32] In the second sura, "those who are mindful of God" are said to be those "who believe in the unseen."[33] In the sixth, God is said to hold "the keys to the unseen: no one knows them but Him."[34] The ineluctable unknown of *al-Ghaib* is an indispensable part of the awe-struck posture of submission that is so central to Islam and also arguably the core of the Muslim sense of the sublime. We might also take faith in *al-Ghaib* as the ground of hope in what may come as it names not only the unseen and unknown but also the future.

If Islam particularly emphasizes the unknowable transcendence of God, it also shares with both Judaism and Christianity a powerful concern with duty toward the neighbor. In fact, in some ways Muslim morality appears to outdo Christianity in its demand for social equality and justice, along with an open hand of solicitude toward fellow human beings in need. The prohibition of usury, for example, has proved more enduring in Islamic nations than among Christians. Moreover, Islam levies upon the wealthy a heavier responsibility for giving to the less fortunate. Whereas the notion of progressive taxation was instituted among Christian democracies only in the twentieth century, the Qur'an already established the basic principle of taxing the well-to-do more than a millennium earlier. According to the Islamic law called *zakat*, the wealthy must make an annual contribution of 2.5 percent to the benefit of the poor, a percentage that applies not only to one's annual income but to one's total holdings.[35]

The Islamic concern for the neighbor is evoked with particular sublimity by the tradition of Sufi mysticism. It is a trend well represented by the poetry of Jalaluddin Balkhi, the thirteenth-century Sufi poet known more colloquially as Rumi. In his verses we also find powerful echoes of the Jesus message that intimately link the mystery and majesty of the divine to the love of the neighbor. Indeed, love itself is the primary theme of Rumi's religious sensibility. "Let yourself be secretly drawn by the strange pull of what you really love," he writes.[36] It is along the path of love, not only the love of God but also the love of a human person, that one is led to the divine. "Be grateful for whoever comes," says Rumi, "because each has been sent as a guide from beyond."[37] Indeed, Rumi comes close to echoing the most radical of Jesus's claims, not fully identifying the divine with love for the fellow human being, to be sure, but locating in love for the human Other a privileged path to God. We thus find him enjoining us to seek the Kaaba that is interior to our neighbor. "Be a pilgrim to the *Ka'ba* inside a human being," he says, "and Mecca will rise into view on its own."[38] The direction of Mecca may be found by looking directly into the eyes of the beloved. Rumi thus directs the religious searcher to turn toward "the *qibla* of the friend's face."[39]

If Islam in these ways displays an impressive opening toward the dimension of *das Ding*, both emphasizing the ineffability of the Godhead and, to a striking extent, directing religious fervor toward relation with the fellow human being, it is also possible to discern in Islam a deeply defensive and symptomatic posture. We arguably glimpse that defensive stance already, as we did in the Christian tradition, in the preference for charity over more direct relations with the Other. But even proper care for charity is part of a larger project: the Islamic aspiration to *complete* the law. Islam seeks to fulfill the promise of the three great waves of revelation that preceded it. As Huston Smith paints the background: "First, God revealed the truth of monotheism, through Abraham. Second, God revealed the Ten Commandments through Moses. Third, God revealed the Golden Rule—that we are to do unto others as we would have them do unto us—through Jesus."[40] It remained for Muhammad to more completely answer the question of how exactly religious duty is to be fulfilled. Jesus pointed in the right direction, but his teaching, Ameer Ali writes, "was left unfinished. It was reserved for another Teacher to systematize the laws of morality."[41] As Smith argues:

> Compared with other religions, Islam spells out the way of life it proposes; it pinpoints it, nailing it down through clear injunctions. . . .

> In addition to being a spiritual guide, [the Qur'an] is a legal com-
> pendium. When its innumerable prescriptions are supplemented by
> the only slightly less authoritative *hadith*—traditions based on what
> Muhammad did or said on his own initiative—we are not surprised to
> find Islam the most socially explicit of the Semitic religions. Western-
> ers who define religion in terms of personal experience would never be
> understood by Muslims, whose religion calls them to establish a specific
> kind of social order. Islam joins faith to politics, religion to society,
> inseparably.[42]

Islamic law is dedicated to exhaustively regulating relations with the
worldly Other, bringing them fully into accord with the will of Allah. This
seamlessness of the Islamic ideal of constant and unreserved devotion
to God is already indicated by the way the Hebrew Sabbath, relegated to
the seventh day of the week, appears in Islam to expand and swallow up
the other six. Not only does the call to prayer pierce the silence every day
of the week, but it does so no fewer than five times. The comprehensive-
ness of the Islamic system of life regulation is thus complemented by the
demand that worshipful devotion to God cannot be relegated to a single
day of the week but must be daily, even hourly, reaffirmed.

If such pervasive regulation of life hints at the underlying defensive
posture of Islamic religiosity, that posture is powerfully reinforced by the
separation between believers and unbelievers. In this respect, Islam appears to up the ante on the Christian investment in orthodox belief, as
well as on a willingness to energetically condemn those who do not accept the creed. The opposition between believers and disbelievers thus
becomes a major theme of the Qur'an. The bottom line is laid out in the
opening paragraph of the second sura.

> This is the Scripture in which there is no doubt, containing guidance
> for those who are mindful of God, who believe in the unseen, keep up
> the prayer, and give out of what We have provided for them; those who
> believe in the revelation sent down to you [Muhammad] and in what
> was sent before you, those who have firm faith in the Hereafter. Such
> people are following their Lord's guidance and it is they who will pros-
> per. As for those who disbelieve, it makes no difference whether you
> warn them or not: they will not believe. God has sealed their hearts and
> their ears, and their eyes are covered. They will have great torment."[43]

We have already examined the function of belief in Christianity,
pointing to the way the embrace of orthodoxy implicitly divides the social
body and functions to distance the subject from the uncertainty incar-

nated by the Other-Thing. Inside the community of the faithful, believers are reassured of being of one mind with one another. Yet they can be almost equally sure of what the disbeliever thinks, if only by virtue of being a mere negation or rejection of the orthodox position.[44] For a number of reasons, however, the tension between believer and disbeliever appears to be heightened in Islam. First, the disbeliever, or *kafir*, tends to be posed as an active danger to the faithful. Disbelief is presented as a positive temptation to be vigilantly guarded against. Special appeal to Allah is therefore not inappropriate: "You are our Protector," goes one prayer, "so help us against the disbelievers."[45] Moreover, the Qur'an lays down ominous warnings about the intentional falseness of disbelievers, who cynically attempt to pass themselves off as truly faithful while remaining secretly attached to their disbelief. In the second sura, immediately after the opening passage quoted above, we find it said of the disbelievers: "When they meet the believers, they say, 'We believe,' but when they are alone with their evil ones, they say, 'We're really with you; we were only mocking.'"[46] Attributing such stealth and deviousness to the disbelievers massively inflates the menace they pose to the faithful, thereby energizing the tension between the two groups.

If suspicion of irreligious hypocrisy threatens to make ceaseless distrust of Others the handmaiden of piety, the Islamic posture toward disbelievers is further jaundiced by some passages of the Qur'an that present them as beyond retrieval. In the verses quoted above it is God himself who has "sealed their hearts and their ears."[47] God, it appears, has already passed judgment on the infidels. "God rejects those who disbelieve."[48] Efforts to make the disbelievers see the error of their ways are therefore likely to be fruitless. "If God intends some people to be so misguided," says the Qur'an, "you will be powerless against God on their behalf. These are the ones whose hearts God does not intend to cleanse."[49]

In response to the recent rise of militant fundamentalism among some Muslim groups, far too much has recklessly been said about the inherent violence of the Islamic religion. Nevertheless, the drumbeat in the Qur'an about dangers posed by disbelievers makes it somewhat unsurprising that some passages appear unhesitatingly to advocate violence against them. The second sura is particularly blunt: "God does not love those who overstep the limits. Kill them wherever you encounter them."[50] The ninth sura instructs that "wherever you encounter the idolaters, kill them, seize them, besiege them."[51] And the forty-seventh: "When you meet the disbelievers in battle, strike them in the neck, and once they are defeated, bind the captives firmly."[52]

Despite the threatening tone of such passages, the history of Islam can boast at many points of an impressive record of religious tolerance.

The Ottoman Sultanate at Constantinople, for example, extended a respectful forbearance to diverse faiths. When Umar al Khattab conquered Jerusalem in 637 Christians feared for their lives, but Umar ordered protection for "their possessions, their churches and crosses."[53] Moorish Spain was far more open and tolerant than the Christian period that succeeded it. Nor is such respect for other religious traditions wholly absent from the Qur'an. At 22:40, for example, God is said to protect all "monasteries, churches, synagogues, and mosques, where God's name is much invoked."[54] It remains to be seen if current trends toward fundamentalist violence among a minority of Islamic sects in the early twentieth-first century will show themselves to be a passing phase or whether they will spread and intensify.

We have already described the history of Christianity as dominated by a defensive reaction toward the radical love gospel of Jesus. But Islam, too, has arguably stepped away from the call to unrestrained love pronounced by Jesus. If there is a major religion that could compete with Christianity for being most symptomatically tensed between an opening toward *das Ding* and defenses arrayed against it, Islam might be the most powerful contender.[55] We earlier reduced the essential teaching of Jesus to two challenging propositions:

1. God is among and between you.
2. The only law is love.

Islam tends quite powerfully to countermand both points, passionately retranscendentalizing an infinite and all-powerful divinity while emphatically expanding and intensifying the letter of the law. If Muhammad is the fourth prophet in the line extending from Abraham to Moses to Jesus, he arguably downplays the gospel of the third in favor of reinforcing the devotionist legacy of the first and the legalist tradition of the second.

Cash Is the Thing!

Ever agitated, the critic interrupts. "There's still something that bothers me about your whole approach in this book. As you admit, your treatments are almost scandalously brief, but what really troubles me is the way you reduce all religions to an opening to the real and defensive measures against that opening. Isn't that formula an oversimplification?"

There's no question that my analyses are almost ridiculously brief. At multiple points, they cry out for book-length treatments of their own. But I'll make no apology for the way those analyses are unfolded with an eye to a single schematic. The heart of my argument is the idea that religion, even allowing for its dizzying range of cultic, symbolic, moral, and social expressions, with all their complexities and differences, is at bottom a symptomatic formation centered on the relation to the unknown Thing in the Other. We have gods to help manage our fundamentally anxiety-producing relations with our fellow human beings. So, yes, I am asserting that beneath the welter of what William James called "the varieties of religious experience" we can discern an essentially bifold dynamic structured around the subject's profoundly ambivalent relation to the unknown of the neighbor-Thing.[56]

But perhaps it will help my case to clarify how that dynamic can be discerned in a last example, pertinent to the distinctive religion of industrialized modernity. Walter Benjamin did not hesitate to identify a fourth great religion of the West: free market capitalism.

> One can behold in capitalism a religion, that is to say, capitalism essentially serves to satisfy the same worries, anguish, and disquiet formerly answered by so-called religion. Capitalism is a pure religious cult, perhaps the most extreme there ever was. . . . Methodologically, [it] would be [productive] to first examine what associations money has adopted with myth in the course of history—until it could draw from Christianity enough mythical elements in order to constitute its own myth.[57]

To confirm Benjamin's thesis in the perspective we have developed, the key will be to recognize how the unique power of capitalism is based on the phantasmatic equation of money with *das Ding*. In the culture of capitalism, we can literally say, *cash is the Thing*. But how exactly? In what way does money incarnate *das Ding*? And how does that incarnation structure relations with our fellow human beings in the social (dis)order of capitalism?

It has long been recognized that money is a strange substance, in fact perhaps uniquely strange. It possesses a peculiar, contradictory status. Money appears supremely to embody the paradox of Marx's definition of the commodity as a "sensuous supra-sensuous thing" (*ein sinnlich übersinnliches Ding*).[58] On the one hand, money is wholly incidental to the things it allows its possessor to buy. It would seem to have no substantial reality of its own. And yet money is in another sense the ultimate substance, second to no other and master of them all. One indication of this strange contradiction is the fact that having wealth, far from satisfying the hunger for lucre, seems only to intensify it. As Solon had already observed in antiquity: "Of wealth, there is no limit that appears to men. For those of us who have the most wealth are eager to double it."[59]

And yet, circling around again, money and wealth continually seem to dissolve into vaporous indeterminacy. While ostensibly a mere instrument for the acquisition of other objects, money becomes a thoroughly magical substance, sucking up into itself the entire motive force of human desire. It is in the first place this uncanny indeterminacy that links money with *das Ding*. Money is at once self-externalizing, ceaselessly implicating the world over and beyond itself, but also, precisely for that power of implicating everything other than itself, money continually reanimates its own deeply mysterious character. Money seems excessive in and of itself, always and intrinsically holding in reserve an inarticulate promise of something infinitely more. As Lacan observes of these conundrums:

> Where things are more enigmatic, is when it is no longer a commodity that is at stake but the fetish par excellence of money. In that case, this thing which has no use value, which has only exchange value, what value does it preserve when it is in a safe? It is nevertheless quite clear that it is put there and that it is kept there. What is this inside that seems to make what is locked up in it completely enigmatic? Is it not in its way, with respect to what constitutes the money, is it not an inside that is altogether outside, outside of what constitutes the essence of the money?[60]

This remark strikingly dovetails with Lacan's theory of *das Ding*. The inside-outness of money foreshadows the notion of "extimacy" that Lacan associated with the Thing. Moreover, the question Lacan here poses about the enigmatic interior of the safe in which money is secreted away points suggestively to the way we are *haunted* by money, both the money belonging to Others and even our own money. Exactly like *das Ding*, money harbors something essentially unknown and inaccessible.

To these suggestive points we might add the way money is linked to the dynamic of the unknown in the Other at the primal site in which Lacan locates the upsurge of *das Ding*: the mother's constant fussing with the infant's feces. The whole process of acculturation is rooted in the drama of toilet training: the division between the proper and the improper, the clean and the dirty, the pure and the defiled, the yes of approval and the no of rejection. Money is the symptomatic intersection of the two domains, the substance that is capable of representing both. From this point of view, money emerges as an all-encompassing primal signifier, the signifier that signifies everything and nothing. Freud, too, had observed the strange all-and-nothing character of money, simultaneously the sign of supreme value and utter valuelessness. Money is always in danger of collapsing into pure waste, pure excrement. At a deep level, we are convinced that money is shit. We don't call it "filthy lucre" for nothing. This paradox of being both treasure and trash, desirable and disgusting, is somehow essential to the meaning of money.

As many commentators have suggested, this profound unconscious ambivalence toward money is at play in the ever-accelerating frenzy of consumption that fuels capitalist economies. Todd McGowan has noted with particular clarity the familiar experience of shoppers that the commodity, once bought, almost inevitably becomes strangely disappointing.[61] It is as if once money has been traded for a tangible commodity, the sublimity of money vanishes, only to be replaced by a distinct whiff of its excremental dimension. The enticingly vacant horizon of desire that the possession of money previously held open suddenly shrinks to the contour of *this mere object of purchase*. The consumer experiences the very opposite of sublimation. The object is not raised to the dignity of the Thing. On the contrary, when money has been traded for the commodity, *das Ding* is degraded to the status of a pathetic object.

Taking note of the strange deflation and disappointment that so predictably accompanies the purchase of a commodity, money steps forward as the postindustrial god who, perversely imitating a more traditional separation of the earthly and the heavenly, divides the world in a new way between the here below, defined by the objects of the marketplace, and the pure, truly transporting light of the divine above, which reposes in pure capital. Yet the preceding points, valid though they may be, do not yet allow us to glimpse the most important function of money as the lifeblood of capitalism. That function resides in the power of money as a *social atomizer*.

Turning to this crucial effect of money as social separator, we need to resist the first and most obvious picture of wealth and poverty as forming the crudest partition of class identity. Of course, it is perfectly true not only that such a partitioning exists and that the possession of money (or the illusion of that possession) is its pivotal factor. Bourgeois society has replaced the more traditional structuration of social order determined by birth and filiation with an order based on access to capital. In what follows, however, I want to argue that the even more determinative if much more hidden effect of money in capitalist society resides not in the *wealth* wielded by the owner but in the *wage contract* that binds the worker. And in making this point, we need again to resist the more obvious reading: it is not a matter of the *inequality* between the factory owner's prodigious wealth and the worker's piddling wage. The crucial factor is paradoxically a certain function of *equality* between the two. To lay out this violently counterintuitive interpretation, we will lean upon two very different points of reference: the work of David Graeber and that of Louis Althusser.

In God We Trust: To Whom (or to What) We Are Indebted

One of the core aims of David Graeber's monumental study *Debt: The First 5000 Years* is to draw on the lessons of anthropology to debunk the central article of faith among classical economic theorists, what Graeber calls "the myth of barter." That myth assumes that the most elemental economic act, perhaps the most primal human act altogether, is the exchange of objects between one person and another in the service of satisfying needs. In this view, the modern marketplace is taken to be continuous with the entire history of the human race and to be fully consistent with the inner, immutable nature of the human being. This means, among other things, that insofar as money is conceived to be merely a more convenient means of transacting exchange than trading, the myth of barter elevates money to the status of the pivotal reality of human existence. Money in some form must have always existed. In effect, when one caveman traded an extra club for another caveman's fur, the club and the fur themselves merely acted in the place of money.

What the myth of barter misses is the distinction between the market economy, modeled on barter-exchange, and what Graeber calls the human economy, which is something else altogether. Graeber lays out the majority judgment of anthropologists that most of the history of exchange among human beings, however connected to the fulfillment of bodily needs, was even more deeply motivated by the service of kinship, status, and prestige. Relations between people didn't exist to make exchange possible but rather the other way round. Exchanges served the end of defining and regulating human relations. The primordial interhuman act was neither a *trade* nor a *purchase* but a *gift*.

Consider the difference. In the market economy of trade or purchase—either the barter of one object for another or the purchase in which a certain sum of money stands in for a bartered object—the deal is closed when the exchange is complete. This for that. Both parties are free to go home and think no more about it. In the human economy, by contrast, accepting a gift, far from being the end of things, opens up a whole range of future obligations, all accompanied by special worries and uncertainties. From whom was the gift received? And in consideration of their status in the group, what sort of gift in return would be appropriate? To give a corresponding gift of lesser value might be an insult, but then again a gift of greater value might insult even more, as if the intention of the gift in return aimed to one-up the generosity of the original giver with something more extravagant. And *when* exactly should a return gift be offered? In waiting too long one might appear ungrateful or even dismissive. Yet to give something too quickly might seem disrespectful in a different way, as if the receiver were motivated by a wish to prematurely shed the posture of humble appreciation.

The upshot, argued for by Graeber in examples from a wide range of cultures, is that the human economy is a grand game of social status in which the circuit of gift exchanges cements the bonds between people in a community. Of crucial importance is the way such exchanges, far from being limited to a momentary tit-for-tat, entwine giver and receiver in a drawn-out dance of recognition and respect.

But we now come to the crucial point for our purposes, a point only implicitly articulated by Graeber's analysis. Across the web of reciprocating exchange, the life of the human economy continually reenlisted people in worrying about the other persons to whom they found themselves indebted. The receipt of gifts always entangled recipients in considerations of social status but also of the whole subjective life of the giver, not only of their basic needs but also their vaguer intentions, hopes, fears, sources of pride and shame, occasions of joy and sorrow, and so on. Human economies were webs of indebtedness, everywhere inflected by subtle concerns of relationship to Others, sensitively attuned to what could be supposed about their social position and expectations. Translated into the theoretical frame we have relied upon in this book, human economies functioned to enlist all members of a community in ceaseless awareness of the inner life of Others. The human economy of "primitive" societies was a kind of never-ending chess game with *das Ding*.

"But wait," says the critic. "You're now claiming that prehistoric cultures were ceaselessly devoted to second-guessing the feelings and intentions of the Other in some subtle game of gift giving. Doesn't this argument ignore the Other-Thing as the primal source of anxiety and contradict your emphasis on the need for psychic defense against it?"

The question gives me the occasion to repeat a crucial clarification relevant to my whole outlook in this book. When Lacan places *das Ding* at the center of gravity of the unconscious, girded around in all directions by various repressions and symptoms, the conclusion to be drawn is not that *das Ding* is everywhere completely avoided and repressed, that we try never to think about it. It would be closer to the truth to say that *we think of little else*. What we have in Graeber's human economy is a whole cultural order in which the carefully deliberated practices of gift giving and exchange continually reengaged each individual in an unending entanglement of concern for everyone else's hidden thoughts and feelings. Poker does the same thing in a more focused way. As every decent player knows, the game of poker depends not on the cards you are dealt but on the success of your attempts to guess your opponents' perceptions and intentions. The famous poker "tell" is the trivial tic or detail in the Other that gives those perceptions or intentions away.

This clarification opens the way to our main point. Where Graeber's human economy continually required engagement with the unknown desire of the Other, the market economy tends to excuse us from having to deal with it. Particularly in modern markets in which prices are standardized, the reliance on money to manage the exchange of goods exempts the participants on both sides from having to otherwise deal with one another. One need not wonder about the status, motives, or character of the Other, but simply to ask oneself whether the price is right. We are thus led to ask whether, in modern market economies, the role of the unknown Thing in the Other has been displaced, or perhaps even subsumed, by money itself.

Producing the Subjects of Ideology

If Graeber's work alerts us to a fundamental shift in human relations that accompanies a money-driven economy, we can draw on the thought of Louis Althusser for a clue to filling out the picture. In what is probably his best-known work, "Ideology and Ideological State Apparatuses," Althusser augments the basic Marxist understanding of ideology and how it works to sustain the ruling order. His first move is to double down on Marx's materialist assumption, in the perspective of which ideology always follows as a consequence, a mere "superstructure" of the material base. "Life, as Marx wrote, "is not determined by consciousness, but consciousness by life."[62] Althusser's innovation is to identify, in parallel with state apparatuses of control and repression (principally the army and the police), what he calls ideological state apparatuses (like churches and schools), which solidify the power of the state not by physical force but by cultivation and manipulation of consciousness. And yet, while aiming to affect formations of consciousness, such ISAs remain fully material inasmuch as they are undergirded by practices. "Ideology," as Althusser says, "always exists in an apparatus, and its practice, or practices. This existence is material."[63] He compares the basic idea to the advice of Pascal: "Kneel down, move your lips in prayer, and you will believe."[64]

Having sketched this picture of the fully material scaffold of ISAs that form and control consciousness in accordance with the interests of the state, Althusser then raises a question about how exactly particular individuals get truly inscribed in such ideological formations. His answer is that they must undergo "interpellation," by which he means that they must come to understand themselves as somehow directly addressed by the compelling force of ideology. Mere individuals, Althusser insists, must become *subjects* of ideology, actively and personally involved with it. As Althusser puts it, "Ideology 'acts' or 'functions' in such a way that it 'recruits' subjects among the individuals (it recruits them all), or 'transforms' individuals into subjects (it transforms them all) by that very operation which I have called interpellation or hailing, and which can be imagined along the lines of the most commonplace everyday police (or other) hailing: 'Hey, you there!'"[65] Althusser insists that such "hailing" is indispensable to the functioning of ideology. In fact, he claims that "the existence of ideology and the hailing or interpellation of individuals as subjects are one and the same thing."[66] Ideology must enlist the individual in its demand for conformity of thought and action in such a way that individuals feel that their own being is at stake and their own active participation is called for. It is by such interpellating recruitment that the individual becomes a willing actor in furthering the aims of the ideology. The subject henceforth heartily *volunteers* for duty. The Lacanian background of Althusser's idea here becomes evident when he asserts, with special emphasis, that the process of interpellation enlists subjects in *the imaginary*. Interpellation is the means for the production of self-conforming *egos*.

So what does interpellation look like in practice? Reminding us that "the formal structure of ideology is always the same," Althusser turns to "a single example, one accessible to everyone, that of religious ideology"—specifically, Christian religious ideology. "It says: This is who you are: you are Peter! This is your origin, you were created by God for all eternity, although you were born in the 1920th year of Our Lord! This is your place in the world! This is what you must do! By these means, if you observe the 'law of love' you will be saved, Peter, and will become part of the Glorious Body of Christ! Etc."[67] To this baseline of address to the individual, singling him or her out for divine election, Althusser notes the crucial factor of God's presentation as an *Other Subject*, a kind of duplication of the subject who is interpellated. Thus "the interpellation of individuals as subjects presupposes the 'existence' of a Unique and central Other Subject, in whose Name the religious ideology interpellates all individuals as subjects."[68] This view resonates with our earlier discussion of the way personification tends to yield a symbolic big Other as guarantor of meaning, along with master signifiers that anchor imaginary identities defined within that universe of meaning. Althusser puts special emphasis on this imaginary character.

> We observe that the structure of all ideology, interpellating individual as subject in the name of a Unique and Absolute Subject is *speculary*, i.e. a mirror-structure, and *doubly* speculary: this mirror duplication is constitutive of ideology and ensures its functioning. Which means that all ideology is *centred*, that the Absolute Subject occupies the unique place of the Centre, and interpellates around it the infinity of individuals into subjects in a double mirror-connexion such that it *subjects* the subjects to the Subject.[69]

It would be easy at this point to lose ourselves in the obvious resonances of this theory with various details of religious tradition, say, of Abram's encounter with Yahweh that leads to his transformation into Abraham, of Moses's exchange with the voice from the burning bush, of the age-old metaphor of religiosity as a matter of *vocation* or *calling*, of the human being created in the *image* of God, and so on. But I will leave that temptation aside in service of a larger objective. Crucial for our purposes at the moment is to step back in some astonishment that the only example of ideological interpellation Althusser offers is drawn from the Christian religion. He focuses, that is, on the ideology of medieval feudalism. The question immediately arises: how might Althusser's account of interpellation apply to the bourgeois epoch of modern capitalism? What is the interpellating agency in our contemporary context? Althusser doesn't provide one. To which my answer is that the omnipotent recruiter, the veritable God that accomplishes interpellation in contemporary society, is *money*.

The Money God

Put in a single word, the ideological framework of modern bourgeois culture is provided by the Enlightenment, the eighteenth-century affirmation of freedom, equality, individualism, reason, progress, and science. There is, of course, something deeply paradoxical about the fact that the ideological alibi for capitalism, a system founded upon exploitation and productive of massive inequality, is provided by the values of freedom and democracy, the ideals of the great modern revolutions of liberation. Yet that very paradox makes the distorting mirror of capitalist ideology all the more effective. Who would suspect that one of the greatest enemies of freedom might reside in the ideal of freedom itself? To see the paradox at work, consider this excerpt from the presidential inauguration speech of George H. W. Bush, delivered in 1989 against the backdrop of the declining power of the Soviet Union under Mikhail Gorbachev:

> The totalitarian era is passing, its old ideas blown away like leaves from an ancient, lifeless tree. A new breeze is blowing, and a nation refreshed by freedom stands ready to push on. . . . We know what works: Freedom works. We know what's right: Freedom is right. We know how to secure a more just and prosperous life for man on earth: through free markets, free speech, free elections, and the exercise of free will unhampered by the state. For the first time in this century, for the first time in perhaps all history, man does not have to invent a system by which to live. We don't have to talk late into the night about which form of government is better. We don't have to wrest justice from the kings. We only have to summon it from within ourselves.[70]

The fundamental axis traced by Bush's speech is the opposition between governmental regulation of economy and society, here simply branded "totalitarianism," and free markets "unhampered by the state." The choice between the two, Bush proclaims, has been conclusively settled by history. No longer is debate about the road to the good life necessary. "We know what works: Freedom works." But it is no accident that the first form of freedom mentioned is that of *free markets*. The really crucial freedom at stake is the freedom of capital itself, which means freedom for private enterprises to operate for maximum profit unrestricted by regulation or taxation enacted in the interest of the public good.

Here we arrive at the crux of the issue. The basic ideological swindle of the capitalist epoch—the championing of individual freedoms that actually ends up disadvantaging the majority of individuals—works so effectively because appeal to the ideal of freedom registers with voters on the level of what they imagine to be their own individual liberties. The rhetoric of freedom repeatedly calls up the repulsive specter of an intrusive governmental Big Brother. But the ideological lure here effects a kind of bait and switch. The average Joe may bristle at the infringement of freedom by imagining the curtailment of his own enjoyments, but the real rubber hits the road elsewhere: protecting the freedom of investors to pursue profit without constraints imposed upon them in the public interest.

The same ideologically induced confusion operates in rhetoric about equality. The majority of Americans will vigorously defend the notion of everyone being treated equally. The very phrase "special interests" tends to rankle left- and right-leaning minds alike. But how many voters, adamant about the value of equal treatment, stop to consider the massively unequal distribution of wealth and privilege that has always divided the body politic and tends overwhelmingly to reproduce itself from generation to generation? To ignore such preexisting differences—differences that advantage the rich kid and hamstring the poor from cradle to grave—is to make a mockery of the ideal of equality. A related example is the way the so-called flat tax favored by conservatives is sometimes touted as merely a "fair tax," as if asking the single mom living at the poverty line to pay the same percentage as the billionaire aboard his megayacht is simply a matter of equal treatment.

Appeals to the value of individualism, especially when it comes to individual initiative and responsibility, also function ideologically. We're led to accept the false premise that everyone is equally well equipped to assume such initiative and responsibility. Yet the effect is even more pernicious at a more general level, as celebrating individualism tends to obscure the ways individuals are inseparable from the larger communities of which they are a part. Moreover, singing the praises of individualism inclines us toward forgetting about the ways collective action and socially affirmative public policy—the very opposite of go-it-alone individualism—may be crucial parts of what enables individuals to realize themselves as individuals.

The point of rehearsing these few examples of ideologically distorted consciousness in our time is to pose a larger question that reaches over and beyond them. Where in all this is the necessity of interpellation? Aren't the sorts of confusions and bait-and-switch appeals that we just sketched sufficient to provide the existing order with its enabling ideological fig leaves? Where, and *why*, would an Althusserian operation of interpellation need to play a role? The question is all the more vexing as Althusser's own example, appealing as it does to the classical big Other of the Christian God, seems more or less irrelevant in the contemporary context. The whole tenor of postmodern life tends to obviate that sort of big Other. In the present age, we live in the twilight of master signifiers.[71]

The answer is that the ideological constellation of freedom, equality, and individualism *is* in fact undergirded and reinforced by a powerful form of interpellation, though in a form very different from the one imagined in Althusser's example. On this point, we have to say, Althusser misses his own train. The interpellating agency of modern society is the ubiquitous power of money. Money is the force that interpellates subjects, though unlike Althusser's own example, it does so anonymously, precisely by *not* directly addressing them. There is no need to call or hail subjects to assume their responsibility in obeisance to an Ultimate Subject. On the contrary, money interpellates all of us, soliciting us all as an aggregate of supposedly free and independent individuals in the capitalist marketplace, which appears less as a prison house of obedience than a wonderland of earthly delights. This interpellation into freedom is all the more effective as it tends to conceal from those it interpellates the wretched unfreedom that is in fact their lot.

Capitalist interpellation is effected by *the implicit meaning of the wage contract*. To see how, we have to take a crucial step beyond the familiar notion that workers under capitalism are human beings turned into mere objects, a central point in Marx's analysis. Especially in the 1844 manuscripts, Marx emphasizes the way the worker becomes just another part of the industrial machine. The basic idea is far from being wholly false. Workers everywhere are routinely objectified and mechanized in various ways. Nevertheless, we need to see that the wage contract produces not objects but *subjects*. It does so for the simple reason that workers who accept the wage contract implicitly authorize themselves as free, choosing agents. Of course, the "freedom" implied by the wage contract is far from being real freedom. On the contrary, the wage that is "freely" agreed upon is not only completely consistent with reduction of the worker to the status of an object but redoubles the burden of the worker's alienation. The injury of selling one's labor power for a wage, a wage inevitably smaller than the total value that labor produces, is augmented by the insult of the assumption that one does it voluntarily. By accepting the wage contract, workers implicitly constitute themselves as free agents.

We now come to the strangest and most important feature of the uniquely capitalist mode of interpellation effected by the exchange of money. The most important addressee of interpellation is not the worker but the members of the larger community. Few workers mistake themselves for freely choosing actors. It is *the rest of us* who are lured to make that mistake. The worker's voluntary acceptance of the wage contract is merely *supposed by everyone else*. On the model of the Lacanian analyst as the subject supposed to know, the capitalist employee is *the subject supposed to consent*. The assumption is that every worker is a subject *who freely signs on for the job*.

It is at this point that we recover Althusser's central insight about interpellation rendering individuals as subjects, though with a crucial difference. In Althusser's Christianized example, subjectivizing interpellation yields the subject's realization *"Yes, it really is me!"*[72] The aim of the religious calling is to enlist solitary subjects in the commitment of faith. By contrast, the capitalist interpellation achieved by the wage contract is not really aimed at the worker at all but rather at the larger community. The anonymous interpellating effect of money draws everyone into its thrall. Money interpellates *all of us* in implicit support for the essential capitalist ideology insofar as it enlists all of us in believing in the free autonomy of every subject. It is this belief that is the sine qua non of capitalist society. Such is the foundational illusion of modern democracy: all individuals are on their own, responsible for themselves. The result is that the social body is thoroughly atomized. By this means, the only truly effective counterweight to the self-serving dominance of capital—self-conscious collective action in the spirit of solidarity—is rendered moot from the get-go.

Money is the magic substance that interpellates every member of capitalist society. And in that system, money really does become a kind of god, though a god that is unmistakably different from the traditional one. The first difference is that money is a completely anonymous, faceless, utterly impersonal god. It is a god who doesn't speak—indeed, who need not speak. The reason is grounded in another crucial difference from the traditional God featured in Althusser's paradigmatic example. If money acts as a new god, it is the first god in history that is not regarded with fear. Relation with every other god came at the price of sacrifice, obedience, and courage in faith. Even the god of love propounded by Jesus aroused the fear of living up to the extraordinary demand of unrestrainedly loving even one's enemy. Yet the only fear relevant to money is the fear of being without it. Money is an object not of fear but of unlimited, covetous desire. Like all gods, money is an incarnation of something unknown, but in the case of money, as with no other god, the void of the unknown is completely colonized by lust.

What makes us available to be interpellated by money is *our own desire for it.* This is the unique aspect of money's role as a stand-in for *das Ding.* Our assumption that agreeing to work for a given quantity of money is a free choice by a self-determining subject is ultimately grounded in our own relation to money. In the thrall of our desire for money, it is almost impossible for us to understand acceptance of money in payment for work performed as anything but the voluntary choice of a free subject. After all, don't we ourselves do things in exchange for money that we don't really want to do?

As a consequence, the interpellating power of money does not require issuing a threatening, imperious command. In the case of money, itself the very materialization of desire, we have always already signed up to be commanded. Money interpellates us by the force of its own intrinsic desirability.

A central thesis of Georg Simmel's classic study, *The Philosophy of Money,* is that money functions as a connector between people. Money is the interstitial tissue that binds communities together in networks of trustworthy yet fluid exchange. Though Simmel surely has a point, the conclusion of our examination here is more nearly the opposite. Money is the great separator, and not merely because wealth in capitalist societies tends overwhelmingly to be accumulated by the few. Money separates not only along the lines of actual ownership but also by reinforcing the sense that we are all separate entities. Money is the great atomizer. In the society mediated by money, there is no integrated whole. No whole, that is, but the free market economy in which we are all supposed to be separate, self-determining entities.

On the side of their defensive function, virtually all conventional gods provide some safe distance from our fellow human beings. Gods triangulate our relation with Others by taking up into divinity itself the anxious potential of *das Ding*. In this sense, money is the most powerful god that has ever existed. It assumes the position of an overmastering force whose power transcends the world of finite objects by virtue of its capacity to *buy* them. Moreover, money succeeds in individuating the mass of persons, establishing to an unprecedented degree the rule of "to each its own." Isolation is the flip side of the blessing of freedom, at least when freedom is understood in its crudest, most individualistic sense.

The money god is thus a perfect anti-Christ. It divides and insistently individuates where Jesus called upon his followers to join together in heartful, loving solidarity. Indeed, the analysis just pursued about the ideological power of money raises from a new angle the question of Jesus's marked antipathy toward lucre. We're led to wonder whether, when Jesus overturned the tables of the money changers in the temple, he wasn't reacting to the way money both separates us from Others and continually motivates us to chase private satisfactions to be enjoyed by ourselves alone. The itinerate preacher from Nazareth precociously sensed that money incarnated the very antithesis of his own vision of finding God in and through embracing the Other in love.

8

Conclusions

> Among the modes at man's disposal for posing the question
> of his existence in the world, and beyond, religion, as a mode
> of subsistence of the subject who interrogates himself, is to be
> distinguished by a dimension that is proper to it, and which is
> struck by a kind of oblivion.
> —Jacques Lacan

Our discussions have increasingly focused on the defensive role of religion. Yet the larger aim of this book is to make the opposite point, audible in an often-proposed etymology of the word "religion" as *re-ligare*. From a Lacanian standpoint, religion is indeed a relinking—a relinking above all to the unknown Other-Thing. For Lacan, that linkage is the core challenge of human existence. Beneath the defensive tendency that almost always accompanies it, the experience of the sacred is centered on a locus of the enigmatic real that is primordially encountered in the fellow human being.[1]

The distance between Freud and Lacan concerning religion reflects the two sides of that divide. Freud focused almost exclusively on the defensive, essentially repressive dimension. Lacan, by contrast, is most concerned with the engagement with the unknowable real that kicks those defenses into motion. For Lacan, as for Rudolf Otto, the religious sensibility is oriented toward a *mysterium tremendum*, though with the crucial qualification that the mystery involved is less about the celestial orbs whirling above our heads than about our tense relations with the human Other who is sitting beside us.

The upshot is that human desire is a ceaseless orbit around an anxious vortex of something incomprehensible. Yet the human subject also remains positively and ineluctably *attracted* to that locus of unknowing. Once this point is properly appreciated, both Freud and Lacan can be seen, from different standpoints, to critique the reassuring certainties of religious belief in favor of a broader embrace of unknowing. Among the more positive takeaways of this perspective is that it becomes possible to see how, at the most elemental level, we all worship the same Thing. Or rather, the same No-thing.

We are left to wonder whether or to what extent religion might someday be able to accept more consciously and deliberately its own internal conflict. Is it possible for a religion of the future to own up more robustly to its core engagement with unknowing? Perhaps we already glimpse something of that movement in current New Age and spiritualist trends. Though even if that is so—indeed, precisely if that is so—the future of religion immediately faces another sticky question: will it be possible for religious communities to reengage unknowing without reinforcing one or another simple-minded rejection of science? Here again, we rejoin one of Freud's greatest fears, that of the religious embrace of willfully blind, antiscientific ignorance.

I will not attempt answers to these questions. My aim in this book has been to sketch an account of the religious that allows them to be asked in a new way. In that spirit of merely framing the questions, let us conclude with a few final, open-ended notes.

Rethinking the Foundations of Psychoanalytic Theory

A Lacanian interpretation of religion recasts the fundamental premises of Freud's theory of the unconscious. We recognize one of the primary stakes of that reconceptualization when we return to Freud's famous exchange with Romain Rolland about Freud's reduction of the religious to a wish-fulfilling illusion. Had he not missed an alternative reading, centered on an "oceanic feeling" of oneness with everything?[2] After rather glibly dismissing the idea as foreign to his own experience, Freud doubles down on the father's role in the Oedipus complex. In doing so, despite acknowledging that Rolland's "oceanic feeling" could be read psychoanalytically as a vestige of the infant's original fusion with the mother, Freud fails to consider the possibility that the two dimensions—an oceanic fusion with the maternal, on the one side, and the paternal law of separation, on the other—might be connected.

From the standpoint of the Lacanian Thing, the connection becomes unmistakable. At stake is the pivot of Lacan's whole notion of the paternal metaphor and the inner meaning of his dictum about human desire as the desire of the Other. The ego and the outside world—including above all the figure of the mother—are originally undifferentiated. For the first months of its life, the infant doesn't distinguish its own body from that of the mother. It is only later, Freud says, that "the ego detaches itself from the external world."[3] For Lacan, that detachment is motivated by the infant's increasingly anxious awareness of something unknown in the maternal Other. To assuage that emerging anxiety the child turns to the third position of the father, along with the whole machinery of the signifier that elaborates it.

On the basis of this unfolding of the paternal metaphor we might venture a division of the religious phenomenon between a maternal dimension (based on an original but problematic fusion) and a paternal counterpart (the deployment of a defensive architecture of separation). The first corresponds to the sense of communion with the maternal embrace—Rolland's "oceanic feeling"—that becomes destabilized by the experience of the uncognized dimension of the Other's desire, the specter of *das Ding*. The second valence aligns with the more familiar Freudian image of the stern father-god who prohibits a regression to an oceanic fusion with the maternal. In one way or another, virtually all religions are uncomfortably stretched between these two poles of symptomatic tension.

This account finds some suggestive confirmation relevant to the Christian tradition in the twentieth-century discovery of the Nag Hammadi Codex, a trove of radically alternative gospels dating to the third and fourth centuries.[4] At least some of the Nag Hammadi texts are conspicuous for their emphasis on the primally feminine character of divinity. An especially striking example can be found in the text titled "Thunder, Perfect Mind." In that alternative gospel, the rolling din of thunder, consistently associated by Greeks, Jews, and most Christians with a masculine deity, is understood as the voice of a distinctly feminine power. That female force is presented as the most absolutely elemental power of divinity. In the "Thunder" text, it is as if the maternal Thing speaks for itself, or rather, herself.

> I am the first and the last.
> I am the one who is honored, and the one scorned;
> I am the whore and the holy one . . .
> I am the incomprehensible silence,
> and . . . the voice of many sounds, the word in many forms;
> I am the utterance of my name . . .
> Do not cast anyone out, or turn anyone away . . .
> I am the one who remains, and the one who dissolves;
> I am she who exists in all fear,
> and strength in trembling.

I am she who cries out . . .
I am cast forth on the face of the earth . . .
I am the sister of my husband,
and he is my offspring . . .
but he is the one who gave birth to me . . .
I am the incomprehensible silence
and the thought often remembered . . .
I am the one who has been hated everywhere,
and who has been loved everywhere.
I am the one they call Life, and you have called Death.
I am the one whose image is great in Egypt,
and the one who has no image among the barbarians . . .
I prepare the bread and my mind within;
I am the knowing of my name.
I am the thought that lives in the light.
I live in everyone, and I delve into them all . . .
I move in every creature. . . .
I am the invisible one in all beings . . .
I am a voice speaking softly . . .
I am the real voice . . the voice from the invisible thought . . .
It is a mystery . . . I cry out in everyone . . .
I hid myself in everyone, and revealed myself within them,
and every mind seeking me longs for me . . .
I am she who gradually brought forth everything . . .
I am the image of the invisible spirit . . .
The mother, the light . . the virgin . . the womb, and the voice . .
I put breath within all things.[5]

Sex and the Sacred

Rolland's challenge to Freud hints at the profound and enduring role of
the maternal Other in the unconscious. The astonishing "Thunder" codex gives it voice. The implication for our inquiry is that the bifold, symptomatic structure underlying the religious phenomenon is profoundly
aligned with sexual difference. That linkage becomes more interesting
when we remember how often the ancients identified the origin and
order of the universe with sexual difference and sexed reproduction. The
aboriginal mind, it seems, could not resist conflating *cosmos* with *coitus*.
But the connection becomes most suggestive when we remind ourselves
of the way gender plays such a central and sensitive role in the major-

ity of religious traditions. Devotional traditions throughout history and around the globe typically subject women to restrictions and prohibitions from which men are exempt. The litany is familiar: women cannot become priests or officiate at services, they must be concealed beneath veils or full-length robes, they cannot enter the sanctuary or must sit in designated places, when menstruating they must be banished altogether, they must give up their name and their property when married, they must walk a discreet distance behind their husbands, and so on and so forth.

But how to further clarify this sacralizing of sexual prejudice? Among the most important and influential features of Lacan's late teaching are his formulas of sexuation, his gloss on Freud's famous question "What does a woman want?" Lacan's scheme is based on two modes of relating to the universal. The masculine position defines the universal by reference to the exception. As Freud's formulation put it, all men are subject to castration only because one man, the primal father, wasn't. For the masculine subject, the law is founded upon the point of its transgression. The masculine structure thus tends to be oriented toward prohibition, on the one hand, and the fantasy of violation, on the other. The feminine position, by contrast, asserts the totality of the universal without reference to the exception, but with the crucial proviso that the whole is internally incomplete, or non-all (*pas-tout*).[6] As non-all, being itself is excessive, in itself more than itself. The real is the ontological exception of Being to itself.

Lacan relies on these two options—what might be called external exception versus internal excess—to posit two forms of enjoyment, so-called phallic *jouissance* versus a feminine *jouissance* that Lacan calls the "*jouissance* of the Other." Put in crude terms, and those relevant only to sexual desire, Lacan's view helps explain why masculine desire is so typically aroused by a fetishistic focus on part objects, a tendency to immerse itself in the brute details of the sex act, while the feminine subject tends to remain more attuned to the larger context and situation, sensitive to the whole milieu of seduction and relationship. On the basis of this and other structural differences, Lacan posits an irresolvable antagonism between the sexes, tersely expressed in his dictum: *Il n'y a pas de rapport sexuel*, "There is no sexual relation."

Lacan's formulas of sexuation shed new light on the larger thesis of this book. If religious life is tensed by a symptomatic conflict between an opening upon the real of *das Ding* and various imaginary or symbolic strategies of defense against that opening, it now becomes possible to assert that the two sides of the tension are deeply gender-relative. Lacan's notion of the feminine non-all can be read as a gender-linked update of his earlier concept of *das Ding*. The Thing is the internal excess, the uncanny leftover. Moreover, the Thing is expressly identified with the *jouissance* of the Other. The masculine logic of exception then appears as essentially defensive, in fact, as the very paradigm of symptomatic defense.[7] As Lacan says of it, "*Jouissance*, qua sexual, is phallic—in other words, it is not related to the Other as such." As we saw in our examination of the appeal to the big Other in the dynamics of perversion, the game of transgression is at every point dependent upon some prior assertion of the law. In posing himself as the dutiful servant of the big Other, the pervert merely *appears* to violate the existing order. He has only to insert himself into that order, making of himself and his own act the exception that proves the rule.

The logics of the "exception" and the "non-all" that inform the dichotomy between phallic and feminine *jouissance* can be seen to inhabit Christianity in a particularly striking way, not because Christianity is to be linked to one side or the other but rather precisely because of the way it uncomfortably straddles the two. The reason is that the figure of Christ himself is deeply ambiguous. From one point of view, Christ can be taken to stand for the ultimate exception, the perfected human subject by whose measure all others are to be judged. The Pauline interpretation depends upon identifying Christ as this exception. The Christ exception stabilizes the law—not, to be sure, by the negative measure of transgression, but rather by offering an impossible exemplar of moral perfection. Of course, this inversion of the role of the exception from its more familiar form of violation or transgression is anything but trivial. It is by means of that inversion that Christianity achieves the universalization of moral failure, establishing a democracy of sin. Compared with the Lamb of God, we are all tainted. It is also by this means, as Nietzsche recognized, that Christianity brings to completion the Judaic invention of bad conscience.[8] Mindful of Christ's perfection, we are all condemned to ceaseless self-recrimination. Nevertheless, the logical form of the relation between the universal and the exception is precisely that described by the masculine formula of sexuation.

According to this first reading, Christianity repeats a traditional assertion of God as furnishing a master signifier. The organization of the church as a hierarchy of authority that defends doctrinal orthodoxy follows with perfect consistency. The sign of the cross becomes the signifier of an impossible exception that establishes the law before which we must all genuflect.

And yet, a second point of view leads us to an opposite conclusion, as Christ can also be taken to instantiate the ultimate denial of all exception. The figure of Jesus inaugurates a new and unprecedented universalism based on his identifying the divine with the love relation between human beings. Said otherwise, he affirms the non-all of humanity, its own constitutive excess. What makes this second view distinct from the first is the way it unfolds the full implications of the Christian notion that every human being is inhabited by infinity. The radical equality of all persons is less a matter of the sinfulness of every human being than of the fact that every human incarnates something of the divine. This new assertion of the universal, asserting the sublime unity of the divine and the human alluded to by the mystics, is to be aligned with Lacan's logic of the feminine. Christ becomes what is "in me more than me," a tincture of the divine. Paradoxically, what makes us all human is less a limitation than a kind of constitutive excess.

Jesus's injunction to embrace the enemy as the friend is the perfect embodiment of the feminine logic of the non-all. The force of that injunction faces us with an intrinsically excessive demand, a demand to extend oneself into a zone of surplus, to forgive what is excessive in the Other and in oneself. Perhaps it is on this basis that Lacan intimately links the divine with the feminine. "Why not interpret one face of the Other, the God face, as based on feminine *jouissance*," he asks. "It is in the opaque place of *jouissance* of the Other, of this Other insofar as woman, if she existed, could be it, that the Supreme Being is situated."[9]

It is also in the context of this discussion that we can make sense of Lacan's evocation of a God who doesn't know. On the side of Christian doctrine that links Christ with the masculine logic of exception, God remains omniscient. God is fully *sujet supposé savoir*. "God only knows," as the familiar saying puts it. Christ's crucifixion was all part of the divine plan, foreordained from eternity. But according to a more radical notion of incarnation, the suffering God is identified with all who suffer, and Christianity marks an opening upon the feminine logic of excess, an Other *jouissance* that is not knowable.[10] The big Other is no longer identifiable with a subject supposed to know, but is, on the contrary, found to be inhabited by an irradicable vacuity or gap. From this point of view, Christian divinity ceases to be immutable or impassible. It is for this reason that Lacan's twentieth seminar continually flirts with the notion of an unknowing God, a suffering and kenotic being whose majesty consists precisely in a sublime form of weakness. Lacan thus risks a radical reassessment of divinity, provoking us with the conclusion that "one can no longer hate God if he himself knows nothing."[11] As Slavoj Žižek has argued, this assertion of a God who does not know can be seen as a necessary correlate of identifying God with love. As Žižek puts it: "Only an imperfect, lacking being loves: we love because we do *not* know everything. On the other hand, even if we were to know everything, love would still be higher than complete knowledge. Perhaps the true achievement of Christianity is to elevate a loving (imperfect) Being to the place of God."[12]

The Heart of the Matter

The critic unexpectedly breaks in a last time: "I was resolved not to make any more trouble for you, but I can't suppress a question about the larger implications of these conclusions. Does religion gain a certain legitimacy from Lacan's point of view? Is he even a strange kind of believer?"

With regard to Lacan himself, answering this question is a slippery business. He more than once affirms his atheism. Perhaps even more telling, he virtually defines the aim of psychoanalysis as a matter of coming to realize that the big Other—for which the law-giving, all-seeing God is a ready stand-in—does not exist. On the other hand, Lacan clearly regarded the religious phenomenon as an exceptionally subtle and complicated problem. Correlatively, Lacan suggests that we underestimate the staying power of God. In his twentieth seminar, he remarks about "people who complimented me for having been able to posit in one of my last seminars that God doesn't exist," to which he adds: "Obviously, they hear (*entendent*)—they hear, but alas, they understand, and what they understand is a bit precipitate. So today, I am instead going to show you in what sense the good old God exists."[13] If Lacan was an avowed atheist, there's surely room to suspect that his was a very strange species of atheism.

For what it may be worth, we might note that the Lacanian theory presented in these pages need not necessarily lead to an atheistic conclusion. While there is no positive evidence for doing so, there is also nothing whatever preventing the wholly psychological argument unfolded here from being carried over into the ontological domain. Were one inclined to draw the most extreme conclusion from the Lacanian view I have presented, the result might fairly be called the most radical possible theology. Such an extrapolation would take a quantum leap beyond the merely unknowable character of God supposed by negative theology toward identifying the divine with negativity itself. Such a leap would intersect with the most shocking conclusion of Eckhart's mystical intuition, in which the Godhead is identified with perfect Nothingness, an infinity of kenotic Non-being. There is more than one indication that Hegel agreed with such a view. On that reading, the role of the negative in Hegel's thought, what he called "the tremendous power of the negative" that underlies the dialectical interconnectedness of everything, is ultimately to be identified with what has traditionally been called God.

Yet wondering about Lacan's personal religiosity or lack of it seems to me less interesting than drawing out the implications of his theoretical stance for what Freud considered the key problem: the relation between religion and science. We can start with three key points:

1. While it doesn't wholly set aside Freud's charge of wish-fulfilling illusion, a Lacanian perspective grounds religion in something much more fundamental. To be sure, Freud's notion of wish fulfillment is much more nuanced than the banality of our ordinary conception. What Freud meant by *Wunsch* touches the most obscure depths of the human psyche. One might even say that there is room in the Freudian sense of *wishing* to accommodate everything we have compassed in this book. Nevertheless, the sense of wish fulfillment foregrounded in *The Future of an Illusion*— that of a collection of childish fictions that flatter our fondest wishes with saccharine fantasies—is certainly not the origin of the religious impulse as Lacan interprets it. On the contrary, for Lacan the reassurance of such fictions should itself be interpreted as a defense from the openness to the real that constitutes the more elemental tropism of the religious.

For Lacan, the experience of the sacred echoes what is unknown and uncanny in the Other. But on that view, religion is not a tissue of wishful fantasy that veils the terrifying depths of existence. On the contrary, the door to the religious is opened by an obscure longing for those very depths. The compulsive force of the religious urge emanates from the ecstatic core of the human being, the most primitive ground of subjectivity, which derives from the archaic experience of the Other as a perpetually unsettling enigma.

2. The religious phenomenon is tensed by powerful defenses against its own deepest motive. A key assertion of this book is that Lacan's conception of *das Ding* positions it as the originary pivot point of ambivalence. On the one hand, we are drawn to the unknown Thing. Precisely that unnerving and anxiety-producing unknown, the unthinkable *jouissance* of the Other, is what most ineluctably lures us. The religious posture is thus inseparable from longing for a destabilizing *jouissance*. Religious fervor always reaches into what is beyond the pleasure principle. The religious passion is always linked with a passion for a transcendence of self, a passion for death. But if we are attracted to that ecstatic locus, we also defend ourselves against it. The Lacanian view is thus able to explain quite precisely why the Godhead is regarded simultaneously as an object of love and fear. It also accounts for the massive symptomatic architecture that protects the religious enthusiast from too close an encounter with the dreadful Thing.

3. In light of the interpretation I've tried to articulate, the relatively simple opposition Freud posed between religion and science should be

revisited. In Freud's view, that opposition was a stand-off between the dogmatic certainty of religious faith and the resolute fallibilism of science, relying as it does on empirical evidence and probabilistic judgment. A Lacanian interpretation of the religious doesn't flatly reject that assessment. And how could it? We are daily reminded of the ways religious faith obstinately refuses scientific rationality. But it is also possible to argue that Lacan's perspective significantly qualifies the tension between religion and science, hinting at a deep point of contact between them. A relation to the Other-Thing orients the subject toward an enduring sense of something more, of an as-yet-undiscovered excess, originally encountered in the disturbingly open question of the Other's desire.

The fact that this originary sense of unknowing does not correspond to any material, substantial reality does not diminish its power over us. On the contrary, the purely supposed and virtual character of *das Ding* only increases its fascination. Lacan can be said to pose the Thing as the most elemental dimension of what Freud called psychical reality. The Thing establishes the primal field of the virtual. Said otherwise, the Thing is the empty frame of fantasy, a void that begs to be filled with content but can never be satisfied. That insistent void is active even in our experience of everyday physical objects. We cannot avoid anticipating something around the corner, something surprising, for example, that might be hidden behind the couch opposite me in the room. The cinematic evocation of this unnerving but irresistible extra, this uncanny something more, was the key to Alfred Hitchcock's genius, and may in fact be associated with the fascination of the cinematic art form in general. The same profound dynamic animates the wide-eyed wonder of the kid on Christmas morning. What will I find in my stocking? What lies inside that wrapped and ribboned box beneath the tree? What else might Santa have left? And who or what is Santa anyway?

The crucial point comes into view when we realize that the religious impulse to bow toward the locus of the unknown, to venerate in some way what is essentially beyond our comprehension, far from being flatly inimical to the scientific standpoint, must at some point be coincident with it. For Lacan, the ineluctable opacity of the unknown Thing is the invisible, ecstatic pole of the entire structure of subjectivity. On this basis, it is possible to glimpse how religion and science might both be taken to be forms of devotion to *das Ding*. Both dedicate themselves to the shifting horizon of the unknown. Perhaps the difference consists merely in the different forms those devotions assume.

Or is it rather the differing forms of *defense* against what is unknown that most distinguishes religion from science? I break off these discussions with this question: Do religion and science both center upon the unknown Thing but inoculate themselves against its destabilizing potential by different means?[14] We have already surveyed a range of ways by which the religious posture insulates itself from its own proximity to the real. In Greek paganism, it wraps the real in myth and invites the subject to inscribe its acts in the imaginary register of the mythic mise-en-scène. In Judaism, it weaves the real into the warp and woof of the covenantal law, opening the meaning of the law to ceaseless reexamination. In Christianity and Islam, it reassures itself against what is threateningly excessive in the demand for love primarily by relying on the stabilizing trellis of orthodoxy.

At least on first look, the scientist appears by contrast to be the true hero of the real, intrepidly facing the traumatic force of the questionable. Let there be no excuses, no shielding ourselves from the hard lessons of truth! Yet science, too, deploys very effective means of psychical defense. They consist primarily of strict adherence to empirical method and mathematical calculation, both of which provide means for sidestepping the specifically *subjective* position of the investigator. The scientist always works from the safe side of observation, in which the personal stakes of encounter are neutered in favor of a purely "objective" standpoint. The scientific ideal of experimental repeatability assumes the anonymous, indifferent character of the observer while at the same time being fortified by procedures of abstract calculation, mediated by the cold logic of mathematical quantification. We here reencounter Heidegger's critique of modern natural science as "enframing" our relation to Nature, and of domesticating a wilder, potentially traumatic Otherness of existence by means of "calculative thinking."[15] Science, as Heidegger put it, "wants to know nothing of the nothing."[16]

The upshot of these final reflections is to challenge us anew with our relation to unknowing, the question of our openness to something abyssal. In an extraordinary two-page essay titled "The Last Chapter in the History of the World," Giorgio Agamben adumbrates an unheard-of art of unknowing. "It is possible," he proposes, "that the way in which we are able to be ignorant is precisely what defines the rank of what we are able to know and that the articulation of a zone of nonknowledge is the condition—and at the same time the touchstone—of all our knowledge."[17]

Agamben's suggestion inevitably recalls the figure of Socrates, who, unmentioned in the text, surely haunts its every word. For Agamben, the question is one of "maintaining oneself in the right relationship with ignorance, allowing an absence of knowledge to guide and accompany our gestures, letting a stubborn silence clearly respond for our words." The aim of such an art is to awaken and cultivate a positive, active, and engaged sense of what remains beyond knowing. "While humans have reflected for centuries on how to preserve, improve, and ensure their knowledge," Agamben remarks, "we lack even the elementary principles of an art of ignorance. . . . The art of living is, in this sense, the capacity to keep ourselves in harmonious relationship with that which escapes us."

Surely Agamben is right that such an art of unknowing remains largely undreamed of, maybe especially in our contemporary culture of calculation and control. Yet can we not say that Jacques Lacan dedicated his entire career to imagining the elements of such an art? In the light of the Lacanian notion of *das Ding*, we can put the point more clearly. If, as we have suggested, the Jesus event consisted in identifying the divine with an open-armed acceptance of what is anxiously unknown in our fellow human beings, it might with some fairness be said that it waited twenty centuries for another lonely pioneer to advocate a similarly unrestrained opening of oneself to what is alien and threatening in the Other. That man was another Jew, an Austrian neuroanatomist named Sigmund Freud. The attentive openness to the unknown that he recommended— the unknown in the Other and in oneself—was the talking cure of psychoanalysis. The great contribution of Lacan was to reinvigorate that talking cure by radicalizing and renuancing the subject's sense of being unknown to itself.

Perhaps the great question of the future, a question that should be asked as much of science as of religion, will concern our capacity to own more responsibly such a relation to the unknown, perhaps in wholly new ways. Will we manage to preserve psychoanalysis from being swept aside, either, as Lacan predicted it might be, by the proliferation of religious "meaning" or by more "scientific" modes of treatment? Or might we even succeed in evolving richer and more transformative arts of unknowing than that of the Freudian cure? The question at stake will be the degree to which we might someday more honestly, more soulfully, more courageously, more seriously *and* more playfully, accept the depths of unknowing that perpetually haunt our sense of our stable selves and the world in which we breathe.

Notes

Preface

1. Martin Heidegger, "What Is Metaphysics," in *Martin Heidegger: Basic Writings*, trans. D. F. Krell (New York: Harper, 1977), 103.

Introduction

1. Quoted by Mark Edmundson in "Defender of the Faith?," *New York Times Magazine*, Sept. 9, 2007.

2. Jacques Lacan, *The Four Fundamental Concepts of Psycho-analysis*, ed. Jacques-Alain Miller, trans. Alain Sheridan (New York: W. W. Norton, 1977), 59.

3. As Lacan put it, he claims very deliberately to "leave the reader no other way out than in, which I prefer to be difficult." Jacques Lacan, *Écrits*, trans. Bruce Fink, in collaboration with Héloïse Fink and Russell Grigg (New York: W. W. Norton, 2006), 412.

4. Jacques Lacan, *The Seminar of Jacques Lacan: Book XX, Encore: On Feminine Sexuality, the Limits of Love and Knowledge, 1972–73*, ed. Jacques-Alain Miller, trans. Bruce Fink (New York: W. W. Norton,1998), 8. Lorenzo Chiesa comments about this passage that "*l'étrange* must by all means not be confused with *l'être ange*." On the contrary, to introduce a provocative confusion between the merely strange and the angelic seems to be precisely Lacan's intention. The question remains: What conclusion does he mean for us to draw from it? See Lorenzo Chiesa, "Woman and the Number of God," in *Theology after Lacan: The Passion for the Real*, ed. Creston Davis, Marcus Pound, and Clayton Crockett (Eugene, OR: Cascade Books, 2014), 168.

Chapter 1

1. The past twenty years have seen a flurry of commentary on the implications of Lacanian theory for rethinking religion. Among the more notable are Pierre Daviot, *Jacques Lacan et le sentiment religieux* (2006); François Balmès, *Dieu, le sexe et la verité* (2007); Marcus Pound, *Theology, Psychoanalysis, and Trauma* (2007); Creston Davis, Marcus Pound, and Clayton Crockett, eds., *Theology after Lacan: The Passion for the Real* (2014); and Lorenzo Chiesa, *The Not-Two: Logic and God*

in Lacan (2016). But no one has done more to demonstrate how Lacan reopens the field of the religious from a psychoanalytic point of view than Slavoj Žižek. Žižek treats questions of religion and God in many of his books, most directly in *The Fragile Absolute—or, Why Is the Christian Legacy Worth Fighting For?* (2000), *On Belief* (2001), *The Puppet and the Dwarf: The Perverse Core of Christianity* (2003), *The Monstrosity of Christ: Paradox or Dialectic?* (with John Milbank, 2009), and *God in Pain: Inversions of Apocalypse* (with Boris Gunjevic, 2012).

    2. Jacques Lacan, *The Seminar of Jacques Lacan: Book VIII, Transference*, ed. Jacques-Alain Miller, trans. Bruce Fink (Cambridge: Polity Press, 2015), 44. See also Lacan, *Four Fundamental Concepts*, 45.

    3. Jacques Lacan, "Seminar XVI: From an Other to the other," translated for private use from the unpublished French transcript of the seminar by Cormac Gallagher, session of Dec. 11, 1968.

    4. Lacan, *Encore*, 76.

    5. Sigmund Freud, *The Future of an Illusion*, in *The Standard Edition of the Complete Psychological Words of Sigmund Freud*, ed. and trans. James Strachey et al. (London: Hogarth Press and the Institute of Psycho-analysis, 1955), 21:33. Further references to Freud cite *The Standard Edition* with volume and page number.

    6. Freud, *The Future of an Illusion*, 21:16–17.

    7. Freud, *The Future of an Illusion*, 21:17.

    8. Freud, *The Future of an Illusion*, 21:49.

    9. Nietzsche, *The Genealogy of Morals*, in *Basic Writings of Nietzsche*, trans. Walter Kaufmann (New York: Modern Library, 1992), 520.

    10. Nietzsche, *Genealogy of Morals*, 523.

    11. Freud, *Civilization and Its Discontents*, 21:123.

    12. Nietzsche, *Genealogy of Morals*, 523–24.

    13. Freud, "Obsessive Actions and Religious Practices," 9:118.

    14. Freud, "Obsessive Actions and Religious Practices," 9:119.

    15. The classic example is that of obsessive handwashing, presumably produced by a displacement on to the hands themselves from something that might otherwise be done with them.

    16. Freud, "Obsessive Actions and Religious Practices," 9:125.

    17. The three drives Freud mentions here remind us how grossly inappropriate and misleading was the choice of James Strachey to translate Freud's cardinal notion of *Trieb* into English as "instinct." It is highly significant that Freud did not use the German term *Instinkt*. Cannibalism, incest, and lust for killing are all quite clearly not the sort of hardwired responses to stimuli characteristic of biological instinct in animals but rather fantasies.

    18. See Julian of Norwich, *Revelations of Divine Love*, compiled by Roger L. Roberts (Wilton, CT: Morehouse-Barlow, 1982).

    19. Freud, "Obsessive Actions and Religious Practices," 9:126.

    20. See Lacan's 1949 paper "The Mirror Stage as Formative of the I Function," in *Écrits*, 75–81.

    21. I have extensively treated the dynamics of the death drive as reinterpreted by Lacan in two earlier books. See my *Death and Desire: Psychoanalytic Theory*

in Lacan's Return to Freud (New York: Routledge, 1991) and *Freud as Philosopher: Metapsychology after Lacan* (New York: Routledge, 2001).

22. Freud, *Notes upon a Case of Obsessional Neurosis*, 10:292.

23. Lacan, "Instance of the Letter in the Unconscious," in *Écrits*, 419.

24. Lacan, "Instance of the Letter in the Unconscious," in *Écrits*, 419.

25. See Freud, *Notes upon a Case of Obsessional Neurosis*, 10:210.

26. Freud, *Notes upon a Case of Obsessional Neurosis*, 10:213.

27. Freud, *Notes upon a Case of Obsessional Neurosis*, 10:166–67. Italics in the original.

28. Alexandre Leupin, *Lacan Today: Psychoanalysis, Science, Religion* (New York: Other Press, 2004). For other treatments of God as an embodiment of the real, see Frederiek Depoortere, "The End of God's Transcendence? On Incarnation in the Work of Slavoj Žižek," *Modern Theology* 23, no. 4 (Oct. 2007): 497–523; and William Richardson, "'Like Straw': Religion and Psychoanalysis," *The Letter: Lacanian Perspectives on Psychoanalysis* 11 (1997): 1–15.

29. "God is real" declares the title of the final chapter of Alexandre Leupin's *Lacan Today: Psychoanalysis, Science, Religion.*

30. Jacques Lacan, *The Triumph of Religion*, trans. Bruce Fink (Malden, MA: Polity Press, 2013), 76.

31. Rudolf Otto, *The Idea of the Holy*, trans. by John Harvey (London: Oxford University Press, 1923).

32. Lacan, *Encore*, 76.

33. Jacques Lacan, *Le séminaire de Jacques Lacan: Livre IV, La relation d'objet* (Paris: Éditions du Seuil, 1994), 48.

34. Lacan, *Encore*, 83.

35. Lacan, *Triumph of Religion*, 74.

36. Lacan, *Triumph of Religion*, 73.

37. Jacques Lacan, "Radiophonie," *Scilicet*, nos. 2–3 (1970): 65. Quoted in Jean-Luc Nancy and Philippe Lacoue-Labarthe, *The Title of the Letter: A Reading of Lacan*, trans. François Raffoul and David Pettigrew (Albany: SUNY Press, 1992), 46.

38. For a clear, free-wheeling, and highly suggestive introduction to the Lacanian concept of the big Other, see Slavoj Žižek, *How to Read Lacan* (New York: W. W. Norton, 2006).

39. Lacan, "From an Other to the other," session of Apr. 30, 1969.

40. Jacques Lacan, *The Seminar of Jacques Lacan: Book X, Anxiety*, ed. Jacques-Alain Miller, trans. A. R. Price (Cambridge: Polity Press, 2014), 31.

Chapter 2

1. While duly noted by many scholars as an important element in Lacan's contribution to the theory of the unconscious, after its introduction in the seventh seminar the concept of *das Ding* appears later to be eclipsed by the notion of the *objet petit a*, explicitly nominated by Lacan in his last years as his most important contribution to psychoanalysis. I deal with the question of Lacan's relative

silence about *das Ding* after the seventh seminar and of the relation between the Thing and the later notion of the *objet a* in the first sections of chapter 3.

2. Jacques Lacan, *The Seminar of Jacques Lacan: Book VII, The Ethics of Psychoanalysis, 1959–60*, ed. Jacques-Alain Miller, trans. Dennis Porter (New York: W. W. Norton, 1986), 62.

3. Lacan, *Ethics of Psychoanalysis*, 97.

4. Lacan, *Ethics of Psychoanalysis*, 112.

5. Freud, *Project for a Scientific Psychology*, 1:331. The crucial text is as follows: "The complex of the fellow human-being falls apart into two components, of which one makes an impression by its constant structure and stays together as a *thing*, while the other can be *understood* by the activity of memory—that is, can be traced back to information from [the subject's] own body. This dissection of a perceptual complex is described as cognizing it."

6. In connection with my decision to capitalize the word "Other," the following passage from Lacan's third seminar, four years prior to his introduction of *das Ding*, is interesting: "And why [the Other] with a capital O? No doubt for a delusional reason, as is the case whenever one is obliged to provide signs that are supplementary to what language offers. That delusional reason is the following. 'You are my wife'—after all, what do you know about it? 'You are my master'—in point of fact, are you so sure? Precisely what constitutes the foundational value of this speech is that what is aimed at in the message, as well as what is apparent in the feint, is that the other is there as absolute Other. Absolute, that is to say that he is recognized but that he isn't known. Similarly, what constitutes the feint is that ultimately you do not know whether it's a feint or not. It's essentially this unknown in the otherness of the Other that characterizes the speech relation at the level at which speech is spoken to the other." *The Seminar of Jacques Lacan: Book III, The Psychoses, 1955–56*, ed. Jacques-Alain Miller, trans. Russell Grigg (New York: W. W. Norton, 1993), 37–38.

7. Freud, *Project for a Scientific Psychology*, 1:331.

8. Lacan, *Anxiety*, 311.

9. Lacan, *Anxiety*, 279.

10. Lacan, *Anxiety*, 325.

11. Lacan, *Anxiety*, 53–54.

12. See Simone de Beauvoir, *The Second Sex*, tr. H. M. Parshley (New York: Vintage Books, 1989), 195–96.

13. De Beauvoir, *The Second Sex*, 195.

14. Lacan, *Anxiety*, 327. And elsewhere: "It's not longing for the maternal breast that provokes anxiety, but its imminence" (53). "The most decisive moment in the anxiety at issue, the anxiety of weaning, is not so much when the breast falls short of the subject's need, it's rather that the infant yields the breast to which he is appended as a portion of himself" (313).

15. Lacan, *Ethics of Psychoanalysis*, 52, 71.

16. See Lacan, *Anxiety*, 22.

17. Jacques Lacan, *The Seminar of Jacques Lacan: Book XVII, The Other Side of Psychoanalysis*, ed. Jacques-Alain Miller, trans. Russell Grigg (New York: W. W. Norton, 1991), 112.

18. Lacan's treatment of the mother figure here recalls the psychoanalytic theory of Melanie Klein, which similarly centers on the infant's problematic relation to the maternal body, a tradition of which Lacan was well aware.

19. Freud, "Negation," 19:235.

20. Compare Freud, "On the Universal Tendency to Debasement in the Sphere of Love," 11:179–90.

21. Jean-Paul Sartre, *Being and Nothingness*, trans. Hazel Barnes (New York: Washington Square Press, 1971), 255.

22. Sartre, *Being and Nothingness*, 255.

23. Sartre, *Being and Nothingness*, 259.

24. Hegel, "The Philosophy of Spirit (Jena Lectures 1805–6): Part I, Spirit according to Its Concept," https://www.marxists.org/reference/archive/hegel /works/jl/ch01a.htm.

25. Lacan, *Ethics of Psychoanalysis*, 84.

26. It is with this ambivalence in mind that Lacan asks, "Which other is this, then, to whom I am more attached than to myself (*moi*), since, at the most assented to heart of my identity to myself, he pulls the strings." Lacan, *Écrits*, 436.

27. Lacan, *Anxiety*, 63.

28. This quote and the preceding text of the joke are found in Freud, *Jokes and Their Relation to the Unconscious*, 8:115.

29. The fundamental distinction that informs Sartre's analysis in his existential masterpiece, *Being and Nothingness*, is that between mere objects (the *en-soi*, or in-itself of being) and the human being as pure consciousness (that is *pour-soi*, or for-itself, and as such, is essentially nothingness).

30. Lacan, *Anxiety*, 155.

31. Lacan, *Anxiety*, 136.

32. Lacan, *Anxiety*, 129.

33. Slavoj Žižek, "The Thing from Inner Space," in *Sexuation*, ed. Renata Salacl (Durham: Duke University Press, 2000), 216–17.

34. Guy de Maupassant, "The Horla," http://www.eastoftheweb.com/short -stories/UBooks/Horl.shtml.

35. Freud, *The Uncanny*, 17:223.

36. Lacan, *Ethics of Psychoanalysis*, 104.

37. Lacan, *Ethics of Psychoanalysis*, 226.

38. The Thing is not a content of fantasy but, we might say, the empty frame that begs to be filled out by fantasy.

39. The focus in the preceding passages on nudity and on the body as sexually arousing object can fairly be said to point to a generally masculinist posture of desire. For a more nuanced and differentiated discussion of love and sexuality, see "Sex and the Sacred" in the concluding chapter.

40. Lacan, *Four Fundamental Concepts*, 235.

41. Slavoj Žižek, "From Che Vuoi to Fantasy: Lacan with Eyes Wide Shut," in How to Read Lacan, 42.

42. Lacan, *Anxiety*, 47.

43. "Here the *a* stands in for the subject—it's a stand-in in the position of precedent. The primordial, mythical subject, posited at the outset as having to

be constituted in the signifying confrontation, can never be grasped by us, and for good reason, because the *a* preceded it and it has to re-emerge secondarily, beyond its vanishing, marked by this initial substitution. The function of the yieldable object as a piece that can be primordially separated off conveys something of the body's identity, antecedent to the body itself with respect to the constitution of the subject." Lacan, *Anxiety*, 314.

44. Lacan, *Anxiety*, 173.

45. Lacan, *Ethics of Psychoanalysis*, 214.

46. Lacan, *Ethics of Psychoanalysis*, 83.

47. Lacan, *Ethics of Psychoanalysis*, 57.

48. Lacan, *Ethics of Psychoanalysis*, 55.

49. Lacan, "From an Other to the other," session of Mar. 5, 1969.

50. Lacan, *Écrits*, 414.

51. Lacan, *Anxiety*, 134.

52. Lacan, *Anxiety*, 67.

53. Lacan, *Anxiety*, 219.

54. Lacan, *Anxiety*, 313.

55. See Boothby, "Figurations of the Objet a," in *Freud as Philosopher*, 241–80.

56. I return to the question of the relation between *objet a* and the Thing in more detail in the following chapter.

57. Lacan, *Anxiety*, 326.

58. Lacan, *Anxiety*, 232.

59. Hannah Arendt, *The Human Condition* (Chicago: University of Chicago Press, 1971), 1–3.

60. Sue Savage-Rumbaugh, "Kanzi," interview on *Radiolab*, NPR, Feb. 19, 2010.

Chapter 3

1. *Komplex der Nebenmensch* is the phrase Freud uses to designate the general problematic of the child's relation with *das Ding* in *Project for a Scientific Psychology*.

2. Lacan, *Transference*, 309.

3. Lacan, *Anxiety*, 311.

4. In his essay, "Ethics amid Commodities: *Das Ding* and the Origin of Value," Todd McGowan provides an excellent commentary, with special reference to sublimation, on the strange appearance and even stranger (near) disappearance of the notion of *das Ding* in Lacan's seventh seminar. In *Studying Lacan's Seminar VII*, forthcoming from Routledge.

5. There are, in fact, sporadic references to *das Ding* after Seminar VII. Aside from the important mentions of the Thing in Seminars VIII (*Transference*) and X (*Anxiety*), Lacan makes a key reference to it in Seminar IX (on Identification). The very first session is bookended by it, as Lacan first points to "the agony which the Thing requires of us for us to join it," and later cites "the debris that comes back to [the subject] from what his reality undergoes in this Thing." Jacques Lacan, "Seminar IX: Identification," translated for private use from the

unpublished French transcript by Cormac Gallagher, session of Nov. 15, 1961. In Seminar XVI, "From an Other to the other," Lacans links the Thing to the lady of courtly love and to Edvard Munch's *Scream* (session of Mar. 12, 1969). In Seminar XX, *Encore*, he associates it with jealousy (101).

6. For more on this topic, see my essay "Harpo's Grin: Rethinking Lacan's Unthinkable 'Thing,'" in *Žižek Responds!* (Bloomsbury Press, forthcoming).

7. Lacan, "From an Other to the other," session of Mar. 12, 1969.

8. Lacan, *Ethics of Psychoanalysis*, 57.

9. One thinks here of the Rat Man's grin, which Freud attributed to a "*horror at pleasure of his own of which he himself was unaware.*" Freud, *Notes upon a Case of Obsessional Neurosis*, 10:167.

10. Lacan, *Ethics of Psychoanalysis*, 136.

11. Lacan, *Ethics of Psychoanalysis*, 39.

12. Lacan, *Ethics of Psychoanalysis*, 132.

13. Lacan, *Écrits*, 357.

14. Lacan, *Écrits*, 357.

15. See Lacan, *The Other Side of Psychoanalysis*.

16. See Michel Foucault, *History of Sexuality: Vol. 1, An Introduction*, trans. Robert Hurley (New York: Vintage Books, 1980).

17. Lacan, *The Ethics of Psychoanalysis*, 56.

18. Slavoj Žižek, "The Real of Sexual Difference," in *Reading Seminar XX: Lacan's Major Work on Love, Knowledge, and Feminine Sexuality*, ed. Suzanne Barnard and Bruce Fink (Albany: State University of New York Press, 2002), 70–71.

19. Slavoj Žižek, "Neighbors and Other Monsters: A Plea for Ethical Violence," in Slavoj Žižek, Eric Santner, and Kenneth Reinhard, eds., *The Neighbor: Three Inquiries in Political Theology* (Chicago: University of Chicago Press, 2005), 163. For useful comparisons of Lacan and Levinas, see Sarah Harasym, eds., *Levinas and Lacan: The Missed Encounter* (Albany, NY: SUNY Press, 1998); and Mari Ruti, *Between Levinas and Lacan: Self, Other, Ethics* (New York: Bloomsbury, 2015).

20. A broad parallel can be imagined at this point between Lacan's perspective in the relation between the I of the subject and the dual dimensionality of the Other and Martin Buber's reflections about distance and relation to the Other in his deservedly famous book *I and Thou*, trans. Walter Kaufmann (New York: Scribner and Sons, 1970).

21. Nietzsche, *Beyond Good and Evil*, in *Basic Writings of Nietzsche*, trans. Walter Kaufmann (New York: Vintage Books, 1961), 214.

22. Lacan, *Ethics of Psychoanalysis*, 134.

23. Lacan introduces the concept of the paternal metaphor in 1957. See Jacques Lacan, *The Seminar of Jacques Lacan: Book IV, The Object Relation*, ed. Jacques-Alain Miller, trans. A. R. Price (Cambridge: Polity Press, 2020), session 22.

24. Lacan thus remarks that "what we find in the incest law is located as such at the level of the unconscious in relation to *das Ding*." Lacan, *Ethics of Psychoanalysis*, 68.

25. Lacan, "The Freudian Thing," in *Écrits*, 361.

26. Lacan, "The Instance of the Letter in the Unconscious," in *Écrits*, 417.

27. Lacan, "The Instance of the Letter in the Unconscious," in *Écrits*, 417.

28. Lacan, "The Instance of the Letter in the Unconscious," in *Écrits*, 422.

29. Lacan, *Ethics of Psychoanalysis*, 52.

30. Lacan, *Anxiety*, 134.

31. See Roman Jakobson, *On Language*, ed. Linda Waugh and Monique Monville-Burston (Cambridge, MA: Harvard University Press, 1990), 309 and 440.

32. Lacan, "The Instance of the Letter in the Unconscious," in *Écrits*, 419.

33. Lacan began using the term *signifiance* at least fifteen years earlier, referring to "the signifierness of dreams." Lacan, "The Instance of the Letter in the Unconscious," in *Écrits*, 424.

34. Like much of Lacan's acquaintance with Hegel, the precise phrasing "the word as the murder of the thing" was made known to Lacan in the 1950s via the highly influential lectures of Alexandre Kojève. The phrase appears not to have been penned by Hegel himself.

35. Lacan, "From an Other to the other," session of Nov. 20, 1968.

36. As Lacan puts this point in his first seminar, "This language system, within which our discourse makes its way, isn't it something which goes infinitely beyond every intention that we might put into it, and which, moreover, is only momentary?" Jacques Lacan, *The Seminar of Jacques Lacan: Book I, Freud's Papers on Technique, 1953–54*, ed. Jacques Alain-Miller, trans. John Forrester (New York: W. W. Norton, 1988), 54.

37. For Žižek on Lacan's "universal symptom," see "The Real of Sex Difference," 58. Of course, in claiming here a kind of near-universal status for the neurotic symptom, I by no means intend to obviate consideration of other psychic formations, such as perversion or psychosis. But such more extreme structural defenses can and should be viewed against the backdrop of a more neurotic "normalcy."

38. Nietzsche, *Beyond Good and Evil*, in *Basic Writings*, 214.

39. Lacan, *Ethics of Psychoanalysis*, 121.

40. The two levels articulated in this section associated with the division of ego from subject—between an essentially defensive deployment of language in simple *signification* to reinforce imaginary identity and another, more open and volatile dimension of resonance, for which Lacan used the term *signifiance*—can be discerned in the two ways Lacan used the concept of the big Other over the course of his teaching. When Lacan first coins the phrase, in a section from his second seminar titled "Introduction of the Big Other," he uses it to point to the capacity of the signifying chain to open up something beyond the ego-to-ego relation of our everyday interactions, allowing for the eruption, as Lacan puts it, of "exactly what you weren't expecting." This first instance of the big Other thus points toward what is truly Other in the interlocutor or in oneself—exactly the sort of unknown dimension that he later comes to call *das Ding*. This sense of the big Other is congruent with Lacan's early identification of unconscious processes with "the discourse of the Other," and he sometimes reverts to this sense of the term even in much later seminars (the sixteenth seminar, "From an Other to the other," is an especially conspicuous example). But over the course of his teaching, Lacan tends increasingly to use "big Other" to designate the more defensive function that seeks to close down ambiguity and indeterminacy, the big Other that is

the policeman of meaning. This shift reflects two phases of Lacan's thought: an initial phase in which the imaginary is taken to be the regime of alienation for which the resources of the symbolic serve the interests of the unconscious desire of the subject, followed broadly by his middle period, when he realizes that the symbolic, too, plays a key role in the alienation of the subject. It is interesting to note, however, that even in the first mention of the phrase in the second seminar, Lacan notes both valences of the term. He thus remarks that "when we use language, our relation with the other always plays on this ambiguity. In other words, language is as much there to found us in the Other as to drastically prevent us from understanding him. And that is indeed what is at stake in the analytic experience." *The Seminar of Jacques Lacan: Book II, The Ego in Freud's Theory and in the Technique of Psychoanalysis, 1953–54,* ed. Jacques-Alain Miller, trans. Sylvana Tomaselli (New York: W. W. Norton, 1988), 244.

41. Martin Heidegger, "The Thing," in *Poetry Language Thought,* trans. Albert Hofstadter (New York: Harper Collophon, 1971), 165–86.

42. Lacan, *Ethics of Psychoanalysis,* 120.

43. Lacan, *Ethics of Psychoanalysis,* 121.

Part 2

1. Lacan, *Ethics of Psychoanalysis,* 100.

2. Lacan, *Triumph of Religion,* 66.

3. Nowhere is this point more emphatically stated than in Weil's essay "The Love of God and Affliction." See *The Simone Weil Reader,* ed. George Panichas (New York: David McCay, 1977), 439–68.

Chapter 4

1. Lacan, *Transference,* 44.

2. See Martin Heidegger, *The Origin of the Work of Art,* in *Martin Heidegger: Basic Writings,* 143–212.

3. Lacan, *Ethics of Psychoanalysis,* 141.

4. Lacan, *Ethics of Psychoanalysis,* 140.

5. Lacan, *Ethics of Psychoanalysis,* 140.

6. Lacan, *Ethics of Psychoanalysis,* 196.

7. Walter Burkert, *Homo Necans: The Anthropology of Ancient Greek Sacrificial Ritual and Myth,* trans. Peter Bing (Berkeley: University of California Press, 1983).

8. This and the previous quote from Lacan, *Anxiety,* 277.

9. In his *Theogony,* Hesiod provides a charming story to justify this asymmetry of benefits. It originated, he tells us, when Prometheus prepared a feast for gods and men but tricked Zeus and his party of divinities by giving them the bones and gristle wrapped appetizingly in fat, while the men received the best cuts, disguised by being wrapped in the fur-singed hide. This escapade led Zeus to pronounce upon Prometheus his famous punishment of being chained to a

rock, upon which a great bird of prey would alight each day to tear open his belly and consume his liver. The transgression of Prometheus also prompted Zeus to withhold fire from men. If they were to feast on the best cuts, then they would eat them raw. In this way, a cosmic balance of power would be restored. Hesiod, *Theogony*, trans. N. O. Brown (New York: MacMillan, 1988), 69.

10. I have elsewhere offered a more detailed discussion of Lacan's contribution to anthropological theories of sacrifice. See Boothby, *Freud as Philosopher*, 175–89.

11. Homer, *Iliad*, trans. Robert Fitzgerald (New York: Anchor Press/Doubleday, 1975), 26–27.

12. Heraclitus, fragment 48. Quoted in Philip Wheelwright, ed., *The Presocratics* (New York: MacMillan, 1987), 78.

13. Here, I take the liberty of altering Fitzgerald's translation of *mênis*, substituting "rage" for Fitzgerald's "anger."

14. Poseidon complains of Zeus's usurpation of his rightful dominion in Homer, *Iliad*, book 15, lines 220–30.

15. The notion of such an overarching judge that arises from the universal agon of contending forces is audible in the famous pronouncement of Anaximander, said by Martin Heidegger to be the earliest extant fragment of Greek thought: "Whence things have their origin, there they must also pass away according to necessity; for they must pay the penalty and be judged for their injustice, according to the ordinance of time." Quoted in *Early Greek Thinking*, trans. David Farrell Krell and Frank A. Capuzzi (New York: Harper and Row, 1975), 13.

16. Homer, *Iliad*, 45.

17. Hesiod, *Theogony*, 67.

18. Hesiod, *Theogony*, 70.

19. At first glance, a recent book by Peter Struck that explores the depths and complexities of ancient Greek arts of knowing might be taken to contradict my thesis here about the essential unknowability of divine forces, but I would argue that Struck's work actually lends support to my basic point. It was precisely the ultimate unfathomability of the divine for the Greeks that spawned the profusion of divination techniques among the Greeks aimed at giving fleeting glimpses into a perennial darkness. See Peter Struck, *Divination and Human Nature: A Cognitive History of Intuition in Classical Antiquity*. (Princeton, NJ: Princeton University Press, 2016).

20. Quoted in Wheelwright, *The Presocratics*, 160.

21. It might be remarked in passing that Hegel observes the essential unthinkability of force in the section of *The Phenomenology of Spirit* titled "Force and Understanding." Force there functions as a perennial spur to revisions of understanding but is never in itself exhaustively conceived.

22. Lacan, *Ethics of Psychoanalysis*, 172.

23. Quoted in E. R. Dodds, *The Greeks and the Irrational* (Berkeley: University of California Press, 1962), 30.

24. Homer, *Iliad*, 51.

25. Dodds, *The Greeks and the Irrational*, 11.

26. Dodds, *The Greeks and the Irrational*, 15.

27. Dodds, *The Greeks and the Irrational*, 14.

28. Dodds, *The Greeks and the Irrational*, 13.

29. Lacan, *Transference*, 162.

30. Paul Veyne, *Did the Greeks Believe in Their Myths? An Essay on the Constitutive Imagination*, trans. Paula Wissing (Chicago: University of Chicago Press, 1988).

31. Lacan, *Transference*, 52.

32. We are here quite close in more than one way to Hegel's assessment of paganism. Compare his remark, referring to the pagan deities: "The gods thus individualized quarrel with one another in a comic fashion. All that presides over them and over men is the unintelligible power of necessity." G. W. F. Hegel, *The Phenomenology of Spirit*, trans. A. V. Miller (Oxford: Oxford University Press, 1977), 583.

33. "For the highest images in every religion there is an analogue in a state of the soul. The God of Mohammed—the solitude of the desert, the distant roar of a lion, the vision of a terrible fighter. The God of the Christians—everything that men and women associate with the word 'love.' The God of the Greeks—a beautiful dream image." Friedrich Nietzsche, *The Portable Nietzsche Reader*, trans. Walter Kaufmann (New York: Viking Press, 1968), 49.

34. Homer, *Iliad*, 115.

35. Homer, *Iliad*, 95.

36. In this case, the baseness of the archer's arrow in the archaic Greek ethos is perfectly parallel to that of the firearm in the samurai fable depicted in Kurosawa's classic film, *The Seven Samurai*.

37. The reference here, of course, is to Hemingway's *Death in the Afternoon*.

38. See A. L. Kennedy's exceptional essay *On Bullfighting* (London: Yellow Jersey Press, 1999).

39. Homer, *Odyssey*, trans. Robert Fitzgerald (New York: Anchor Press/Doubleday, 1961), 212–13.

40. Homer, *Iliad*, 496.

41. In *The Best of the Achaeans*, Gregory Nagy poses the question of whether Achilles or Odysseus best exemplifies the true hero. Is archaic Greek heroism best embodied by body or mind, by Akhilleus's exertion of sheer force or the craftiness of Odysseus? From the standpoint adopted here, however, both postures meet in the middle insofar as the hero always pits himself—physically, mentally, or both—against the larger, ultimately unknowable forces arrayed against him. See Gregory Nagy, *The Best of the Achaeans: Concepts of the Hero in Archaic Greek Poetry* (Baltimore: Johns Hopkins University Press, 1979).

42. In Edmond Rostand's play *Cyrano de Bergerac*.

43. It is held by some classical scholars that the Dolon episode is a later addition to the Homeric poem, but I would contend that the essential point it illustrates remains true to the overarching ethos of the Homeric sensibility.

44. At this point we can link the Greek hero cults in which worship was extended to outstanding mortals like Heracles, Theseus, and others, to the role played by saints in the Christian religion. See Walter Burkert, *Greek Religion*, trans. John Raffan (Cambridge, MA: Harvard University Press, 1985), 203–7.

45. Lacan, *The Ego in Freud's Theory*, 229.

46. Lacan, *Transference*, 100.

47. Lacan, *The Ego in Freud's Theory*, 229.

48. See Lacan, *Écrits*, 81.

49. C. Fred Alford, *The Psychoanalytic Theory of Greek Tragedy* (New Haven, CT: Yale University Press, 1960), 189–90.

50. Friedrich Nietzsche, *The Birth of Tragedy*, in *Basic Writings of Nietzsche*, trans. Walter Kaufmann (New York: Modern Library, 1992), 74.

51. See Martin Heidegger, *Introduction to Metaphysics*, trans. Gregory Fried and Richard Polt (New Haven, CT: Yale University Press, 2004).

52. Heidegger's opposition between beings (*Seiende*) and Being (*Sein*) roughly parallels that between appearances and the underlying reality that gives rise to them.

53. Susan Sontag, *Against Interpretation* (New York: Farrar, Straus, and Giroux, 1966), 7.

54. I refer here to Plato's dialogue *Meno*, in which Socrates succeeds in eliciting from an illiterate slave boy a quite sophisticated understanding of mathematics.

55. I treat the question of gender in relation to the Pythagorean opposites at greater length elsewhere. See Boothby, *Sex on the Couch: What Freud Still Has to Teach Us about Sex and Gender* (New York: Routledge, 2005), 137–39.

56. De Beauvoir, *The Second Sex*, 149–50.

57. De Beauvoir, *The Second Sex*, 165–66.

58. There were, of course, women who were specifically authorized to know the dark secrets of things; among divinities there were the Muses, among mortals, the Pythian priestesses of Delphi, and so on. But these were the exceptions that proved the rule. That men in the Homeric culture harbored a fear of what women know, far from being refuted by such "authorized" exceptions, is arguably demonstrated by them.

59. Sophocles, *Oedipus the King and Antigone*, trans. and ed. Peter Arnott (Arlington Heights, IL: Harlan Davidson, 1960), line 1034.

60. In Greek, Oedipus means "swollen foot."

61. Sophocles, *Oedipus the King*, lines 943–49.

62. Sophocles, *Oedipus the King*, line 1172.

Chapter 5

1. Lacan, *Encore*, 83.

2. Lacan, *Anxiety*, 271.

3. It is interesting to note, as Burkert does, that the Greek word *theos* was generally used not to name a deity ("*theos* in the singular does not have a normal vocative"), but rather as a predicate that describes the force of influence upon a mortal man exerted by one or another god, the way in which one is *en-theos*. Burkert, *Greek Religion*, 271–72.

4. Lacan, *Transference*, 179.

5. Dodds, *The Greeks and the Irrational,* 35.

6. In some communities, the *kippah* is sometimes worn by women as well.

7. Exodus 24:18.

8. Talmud, Tractate Shabbat, 156b.

9. The devout modesty of Jewish culture differs markedly from the Greek embrace of open nudity. It is even tempting to think of Greek pride in nudity, contrasted by Pericles in his funeral oration with Persian shame at nakedness, as a form of willing exposure to the divine gaze and therefore in itself an emblem of Greek heroism.

10. In the historical context, of course, the requirement of circumcision would not have seemed so strange. There is good evidence that circumcision was widely practiced in Egypt before it was adopted by the Jews.

11. See Joseph Walsh, ed., *What Would You Die For? Perpetua's Passion* (Baltimore: Apprentice House, 2005).

12. My aim is to contrast the Greek pagan outlook to the Hebrew, not with regard to any historical interaction or derivation but rather with regard to their differing internal structures. Nor am I claiming that the polytheistic religions of the ancient Middle East were exactly comparable to the Greek example. As Jan Assmann points out, "Greece, with its elaborate aestheticized mythology, seems to be a rather special case that does not lend itself to generalizations." Jan Assmann, *Of God and Gods* (Madison: University of Wisconsin Press, 2008), 9.

13. As Lacan remarks, "This first attempt [of Akhenaton] at a rationalist vision of the world, which is presupposed in the unitarianism of the real, in the substantive unification of the world centered on the sun, failed. . . . One man keeps the flame of this rationalist cause alight, Moses the Egyptian." Lacan, *Ethics of Psychoanalysis,* 173.

14. Compare the comment by Kenneth Reinhard and Julia Lupton: "It is the scandal and the gift of monotheism that it not only creates moments of traumatic singularity, but also thinks the singular as trauma, rending the fabric of an animistic nature which would unite every polarity of being in the fullness of a sexual relation. Unlike the gods of Greek philosophy, the monotheistic God is not part of the nature he creates." "The Subject of Religion: Lacan and the Ten Commandments," *Diacritics* 33, no. 2 (Summer 2003): 71.

15. Lacan, "Seminar XVI: From an Other to the other," session of Dec. 11, 1968.

16. The distinction here is usually translated "the subject of the enunciation" or "enunciated subject" vs. "the enunciating subject." It might also be rendered "the subject who has been spoken for" versus the "subject who speaks."

17. Lacan, *Anxiety,* 245.

18. Lacan, *Anxiety,* 249.

19. Compare Amos 2:6.

20. See Exodus 19:16–18 and 20:19.

21. Mladen Dolar, *A Voice and Nothing More* (Cambridge, MA: MIT Press, 2006).

22. That the shofar is comparable, as Lacan himself notes, to the *objet a* yet

also, as we do here, to *das Ding*, offers a good example for explicating the relation between the two. The *objet a*, we might say, is the material trace—in this case, the pure sounding—of something that remains uncannily concealed behind it.

23. Lacan, *Anxiety*, 251

24. Lacan, *Anxiety*, 251

25. Lacan, "Seminar XVI: From an Other to the other," session of Dec. 11, 1968.

26. Exodus 20:1–3.

27. Reinhard and Lupton, "The Subject of Religion," 75.

28. Reinhard and Lupton, "The Subject of Religion," 75.

29. Reinhard and Lupton, "The Subject of Religion," 78.

30. Lacan, *Ethics of Psychoanalysis*, 174.

31. Lacan, *Ethics of Psychoanalysis*, 81.

32. As many commentators have pointed out, the commandment about the Sabbath occupies a special place as it is last of the first five commandments, which are devoted to the love and duty to God, and therefore forms the pivot to the second five, concerned with relations with one's fellow persons.

33. One is tempted to say that if God rested on the seventh day of Creation in order to make room for humanity, the Sabbath day of rest to humanity is then granted in order to make room for God.

34. Lacan, *Ethics of Psychoanalysis*, 81.

35. Lacan, *Écrits*, 420–21.

36. As Reinhard and Lupton put the main point: "The weekly punctuation of the Sabbath casts Redemption not as an imaginary conclusion to the historical process, but as an ever-present opening in the signifying chain, the self-difference of every moment produced by the anxious expectation of time's end." "The Subject of Religion," 87.

37. Lacan, *Écrits*, 414.

38. At the close of 2021, Jews had won 232 out of a total of 962 Nobels, according to Wikipedia.

39. It is reasonable to group the fifth commandment about honoring thy father and mother with those dealing with relation to God.

40. Lacan, *Ethics of Psychoanalysis*, 81–82.

41. Lacan, *Ethics of Psychoanalysis*, 82.

42. Lacan, *Ethics of Psychoanalysis*, 82.

43. Letter to the Romans, 7:7–8.

44. All three quotes from Lacan, *Ethics of Psychoanalysis*, 82–83.

Chapter 6

1. Lacan, *Triumph of Religion*, 66.

2. Lacan, *Triumph of Religion*, 64. See also Lacan's remark on p. 67: "Humanity will be cured by psychoanalysis. By drowning the symptom in meaning, in religious meaning naturally, people will manage to repress it."

3. Lacan, *Triumph of Religion*, 64–65.

4. Here, we are essentially retracing the analysis pioneered by Slavoj Žižek, who remarks upon "the overwhelming argument for the intimate link between Judaism and psychoanalysis: in both cases the focus is on the traumatic encounter with the abyss of the desiring Other—the Jewish people's encounter with their God whose impenetrable Call derails the routine of daily existence; the child's encounter with the enigma of the Other's jouissance." Slavoj Žižek and John Milbank, *The Monstrosity of Christ: Paradox or Dialectic?*," ed. Creston Davis (Cambridge, MA: MIT Press, 2009), 37.

5. There is, of course, a profound tension here, as what for Jesus himself lies clearly open in plain sight remains stubbornly invisible to those who struggle to follow his teaching. Or, to put it in another way, it is precisely when Christ most clearly reveals himself that the question presses most powerfully: "Yes, but here there surely must be something more."

6. Christianity has been charged with being idolatrous at different times by both Jewish and Islamic critics.

7. The word "crucifixion" is capitalized in Christian literature as a result of Paul's interpretation, a half century after the fact, that elevated the death of Jesus into the cosmic event of sacrifice that redeemed creation. In keeping with the very different interpretation of Jesus's teaching in this book, I generally leave the word uncapitalized.

8. As Galatians 5:14 puts it, "The whole law is fulfilled in one word, 'You shall love your neighbor as yourself.'" Here and subsequently unless otherwise noted, translation from the Revised Standard Version.

9. Compare also Luke 10:27, Mark 12:30–31.

10. Matthew 22:36–40.

11. Matthew 19:16–19.

12. Matthew 18:20.

13. Luke 17:20–21. "And when he was demanded of the Pharisees, when the kingdom of God should come, he answered them and said, The kingdom of God cometh not with observation: 21 Neither shall they say, Lo here! or, lo there! for, behold, the kingdom of God is within you" (King James Version).

14. Matthew 25:40.

15. Freud, *Civilization and Its Discontents*, 21:109.

16. Lacan, *Ethics of Psychoanalysis*, 186.

17. Lacan, *Ethics of Psychoanalysis*, 187.

18. Tracy McNulty has offered an illuminating if somewhat different Lacanian perspective on Jesus's exhortation to love the enemy. See Tracy McNulty, *Wrestling with the Angel: Experiments in Symbolic Life* (New York: Columbia University Press, 2014), esp. 111–20.

19. Lacan, *Ethics of Psychoanalysis*, 186.

20. Leviticus 19:9 reads: "When you reap the harvest of your land, you shall not reap your field to its very border, neither shall you gather the gleanings after your harvest."

21. Leviticus 19:33–34.

22. Lacan, *Ethics of Psychoanalysis*, 187.

23. Galatians 3:28.

24. Nikos Kazantzakis clearly understood the meaning of this connection between Jesus and Mary Magdalene and exploited it to maximum effect in his novel *The Last Temptation of Christ*. It is clear, however, that many Christians regarded this connection as a bridge too far. The release of Martin Scorsese's film version of Kazantzakis's novel led to the firebombing of at least one theater in France.

25. Nietzsche, *Beyond Good and Evil*, 61.

26. The larger quote from which this citation is taken makes it clear that Lacan is here talking specifically about rites of passage and initiation. See Jacques Lacan, *Desire and Its Interpretation*, session of May 20, 1959.

27. It was in this sense that Lacan, especially in his early work, posited the phallus as a master signifier, a signifier with no clear signified.

28. Matthew 16:24.

29. Lacan, *Anxiety*, 220–21.

30. See Žižek's *The Puppet and the Dwarf*.

31. Matthew 16:24–25.

32. Todd McGowan, *Emancipation after Hegel: A Contradictory Revolution* (New York: Columbia University Press, 2019), 113.

33. Hegel, *Phenomenology of Spirit*, 19.

34. McGowan, *Emancipation after Hegel*, 105.

35. Hegel, *Phenomenology of Spirit*, 19.

36. To quote Hegel: "The wish to live eternally . . . is only a childlike representation. . . . [H]uman being as a single living thing, its singular life, its natural life, must die. . . . The fact of the matter is that humanity is immortal only through cognitive knowledge, for only in the activity of thinking is its soul pure and free rather than mortal and animallike." G. W. F. Hegel, *Lectures on the Philosophy of Religion*, ed. Peter Hodgson, trans. R. F. Brown, P. C. Hodgson, and J. M. Stewart (Berkeley: University of California Press, 1984), 3:303–4.

37. Matthew 7:1–5 (KJV).

38. Lacan, *Transference*, 40.

39. Hegel, *Lectures of the Philosophy of World History*, 449, quoted by McGowan in *Emancipation after Hegel*, 201.

40. J. N. Findlay, "Analysis," in Hegel, *Phenomenology of Spirit*, 586.

41. Lacan is critical of Hegelian dialectic precisely because he takes it to be an embrace of a metaphysical closure, a return-to-self of the Absolute. As he puts it at one point, "It is inadmissible that I should be accused of having been lured by a purely dialectical exhaustion of being." Lacan, "Subversion of the Subject and the Dialectic of Desire," in *Écrits*, 681.

42. Lacan, *Ethics of Psychoanalysis*, 178.

43. Lacan, *Anxiety*, 306–8.

44. 1 John 4:8 and 16 make it explicit: "He who does not love does not know God, for God is love." "God is love, and he who abides in love abides in God, and God abides in him."

45. See Gershom Scholem, *On the Kabbalah and Its Symbolism (Mysticism and Kabbalah)*, trans. Ralph Manheim (New York: Schocken Books, 1996).

46. Matthew 5:17. "Think not that I have come to abolish the Law or the Prophets; I have come not to abolish them but to fulfill them."

47. Lacan, *Ethics of Psychoanalysis*, 84. In this quotation, Lacan explicitly relates "rediscovering the relationship to *das Ding* somewhere beyond the law" to "something that all religions engage in, all mysticisms, all that Kant disdainfully calls the *Religionsschwärmereien*, religious enthusiasms."

48. Lacan, *Encore*, 76.

49. Hadewijch of Brabant, Letter 18: "The Greatness of the Soul," in *Hadewijch: The Complete Works*, trans. Mother Columba Hart (New York: Paulist Press, 1990), 86.

50. Žižek, *Monstrosity of Christ*, 38.

51. Žižek, *Monstrosity of Christ*, 237.

52. Žižek, *Monstrosity of Christ*, 25.

53. I use the *Star Trek* phrase "prime directive" advisedly. As the guiding operative principle for the *Enterprise*'s intergalactic journey "to go where no man has gone before," the prime directive of accepting alien civilizations, seeking to understand and interact with them on their own terms without seeking to dominate or interfere with them, is a profoundly Christian guide to behavior while also apparently being wholly atheistic.

54. Friedrich Nietzsche, *The Anti-Christ*, in *The Portable Nietzsche Reader*, 612.

55. See G. W. F. Hegel, "The Positivity of the Christian Religion," in *Early Theological Writings* (Philadelphia: University of Pennsylvania Press, 1979), 67–181.

56. See Søren Kierkegaard, *Attack on Christendom*, trans. Walter Lowrie (Princeton, NJ: Princeton University Press, 1972).

57. For Nietzsche, the key point concerns *ressentiment*, particularly against the suffering imposed upon us by this life, in the face of which the burdened are led to hope for an escape from suffering in another life. Nietzsche argues that Paul provides the exemplary instance of such an attitude. The less obvious implication is that the teaching of Jesus cut in precisely the opposite direction, affirming the value of love in this life, even at the cost of death.

58. Yuval Noah Harari, *Sapiens: A Brief History of Humankind* (New York: HarperCollins, 2015).

59. Lacan, *Ethics of Psychoanalysis*, 171.

60. Freud, *The Future of an Illusion*, 21:28. To be fair to Tertullian, there is a sense, precisely in terms of the argument I have put forward in this book, namely that following Christ's injunction to love not only the neighbor but the enemy might be called absurd, if only because the benefit to the one who extends that love is anything but immediately obvious.

61. See Augustine, *The Confessions*, trans. R. S. Pine-Coffin (London: Penguin Books, 1961), 50.

62. The source and authenticity of the text in question, the so-called *pericope adulterae*, have been disputed.

63. Compare John 7:53–8:11. The crowd of accusers are in fact a group of scribes and Pharisees who are once again determined to put Jesus to a test of orthodoxy.

64. Matthew 7:1.

65. Raised in a Protestant family but heavily influenced by exposure to Asian thought in the work of Joseph Campbell, Lucas called himself a Buddhist-Methodist.

Chapter 7

1. Of course, such a trajectory is more "essential" than historical for the simple reason that while Judaic monotheism arose in general rejection of polytheism, the origins of Judaism predated the Homeric era of Greek polytheism that is focused upon in this book.

2. Compare Kant's use of the Latin phrase in the opening paragraph of "What Is Enlightenment?" in *Perpetual Peace and Other Essays on Politics, History, and Morals*, trans. Ted Humphrey (New York: Hackett, 1983), 41.

3. As Slavoj Žižek ("Neighbors and Other Monsters," 150) put it, "Christianity simultaneously goes too far and not far enough."

4. Of course, the violent excesses committed in the name of Christianity were by no means always the product of purely religious zeal. The horrific violence perpetrated upon the native peoples of the Americas by the conquistadors, for example, was likely less a product of genuine spiritual piety than an exercise of gross political and economic exploitation carried out and justified beneath a fig leaf of outward religiosity.

5. The categories I list here of love, art, science, or war are not accidentally reminiscent of the four truth procedures enumerated by Alain Badiou.

6. The term "Hindu" is quite ancient, perhaps derived from the Indus River, but as a catchall term that lumps together a huge range of sects and practices, "Hinduism" was introduced during the period of the British colonialization of India.

7. Quoted by Klaus Klostermaier, *A Survey of Hinduism* (Binghamton, NY: SUNY Press, 1994), 1.

8. Lacan, "The Mirror Stage," in *Écrits*, 81.

9. Shankara, *The Crest Jewel of Discrimination* (*Vivekachudamani*), trans. John Richards (n.p.: Freedom Religion Press, 2011), verse 254.

10. Sarvepalli Radhakrishnan and Charles Moore, eds., *A Sourcebook Indian Philosophy* (Princeton, NJ: Princeton University Press, 1973), 23–24.

11. The reference is to Shunryu Suzuki, *Zen Mind, Beginner's Mind*, ed. Trudy Dixon (New York: Weatherhill, 1975).

12. Keiji Nishitani, *Religion and Nothingness*, trans. Jan Van Bragt (Berkeley: University of California Press, 1982).

13. Nishitani, *Religion and Nothingness*, 47.

14. Distinguished at some points as the difference between relative nothingness and absolute nothingness, nihility is characterized by closure, death, and meaninglessness, where the emptiness of *sunyata* offers an opening and ultimately an affirmation. Nishitani thus claims that "the field of *sunyata* is nothing

other than the field of the Great Affirmation." And elsewhere: "Emptiness might be called the field of 'be-ification' (*Ichtung*) in contrast to nihility which is the field of 'nullification' (*Nichtung*)." *Religion and Nothingness*, 131 and 124.

15. Heidegger, "What Is Metaphysics?," in *Basic Writings*, 103. Nishitani is also deeply impressed by Sartre's identification of the human for-itself with nothingness, linking it with freedom, though he is critical of the way Sartre retains a Cartesian duality between being in-itself and the for-itself of consciousness.

16. Nishitani, *Religion and Nothingness*, 153.

17. Nishitani, *Religion and Nothingness*, 123.

18. Nishitani, *Religion and Nothingness*, 149.

19. Nishitani, *Religion and Nothingness*, 148.

20. Nishitani's notion of the "home-ground" of beings (*moto*) is among his most frequently used yet most complex and mysterious references. The term points us simultaneously toward the total nexus of relations and conditions that give rise to any entity, thoughts as well as things, but also toward the absolute emptiness of sunyata.

21. Nishitani, *Religion and Nothingness*, 59.

22. Nishitani, *Religion and Nothingness*, 63. Nishitani later notes that Eckhart "claimed that the ground of God lies within the self, nearer to the self than the self is to itself." 90.

23. Nishitani, *Religion and Nothingness*, 111.

24. Nishitani, *Religion and Nothingness*, 69–70.

25. Nishitani, *Religion and Nothingness*, 71.

26. Nishitani, *Religion and Nothingness*, 275.

27. Nishitani, *Religion and Nothingness*, 251.

28. Nishitani, *Religion and Nothingness*, 106.

29. Nishitani, *Religion and Nothingness*, 139.

30. Following in the path opened up by his teacher Kitaro Nishida, Nishitani explored the paradoxes of knowing and unknowing in a dialogue, both appreciative and critical, with Martin Buber's philosophy of I and Thou.

31. Nishitani, *Religion and Nothingness*, 101.

32. I am grateful to my Egyptian colleague, Tariq Osman, for alerting me to the central importance of *Al Ghaib* in the Qur'an and in Muslim religiosity more generally.

33. Qur'an 2:3. All quotes from the Qur'an use the translation by M. A. S. Abdel Haleem (Oxford: Oxford University Press, 2016).

34. Qur'an 6:59.

35. See Zainulbahar Noor and Francine Pickup, "Zakat Requires Muslims to Donate 2.5% of Their Wealth: Could This End Poverty?," *Guardian*, June 22, 2017, https://www.theguardian.com/global-development-professionals-network/2017/jun/22/zakat-requires-muslims-to-donate-25-of-their-wealth-could-this-end-poverty.

36. Coleman Barks, ed., *The Essential Rumi*, trans. Coleman Barks (New York: HarperCollins, 2004), 51.

37. Barks, *The Essential Rumi*, 109.

38. Barks, *The Essential Rumi*, 328.

39. Quoted by Brad Gooch, *Rumi's Secret: The Life of the Sufi Poet of Love* (New York: Harper Perennial, 2018), 50. A saying commonly attributed to Rumi is strikingly Lacanian: "If you could get rid of yourself just once, the secret of secrets would open to you. The face of the unknown, hidden beyond the universe would appear on the mirror of your perception."

40. Huston Smith, *The World's Religions* (New York: HarperCollins, 1991), 243.

41. Syed Ameer Ali, *The Spirit of Islam* (London: Christophers, 1923) 32.

42. Smith, *The World's Religions*, 243 and 249.

43. Qur'an 2:2–7.

44. As we noted earlier, such "certainty" about the outlook of the disbeliever may possess very little positive content. The believer's conviction about the infidel's position can crystalize as a warrantless certainty, a nearly pure supposition, and can function even more effectively for being unspecified.

45. Qur'an 2:286.

46. Qur'an 2:14. "The hypocrites will be in the lowest depths of Hell" (4:145).

47. Of course, the notion that the capacity for faith is a God-given grace is found in more than one religion, very much including Christianity. Many Christian sects, Calvinism, for example, stress the hopeless irretrievability of the faithless.

48. Qur'an 2:89.

49. Qur'an 5:41. See also: "[Prophet], when you recite the Qur'an, We put an invisible barrier between you and those who do not believe in the life to come. We have put covers on their hearts that prevent them from understanding it, and heaviness in their hearts" (17:45–46). And elsewhere: "You call them to a straight path and those who do not believe in the Hereafter turn away from that path. Even if We were to show [the disbelievers] mercy and relieve them of distress, they would blindly persist in their transgression. We have already afflicted them, yet they did not submit to their Lord: they will not humble themselves until We open a gate to severe torment for them—then they will be plunged into utter despair" (23:73–77).

50. Qur'an 2:191.

51. Qur'an 9:5.

52. Qur'an 47:4.

53. Quoted by Mustafa Akyol, "Would the Prophet Muhammad Convert the Hagia Sophia?," *New York Times*, July 20, 2020.

54. Qur'an 22:40.

55. Viewed psychoanalytically, it is not an accident that the two largest world religions are the most deeply symptomatic. As Freud pointed out, the extremity of symptomatic tensions between competing forces of drive and defense is the most important factor in the subject's passionate attachment to the symptom. The most symptomatic religions are apparently, at least at some level of psychic function, the most satisfying.

56. In fact, there is a great deal in James's analysis in *Varieties* that runs parallel to my argument. What he calls "the reality of the unseen" is broadly coincident with my view of of the religious impulse in relation to *das Ding*.

57. Walter Benjamin, "Capitalism as Religion," trans. Chad Kautzer, in *The Frankfurt School on Religion: Key Writings by the Major Thinkers*, ed. Eduardo Mendieta (New York: Routledge, 2005), 259 and 261.

58. Karl Marx, *Capital: A Critique of Political Economy*, trans. Ben Fowkes (New York: Penguin, 1990), 165.

59. Quoted by Richard Seaford, *Money and the Early Greek Mind: Homer, Philosophy, Tragedy* (Cambridge: Cambridge University Press, 2004), 165.

60. Lacan, "From an Other to the other," session of Apr. 30, 1969.

61. See Todd McGowan, *Capitalism and Desire: The High Price of Free Markets* (New York: Columbia University Press, 2016).

62. Karl Marx and Fredrick Engels, *The Marx Reader*, ed. Robert Tucker (New York: W. W. Norton, 1978), 155.

63. Louis Althusser, "Ideology and Ideological State Apparatuses," in *Mapping Ideology*, ed. Slavoj Žižek (London: Verso, 1994). 126.

64. Althusser, "Ideology and Ideological State Apparatuses," 127.

65. Althusser, "Ideology and Ideological State Apparatuses," 130–31.

66. Althusser, "Ideology and Ideological State Apparatuses," 131.

67. Althusser, "Ideology and Ideological State Apparatuses," 132–33.

68. Althusser, "Ideology and Ideological State Apparatuses," 134.

69. Althusser, "Ideology and Ideological State Apparatuses," 134–35.

70 Inaugural address of George H. W. Bush, Jan. 20, 1989, available at https://avalon.law.yale.edu/20th_century/bush.asp.

71. See Renata Salecl's essay on the disappearing big Other in modern society: "Disbelief in the Big Other in the University and Beyond," *Anglistica* 4, no. 1 (2000): 49–67.

72. Althusser, "Ideology and Ideological State Apparatuses," 133.

Chapter 8

1. The account here elaborated of the unknown Thing in the human Other projected into the space of one or another divinity bears more than a little similarity to the theory of religion put forward by Ludwig Feuerbach. In *The Essence of Christianity*, Feuerbach argues not only that the gods are externalizations of essentially human powers, but also that the broad historical development of religion displays a tendency toward returning those powers to their human origin. Feuerbach therefore argues that in the prehistory of religion, the objects of divinity are at the farthest remove from the human and that Christianity, with its doctrine of incarnation, decisively brings the Godhead back down to earth.

2. Freud, *The Future of an Illusion*, 21:64.

3. Freud, *The Future of an Illusion*, 21:68.

4. The Nag Hammadi papyri appear to have been buried by monks seek-

ing to prevent their confiscation and destruction in the aftermath of their being condemned as heretical.

5. Quoted by Elaine Pagels, *Why Religion? A Personal Story* (New York: Harper Collins, 2018), 179–80, 199.

6. Lacan elaborates the formulas of sexuation in *Seminar XX: Encore*. For useful explications of his theory on this point, see Copjec, Imagine There's No Woman, 201–36; Žižek, "The Real of Sexual Difference," 57–75.

7. Lacan, *Encore*, 9.

8. Nietzsche, *Genealogy of Morals*, 493–532

9. Quotes from Lacan, *Encore*, 77 and 82.

10. We here locate the obverse of our previous discussion of the sufferer's perverse identification with the crucified.

11. Lacan, *Encore*, 98.

12. Žižek, "The Real of Sexual Difference," 61.

13. Lacan, *Encore*, 68. It is significant that in the two pages following this provocative reference to God's enduring appeal, Lacan focuses on the linkage between *jouissance* and *signifiance*. Just a few pages earlier, he had this to say: "The Other, the Other as the locus of truth, is the only place, albeit an irreducible place, that we can give to the term 'divine being,' God, to call him by his name. God (*Dieu*) is the locus where, if you will allow me this wordplay, the *dieu*—the *dieur*–the *dire*, is produced. With a trifling change, the *dire* constitutes *Dieu*. And as long as things are said, the God hypothesis will persist." *Encore*, 45.

14. Lacan also remarks the failure of both: "Neither science nor religion is of a kind to save the Thing or to give it to us, because the magic circle that separates us from it is imposed by our relation to the signifier. Lacan, *Ethics of Psychoanalysis*, 134.

15. For Heidegger's notion of *Gestell*, or "enframing," see his essay "The Question concerning Technology," in *Basic Writings*.

16. Heidegger, "What Is Metaphysics?," in *Basic Writings*, 96.

17. For this and the following two quotations, see Giorgio Agamben, "The Last Chapter in the History of the World," in *Nudities*, trans. David Kishik and Stefan Pedatella (Stanford, CA: Stanford University Press, 2011), 113–14.

Bibliography

Agamben, Giorgio. *Nudities.* Translated by David Kishik and Stefan Pedatella. Stanford, CA: Stanford University Press, 2011.

Akyol, Mustafa. "Would the Prophet Muhammad Convert the Hagia Sophia?" *New York Times,* July 20, 2020.

Alford, C. Fred. *The Psychoanalytic Theory of Greek Tragedy.* New Haven, CT: Yale University Press, 1960.

Althusser, Louis. "Ideology and Ideological State Apparatuses." In *Mapping Ideology,* edited by Slavoj Žižek. London: Verso, 1994.

Ameer, Ali. *The Spirit of Islam.* London: Christophers, 1923.

Arendt, Hannah. *The Human Condition.* Chicago: University of Chicago Press, 1971.

Assmann, Jan. *Of God and Gods.* Madison: University of Wisconsin Press, 2008.

Augustine. *The Confessions.* Translated by R. S. Pine-Coffin. London: Penguin Books, 1961.

Badiou, Alain. *Being and Event.* Translated by Oliver Feltham. London: Continuum, 2005.

Balmès, François. *Dieu, le sexe et la verité.* Paris: Eres, 2007.

Barks, Coleman, ed. *The Essential Rumi.* Translated by Coleman Barks. New York: HarperCollins, 2004.

Benjamin, Walter, "Capitalism as Religion." Translated by Chad Kautzer. In *The Frankfurt School on Religion: Key Writings by the Major Thinkers,* edited by Eduardo Mendieta. New York: Routledge, 2005.

Boothby, Richard. *Death and Desire: Psychoanalytic Theory in Lacan's Return to Freud.* New York: Routledge, 1991.

———. *Freud as Philosopher: Metapsychology after Lacan.* New York: Routledge, 2001.

———. "Harpo's Grin: Rethinking Lacan's Unthinkable 'Thing.'" In *Žižek Responds!* Bloomsbury Press, forthcoming.

———. "The No-Thing of God: Psychoanalysis of Religion after Lacan." In *The Oxford Handbook of Philosophy and Psychoanalysis,* edited by Michael Lacewing and Richard Gipps. Oxford: Oxford University Press, 2018.

———. *Sex on the Couch: What Freud Still Has to Teach Us about Sex and Gender.* New York: Routledge, 2005.

Buber, Martin. *I and Thou.* Translated by Walter Kaufmann. New York: Scribner and Sons, 1970.

Burkert, Walter. *Greek Religion.* Translated by John Raffan. Cambridge, MA: Harvard University Press, 1985.

————. *Homo Necans: The Anthropology of Ancient Greek Sacrificial Ritual and Myth.* Translated by Peter Bing. Berkeley: University of California Press, 1983.

Calimachi, Rukmini. "Freed from ISIS, Yazidi Women Return in 'Severe Shock.'" *New York Times,* July 27, 2017.

Chiesa, Lorenzo. *The Not-Two: Logic and God in Lacan.* Cambridge, MA: MIT Press, 2016.

————. "Woman and the Number of God." In *Theology after Lacan: The Passion for the Real,* edited by Creston Davis, Marcus Pound, and Clayton Crockett. Eugene, OR: Cascade Books, 2014.

Copjec, Joan. *Imagine There's No Woman: Ethics and Sublimation.* Cambridge, MA: MIT Press, 2002.

Daviot, Pierre. *Jacques Lacan et le sentiment religieux.* Paris: Eres, 2006.

Davis, Bret W. *Heidegger and the Will: On the Way to Gelassenheit.* Evanston, IL: Northwestern University Press, 2007.

Davis, Creston, Marcus Pound, and Clayton Crockett, eds. *Theology after Lacan: The Passion for the Real.* Eugene, OR: Cascade Books, 2014.

de Beauvoir, Simone. *The Second Sex.* Translated by H. M. Parshley. New York: Vintage Books, 1989.

De Certeau, Michel. *Heterologies: Discourse on the Other.* Translated by B. Massumi. Theory and History of Literature, vol. 17. Minneapolis: University of Minnesota Press, 2006.

Depoortere, Frederiek. "The End of God's Transcendence? On Incarnation in the Work of Slavoj Žižek." *Modern Theology* 23, no. 4 (Oct. 2007): 497–523.

Descartes, René. *Discourse on Method and Meditations on First Philosophy.* Translated by Donald Cress. Indianapolis: Hackett, 1993.

Dodds, E. R. *The Greeks and the Irrational.* Berkeley: University of California Press, 1962.

Dolar, Mladen. *A Voice and Nothing More.* Cambridge, MA: MIT Press, 2006.

Edmundson, Mark. "Defender of the Faith?" *New York Times Magazine,* Sept. 9, 2007.

Eisenstein, Paul, and Todd McGowan. *Rupture: The Emergence of the Political.* Evanston, IL: Northwestern University Press, 2012.

Feuerbach, Ludwig. *The Essence of Christianity.* Translated by George Eliot. New York: Prometheus Books, 1989.

Freud, Sigmund, *The Standard Edition of the Complete Psychological Words of Sigmund Freud.* 24 vols. Edited and translated by James Strachey et al. London: Hogarth Press and the Institute of Psycho-analysis, 1955.

Foucault, Michel. *History of Sexuality: Vol. 1, An Introduction.* Translated by Robert Hurley. New York: Vintage Books, 1980.

Gooch, Brad. *Rumi's Secret: The Life of the Sufi Poet of Love.* New York: Harper Perennial, 2018.

Graeber, David. *Debt: The First 5000 Years.* Brooklyn, NY: Melville House, 2014.

Hadewijch of Brabant. Letter 18, "The Greatness of the Soul." In *Hadewijch: The Complete Works,* translated by Mother Columba Hart. New York: Paulist Press, 1990.

BIBLIOGRAPHY

Haleem, M. A. S. Abdel, trans. *The Qur'an: A New Translation*. Oxford: Oxford University Press, 2016.

Harari, Yuval Noah. *Sapiens: A Brief History of Humankind*. New York: Harper-Collins, 2015.

Harasym, Sarah, ed. *Levinas and Lacan: The Missed Encounter*. Albany, NY: SUNY Press, 1998.

Hegel, Georg Wilhelm Friedrich. *Early Theological Writings*. Philadelphia: University of Pennsylvania Press, 1979.

——. *Lectures on the Philosophy of Religion*. Edited by Peter Hodgson, translated by R. F. Brown, P. C. Hodgson, and J. M. Stewart. Berkeley: University of California Press, 1984,

——. *The Phenomenology of Spirit*. Translated by A. V. Miller. Oxford: Oxford University Press, 1977.

——. *The Philosophy of History*. Translated by J. Sibree. New York: Dover, 1956.

——. "The Philosophy of Spirit (Jena Lectures 1805–6): Part I, Spirit according to Its Concept." https://www.marxists.org/reference/archive/hegel/works/jl/ch01a.htm.

Heidegger, Martin. *Being and Time*. Translated by John MacQuarrie and Edward Robinson. New York: Harper and Row, 1962.

——. *Early Greek Thinking*, Translated by David Farrell Krell and Frank A. Capuzzi. New York: Harper and Row, 1975.

——. *Introduction to Metaphysics*. Translated by Gregory Fried and Richard Polt. New Haven, CT: Yale University Press, 2004.

——. *Martin Heidegger: Basic Writings*. Translated by D. F. Krell. New York: Harper, 1977.

——. *Poetry Language Thought*. Translated by Albert Hofstadter. New York: Harper Collophon, 1971.

Hemingway, Ernest. *Death in the Afternoon*. New York: Scribner, 1969.

Hesiod. *Theogony*. Translated by N. O. Brown. New York: MacMillan, 1988.

Homer. *Iliad*. Translated by Robert Fitzgerald. New York: Anchor Press/Doubleday, 1975.

——. *Odyssey*. Translated Robert Fitzgerald. New York: Anchor Press/Doubleday, 1961.

Jakobson, Roman. *On Language*. Edited Linda Waugh and Monique Monville-Burston. Cambridge, MA: Harvard University Press, 1990.

Julian of Norwich. *Revelations of Divine Love*. Compiled by Roger L. Roberts. Wilton, CT: Morehouse-Barlow, 1982.

Kant, Immanuel. *Religion within the Limits of Reason Alone*. New York: Harper and Row, 1960.

——. "What Is Enlightenment?" In *Perpetual Peace and Other Essays on Politics, History, and Morals*. Translated by Ted Humphrey. New York: Hackett, 1983.

Kazantzakis, Nikos. *The Last Temptation of Christ*. Translated by Peter Bien. New York: Simon and Schuster, 1998.

——. *Odyssey: A Modern Sequel*. Translated by Kimon Friar. New York: Simon and Schuster, 1958.

———. *Zorba the Greek*. Translated by Peter Bien. New York: Simon and Schuster, 2014.

Kennedy, A. L. *On Bullfighting*. London: Yellow Jersey Press, 1999.

Kierkegaard, Søren. *Attack on Christendom*. Translated by Walter Lowrie. Princeton, NJ: Princeton University Press, 1972.

———. *Fear and Trembling*. Translated by Walter Lowrie. Princeton, NJ: Princeton University Press, 1974.

Klostermaier, Klaus K. *A Survey of Hinduism*. 2d ed. Binghamton, NY: SUNY Press, 1994.

Kojève, Alexandre. *Introduction to the Reading of Hegel: Lectures on the Phenomenology of Spirit*. Assembled by Raymond Queneau, edited by Allan Bloom, translated by James Nichols. Ithaca, NY: Cornell University Press, 1980.

Lacan, Jacques. *Écrits*. Translated by Bruce Fink, in collaboration with Héloïse Fink and Russell Grigg. New York: W. W. Norton, 2006.

———. *The Four Fundamental Concepts of Psycho-analysis*. Edited by Jacques-Alain Miller, translated by Alain Sheridan. New York: W. W. Norton, 1977.

———. "Radiophonie." *Scilicet*, nos. 2–3 (1970).

———. *The Seminar of Jacques Lacan: Book I, Freud's Papers on Technique, 1953–54*. Edited by Jacques-Alain Miller, translated by John Forrester. New York: W. W. Norton, 1988.

———. *The Seminar of Jacques Lacan: Book II, The Ego in Freud's Theory and in the Technique of Psychoanalysis, 1954–55*. Edited by Jacques-Alain Miller, translated by Sylvana Tomaselli. New York: W. W. Norton, 1988.

———. *The Seminar of Jacques Lacan: Book III, The Psychoses, 1955–56*. Edited by Jacques-Alain Miller, translated by Russell Grigg. New York: W. W. Norton, 1993.

———. *The Seminar of Jacques Lacan: Book IV, The Object Relation*. Edited by Jacques-Alain Miller, translated by A. R. Price. Cambridge: Polity Press, 2020.

———. *The Seminar of Jacques Lacan: Book VI: Desire and Its Interpretation, 1958–59*. Edited by Jacques-Alain Miller, translated by Bruce Fink. Cambridge: Polity Press, 2019.

———. *The Seminar of Jacques Lacan: Book VII, The Ethics of Psychoanalysis, 1959–60*. Edited by Jacques-Alain Miller, translated by Dennis Porter. New York: W. W. Norton, 1986.

———. *The Seminar of Jacques Lacan: Book VIII, Transference*. Edited by Jacques-Alain Miller, translated by Bruce Fink. Cambridge: Polity Press, 2015.

———. *The Seminar of Jacques Lacan: Book X, Anxiety*. Edited by Jacques-Alain Miller, translated by A. R. Price. Cambridge: Polity Press, 2014.

———. "Seminar XVI: From an Other to the other." Translated for private use from the unpublished French transcript of the seminar by Cormac Gallagher.

———. *The Seminar of Jacques Lacan: Book XVII, The Other Side of Psychoanalysis*. Edited by Jacques-Alain Miller, translated by Russell Grigg. New York: W. W. Norton, 1991.

———. *The Seminar of Jacques Lacan: Book XX, Encore: On Feminine Sexuality, the*

Limits of Love and Knowledge, 1972–73. Edited by Jacques-Alain Miller, translated by Bruce Fink. New York: W. W. Norton, 1998.

———. "Seminar IX: Identification." Translated for private use from the unpublished French transcript of the seminar by Cormac Gallagher.

———. "Seminar XXII: R.S.I." Translated for private use from the unpublished French transcript of the seminar by Cormac Gallagher.

———. *Television.* Translated by Denis Hollier, Rosalind Krauss, and Annette Michelson. *October* 40 (Spring 1987).

———. *The Triumph of Religion.* Translated by Bruce Fink. Malden MA: Polity Press, 2013.

Leupin, Alexandre. *Lacan Today: Psychoanalysis, Science, Religion.* New York: Other Press, 2004.

Malabou, Catherine. *The Future of Hegel: Plasticity, Temporality, and Dialectic.* Translated by Lisabeth During. London: Routledge, 2005.

Marx, Karl. *Capital: A Critique of Political Economy.* Translated by Ben Fowkes. New York: Penguin, 1990.

Marx, Karl, and Fredrick Engels. *The Marx Reader.* Edited by Robert Tucker. New York: W. W. Norton, 1978.

McGowan, Todd. *Capitalism and Desire: The High Price of Free Markets.* New York: Columbia University Press, 2016.

———. *Emancipation after Hegel: A Contradictory Revolution.* New York: Columbia University Press, 2019.

McNulty, Tracy. *Wrestling with the Angel: Experiments in Symbolic Life.* New York: Columbia University Press, 2014.

Mendieta, Eduardo, ed. *The Frankfurt School on Religion: Key Writings by the Major Thinkers.* New York: Routledge, 2005.

Nagy, Gregory. *The Best of the Achaeans: Concepts of the Hero in Archaic Greek Poetry.* Baltimore, MD: Johns Hopkins University Press, 1979.

Nancy, Jean-Luc, and Philippe Lacoue-Labarthe. *The Title of the Letter: A Reading of Lacan.* Translated by François Raffoul and David Pettigrew. Albany: SUNY Press, 1992.

Nietzsche, Friedrich. *Beyond Good and Evil.* In *Basic Writings of Nietzsche,* translated by Walter Kaufmann. New York: Vintage Books, 1961.

———. *The Birth of Tragedy.* In *Basic Writings of Nietzsche.* Translated by Walter Kaufmann. New York: Modern Library, 1992.

———. *The Genealogy of Morals.* In *Basic Writings of Nietzsche.* Translated by Walter Kaufmann. New York: Modern Library, 1992.

———. *Human All Too Human: A Book for Free Spirits.* Translated by Marion Faber, with Stephen Lehmann. Lincoln: University of Nebraska Press, 1986.

———. *The Portable Nietzsche Reader.* Translated by Walter Kaufmann. New York: Viking Press, 1968.

Nishitani, Keiji. *Religion and Nothingness.* Translated by Jan Van Bragt. Berkeley: University of California Press, 1982.

Nobus, Dany. *The Law of Desire: On Lacan's "Kant with Sade."* Cham, SZ: Palgrave MacMillan, 2017.

Otto, Rudolf. *The Idea of the Holy.* Translated by John Harvey. London: Oxford University Press, 1923.

Pagels, Elaine. *The Origin of Satan.* New York: Random House, 1995.

———. *Why Religion: A Personal Story.* New York: HarperCollins, 2018.

Paul, Robert. *Moses and Civilization: The Meaning behind Freud's Myth.* New Haven, CT: Yale University Press, 1969.

Pound, Marcus. "By the Grace of Lacan." In *Theology after Lacan: The Passion for the Real,* edited by Creston Davis, Marcus Pound, and Clayton Crockett. Eugene, OR: Cascade Books, 2014.

———. *Theology, Psychoanalysis, and Trauma.* London: SCM Press, 2007.

Radhakrishnan, Sarvepalli, and Charles Moore, eds. *A Sourcebook Indian Philosophy.* Princeton, NJ: Princeton University Press, 1973.

Reinhard, Kenneth. "There Is Something of One (God): Lacan and Political Theology." In *Theology after Lacan: The Passion for the Real,* edited by Creston Davis, Marcus Pound, and Clayton Crockett. Eugene, OR: Cascade Books, 2014.

Reinhard, Kenneth, and Julia Lupton. "The Subject of Religion: Lacan and the Ten Commandments." *Diacritics* 33, no. 2 (Summer 2003): 71–97.

Richardson, William J. "'Like Straw': Religion and Psychoanalysis." *The Letter: Lacanian Perspectives on Psychoanalysis* 11 (1997): 1–15.

Ruti, Mari. *Between Levinas and Lacan: Self, Other, Ethics.* New York: Bloomsbury, 2015.

Salecl, Renata. "Disbelief in the Big Other in the University and Beyond." *Anglistica* 4, no. 1 (2000): 49–67.

Sartre, Jean-Paul. *Being and Nothingness.* Translated by Hazel Barnes. New York: Washington Square Press, 1971.

Saussure, Ferdinand de. *Course in General Linguistics.* Edited by C. Bally, Albert Sechehaye with A. Reidlinger, translated by Wade Baskin. New York: McGraw Hill, 1966.

Savage-Rumbaugh, Sue. "Kanzi." Interview on *Radiolab,* NPR, February 19, 2010.

Scholem, Gershom. *On the Kabbalah and Its Symbolism (Mysticism and Kabbalah).* Translated by Ralph Manheim. New York: Schocken Books, 1996.

Seaford, Richard. *Money and the Early Greek Mind: Homer, Philosophy, Tragedy.* Cambridge: Cambridge University Press, 2004.

Shankara. *The Crest Jewel of Discrimination (Vivekachudamani).* Translated by John Richards, N.p.: Freedom Religion Press, 2011.

Simmel, Georg. *The Philosophy of Money.* Edited by David Frisby, translated by Tom Bottomore and David Frisby. London: Routledge, 1978.

Smith, Huston. *The World's Religions.* New York: HarperCollins, 1991.

Sontag, Susan. *Against Interpretation.* New York: Farrar, Straus, and Giroux, 1966.

Sophocles. *Oedipus the King and Antigone.* Translated and edited by Peter Arnott. Arlington Heights, IL: Harlan Davidson, 1960.

Struck, Peter. *Divination and Human Nature: A Cognitive History of Intuition in Classical Antiquity.* Princeton, NJ: Princeton University Press, 2016.

Suzuki, Shunryu. *Zen Mind, Beginner's Mind.* Edited by Trudy Dixon. New York: Weatherhill, 1975.

Veyne, Paul. *Did the Greeks Believe Their Myths? An Essay on the Constitutive Imagination.* Translated by Paula Wissing. Chicago: University of Chicago Press, 1988.

Walsh, Joseph, ed. *What Would You Die For? Perpetua's Passion.* Baltimore: Apprentice House, 2005.

Weil, Simone. *The Simone Weil Reader.* Edited by George Panichas. New York: David McKay, 1977.

Wheelwright, Philip, ed. *The Presocratics.* New York: MacMillan, 1987.

Wittgenstein, Ludwig. *Philosophical Investigations.* Translated by G. E. M. Anscombe. New York: McMillan, 1968.

Žižek, Slavoj. *The Fragile Absolute—or, Why Is the Christian Legacy Worth Fighting For?* London: Verso, 2000.

———. "Hegel and Shitting: The Idea's Constipation." In *Hegel and the Infinite: Religion, Politics, and Dialectic,* edited by Slavoj Žižek, Clayton Crockett, and Creston Davis. New York: Columbia University Press, 2011.

———. *How to Read Lacan.* New York: W. W. Norton, 2006.

———. *The Indivisible Remainder: An Essay on Schelling and Related Matters.* London: Verso, 1996.

———. *Less Than Nothing: Hegel and the Shadow of Dialectical Materialism.* London: Verso, 2012.

———. "Neighbors and Other Monsters: A Plea for Ethical Violence." In Slavoj Žižek, Eric Santner, and Kenneth Reinhard, *The Neighbor: Three Inquiries in Political Theology.* Chicago: University of Chicago Press, 2005.

———. *On Belief.* London: Routledge, 2001.

———. *The Puppet and the Dwarf: The Perverse Core of Christianity.* Cambridge, MA: MIT Press, 2003.

———. "The Real of Sexual Difference." In *Reading Seminar XX: Lacan's Major Work on Love, Knowledge, and Feminine Sexuality,* edited by Suzanne Barnard and Bruce Fink. Albany: State University of New York Press, 2002.

———. *Tarrying with the Negative: Kant, Hegel, and the Critique of Ideology.* Durham, NC: Duke University Press, 1993.

———. "The Thing from Inner Space." In *Sexuatio,* edited by Renata Salacl. Durham:: Duke University Press, 2000.

Žižek, Slavoj, and Boris Gunjevic. *God in Pain: Inversions of Apocalypse.* New York: Seven Stories, 2012.

Žižek, Slavoj, and John Milbank. *The Monstrosity of Christ: Paradox or Dialectic?* Edited by Creston Davis. Cambridge, MA: MIT Press, 2009.

Index

Abram/Abraham: sacrifice of Isaac, 111–12, 116, 134; and Yahweh, 109–11, 128–29, 185

Advaita Vedanta doctrine, 167, 171

Agamben, Giorgio, 201–2

Agamemnon, 77, 78, 87, 109, 112

Akhenaton, 113

Akhilleus, 75, 88–89, 91, 92, 161–62, 213n41

Alford, C. Fred, 93–94

al-Ghaib (unseen/hidden/unknown), the, 173

Ali, Ameer, 174

Allah: and disbelievers, 176; and law, 175; unknowability of, 172–73

Althusser, Louis: on ideology, 180, 183–85; on interpellation, 187–89

ambivalence: and *das Ding*/the Thing, 33–34, 107, 199; and "falsely false," 33–35, 39; and father, 11; toward the feminine, 26; toward money, 180; toward neighbor-Thing, 35, 178

analyst: and *das Ding*, 50–52; judging by, 144–45; as *objet a*, 51; as silent, 62; as subject-supposed-to-know, 51–52, 156, 188; and transference, 149–50

Anaxagoras, 80

Anaximenes, 95

anxiety: and desire, 33–35; in Judaism, 127–28; mother as source of, 25–26, 38; provoked by analyst, 51; Sartre on, 29; of sex 40–41; and stranger, 36; and the void, 91–92

Anxiety seminar (Lacan), 25, 42–43, 48, 115

Aphrodite, 76

Apollo, 76, 94

Apology (Plato), 75

appearance: in Greek polytheism, 78–83, 94, 103; person as, 171

Arendt, Hannah, 100

Ares, 76

Aristotle, 91, 106

atheism: and Christianity, 145–47, 149; and Freud, 9; Lacan's commitment to, 4, 198–99

Athena, 90, 109

Atman (consciousness), 167–68

Attack on Christendom (Kierkegaard), 151

Aufhebung (canceled/negated and preserved/affirmed), 60

Badiou, Alain, 152, 220n5

baptism, 15–16

belief: in capitalism, 189; Christian, 153–58, 160–62; contrast among religions in, 155; and dogma/orthodoxy, 150–51, 165, 175–76; and evil, 161; form vs. content in, 153–54; Freud's critique of, 1–2, 10–11; in Judaism, 123; in myth, 69–70, 83–86; subject and, 9–10; and unbeliever/disbeliever, 157, 161, 175–76, 222n44, 222n47; and unknowing, 191–92; and wish fulfillment, 9–10, 12–13, 192–93, 199

Bernini, Gian Lorenzo, 148

big Other: dogma and, 151–52; God and, 21–22, 198–99; in Greek polytheism, 77–78; and Judaism, 109, 129; and little other, 7, 47, 51, 124, 129, 151; and perversion, 196; as representing symbolic structures, 7, 22, 23, 51–52; and Ten Commandments, 124–25; as term, 210n40

Birth of Tragedy, The (Nietzsche), 94

body image, 16–17, 41, 44

Brahman as cosmic self, 167–68

Buddhism: bearing on Lacan's thought, 20; as nontheistic, 13; as offshoot of